Spring 91

WOMEN'S VOICES

A JOURNAL OF ARCHETYPE AND CULTURE

Fall 2014

SPRING JOURNAL
New Orleans, Louisiana

SPRING: A JOURNAL OF ARCHETYPE AND CULTURE

Nancy Cater, Editor-in-chief
Patricia Reis, Guest Editor

Jungiana Editor: Riccardo Bernardini   Film Review Editor: Helena Bassil-Morozow
Book Review Editor: Emilija Kiehl

Spring is the oldest Jungian psychology journal in the world. Published twice a year, each issue explores from the perspective of depth psychology a theme of contemporary relevance and contains articles as well as book and film reviews by a wide range of authors from Jungian psychology, the humanities, and other interrelated disciplines.

Founded in 1941 by the Analytical Psychology Club of New York, *Spring* was edited by Jane Pratt until 1969. With the 1970 issue, James Hillman became the editor of *Spring* and moved it to Zürich. When Hillman left Zürich and became the Dean of Graduate Studies at the University of Dallas in 1978, he transferred the editing and publishing of *Spring* there. It was edited in Dallas until 1988 when Hillman and *Spring* moved to Connecticut. Hillman retired as Publisher and Senior Editor of the journal in 1997. From 1997 until 2004 *Spring* remained in Connecticut and was edited by Charles Boer. *Spring* moved its offices to New Orleans, Louisiana in 2004 and has been edited by Nancy Cater there since.

Cover Image:
"Tail for blanket and pillow," by Irene Hardwicke Olivieri, oil on wooden panel, 22x19 in.

Cover design, typography, and layout:
Northern Graphic Design & Publishing, info@ncarto.com

© 2014 Spring Journal, Inc.   ISSN: 0362-0522   ISBN: 978-1-935528-66-1

CONTENTS

FILM REVIEW

BOOK REVIEWS

INTRODUCTION

NANCY CATER

For this Women's Voices issue of *Spring*, I was delighted to have Patricia Reis serve as my co-editor. Patricia is the author of *The Dreaming Way: Dreams and Art for Remembering and Recovery*; *Daughters of Saturn: From Father's Daughter to Creative Woman*; and *Through the Goddess: A Woman's Way of Healing*. Her essays and reviews have been published in *Spring, The San Francisco Jung Institute Library Journal* [now *Jung Journal: Culture and Psyche*], and numerous other journals and books. She is the creator/producer of the DVD, *Arctic Refuge Sutra: Teachings from an Endangered Landscape*, and appeared in the film, *Signs Out of Time*, a documentary produced by Canadian filmmaker Donna Read about the life and work of archaeologist Marija Gimbutas with whom Patricia studied, traveled, and worked as an illustrator.

Patricia received her B.A. from the University of Wisconsin, Madison, in English Literature and an M.F.A. from the University of California Los Angeles (UCLA) in Sculpture. In 1986, she earned an M.A. from Pacifica Graduate Institute in Counseling Psychology. She has held positions as faculty, lecturer, and dissertation advisor and has mentored and facilitated many artists and writers in bringing their work to fruition. Patricia divides her time between Portland, Maine and Nova Scotia and is currently focused on writing a memoir.

My and Patricia's inspiration for this volume was the most recent book written by American writer, naturalist, and environmental activist Terry Tempest Williams and entitled *When Women Were Birds: Fifty-four Variations on Voice*. In its opening pages, the author tells us what led her to write this book. When she was in her early 30s, her mother, age fifty-four, died of cancer. Shortly before her death, she told Terry: "I am leaving you all my journals . . . But you must promise me that you will not look at them until after I am gone." It was a tradition in the Mormon faith to which Terry belonged for women to keep journals documenting their lives in the Mormon community. A month after her mother died, Terry found the journals, shelves and shelves of them, all blank. Already a writer herself, Terry did not in her own writing address the inheritance of the blank journals and what that meant to her for over twenty years. She continued expressing her own voice through writing, though, beginning with her seminal first book, *Refuge*, and writing twelve more books over the next two decades.

Only when Terry was fifty-four herself, the age of her mother when she died, did she tackle the subject of voice, and lack of voice, as reflected in her inheritance of her mother's blank journals. She did this through writing *When Women Were Birds* (2013). This book contains fifty-four evocative essays on "What is Voice?" She explores complex and often contradictory subjects that she relates to issues of women expressing themselves (or not): Story, Secrets, Survival, Silence, Solitude, Suffering, Sovereignty, Speaking Up, Sexuality, Shadow.

In our Call for Papers, Patricia and I stated that *When Women Were Birds* was our inspiration for this issue, and set out a number of provocative quotes from the book, each of which we felt could serve as the jumping off point for an article. Included in these were:

"Each voice belongs to a place."

"At the heart of my emerging voice was the belief that nature held the secret to harmony and unity, not just outside us, but inside us, no separation."

"I am writing the creation story of my own voice through the blank pages my mother has bequeathed to me."

"The first voice I heard belonged to my mother."

"When one woman doesn't speak, other women get hurt."

"I am afraid of silence. Silence creates a pathway to peace through pain, the pain of a distracted and frantic mind before it becomes still."

"I fear silence because it leads me to myself, a self I may not wish to confront....Silence leaves me alone in a place of feeling. It is not necessarily a place of comfort."

"Silence introduced in a society that worships noise is like the moon exposing the night."

"(Eve) exposed the truth of what every woman knows: to find our sovereign voices often requires a betrayal."

We also said in the Call for Papers that we were particularly interested in receiving articles that deal with the psychological issues that arise when women attempt to express themselves, the obstacles faced, the obstacles overcome (or not), the creativity that may released. We welcomed clinical articles, as well as personal and more academic papers. From my own perspective, I hoped that this issue could serve to expand the kinds of articles published in *Spring*, as well as the writers who wrote for it, and also reach out to a larger audience.

The response to the Call for Papers was un-precedented in the time that I have served as *Spring*'s editor, with our receiving many more submissions than ever before, making it difficult to select which articles to include.

We are very honored that Terry Tempest Williams herself agreed to be interviewed by Patricia for this volume. Her interview comes first and sets the tone for the articles that follow, as she explores in detail with Patricia issues related to voice that were discussed in *When Women Were Birds*.

In *When Women Were Birds*, Terry Tempest Williams asks, "What needs to be counted on to have a voice? Courage. Anger. Love. Something to say; someone to listen." The sixteen contributors to this volume recognize and demonstrate, directly or indirectly, the truth of Terry Tempest Williams' observation. They come from different places and from different backgrounds. They are writers, poets, teachers, analysts, educators, and theorists. Their writing styles vary accordingly, yet their works share similar themes, from the deeply personal to the cultural and historical, from the literary to the mythological and spiritual. Terry Tempest Williams' statement also implies a necessary bond between speaker and listener, or as in this case, author and reader, and it is our hope that this Women's Voices issue of *Spring* will encourage such a mutually inspired relationship.

We are grateful to Terry Tempest Williams for inspiring us with her work, for her great generosity of spirit, and for engaging with Patricia in a stirring, intimate, and heartfelt interview.

We would like to thank the contributors for responding so fully to our Call for Papers and for delving deep into their experiences with eloquence, honesty, and intelligence.

We express our gratitude to artist, Irene Olivieri Hardwick, for generously providing us with the cover art and the images that appear in Susan Amons' review of her book, *Irene Olivieri Hardwick: Closer to Wildness.*

Patricia would like to thank Nancy Cater for envisioning the Women's Voices issue and inviting her to participate as co-editor. Nancy's dedication and commitment to bringing the highest standards to bear on all aspects of the Journal's production made the experience and the outcome deeply satisfying.

Nancy Cater and Patricia Reis

Photo © Louis Gakumba

Terry Tempest Williams is an American writer, conservationist, and activist. Author of fourteen books, she is the recipient of numerous awards, including a John Simon Guggenheim Memorial Fellowship and a Lannan Literary Fellowship in creative nonfiction. Grounded in her training as a wildlife biologist and the arid landscape of her native Utah where she was raised as a Mormon, she probes the interrelations between ecology and wilderness preservation, women's health, and our relationship to culture and nature, with her signature poetic and spiritual depth.

Refuge: An Unnatural History of Family and Place (1991) has become a classic. In the spring of 1983, Williams learned her mother was dying of cancer. That same season, The Great Salt Lake began to rise to record heights, threatening the herons, owls, and snowy egrets by which Williams, a poet and naturalist, had come to gauge her life. One event was nature at its most random; the other, human intervention at its most horrific: Terry's mother, and Terry herself, had been exposed to the fallout of atomic bomb tests in the 1950s. Written as a memoir, *Refuge* juxtaposes a narrative of family and the natural world, through a season of death and renewal.

When Williams discovers that all her mother's journals, bequeathed to her on her mother's deathbed, are blank, she is confronted with a profound mystery. Twenty years later, she takes up the themes of *Refuge* in *When Women Were Birds: Fifty-four Variations on Voice* (2012). Composed of fifty-four sections, the age of her mother when she died, Terry contemplates a deeper understanding of her mother and her motivations, while charting the evolution of her own voice in relationship to her Mormon heritage, her marriage, the environment, her role as a writer, her place as a woman in the world, and much more.

I recall a bone whistle made from the hands of a desert dweller that now resides in the Natural History Museum of Utah. It was made from the hollow bone of a bird in the aridity of the Great Basin adjacent to Great Salt Lake. I knew the sound of that whistle, "a dangerous and passionate illumination" of both the sorrow and beauty of our lives. My voice is born out of silences bared. Writing has saved my life.

SILENCE

PR: In your work, Silence has many tongues. You make a distinction between privacy and silence, saying, "Mother was a private woman, not a silent one." When I read Variation I in *Birds* about the blank journals, I said, "Wait, wait!" and immediately re-read my worn original copy of *Refuge: An Unnatural History of Family and Place*. Written in 1991, over twenty years ago, *Refuge* tracks the arc of your mother's dying from cancer alongside the apocalyptic rise and fall of the Great Salt Lake and subsequent threat to the Bear River Migratory Bird Refuge. In it, you portray the strong red thread of your maternal lineage, the generations of Mormon women who had minds and thoughts of their own.

In *Refuge*, your mother appears as such a vivid personality, your relationship enviable in its intimacy; she says and writes things to you that are strongly felt and deeply meaningful. And your grandmother, Mimi, is even bolder and more outspoken. You recount a three-way conversation between you, your mother, and your grandmother while looking at your astrological charts. The talk is about giving up personal authority because it's easier, how women have been taught to sacrifice, support, and endure. Your mother comments, "I think I paid a price physically."

Refuge speaks of your dawning awareness of the price paid by being a "downwinder" of the atomic testing done in the desert. Not only had your mother died of cancer, nine women in your family had, including your beloved grandmother. I go back to Hélène Cixous who says, "To begin (writing, living) we must have death." I have always thought that writing *Refuge* must have radicalized you. It feels like a blood relation to *Birds*, because the same themes are woven into its DNA. There are thirty-seven chapters named for birds. And at the close of *Refuge*, you declare yourself to be "a woman with wings," an augur of *When Women Were Birds*.

How has your voice changed in the intervening years between *Refuge* and *Birds*?

TTW: When I chose to cross the line at the Nevada Nuclear Test Site in opposition to the testing of nuclear bombs in the desert and commit civil disobedience in the name of the women in my family, members of The Clan of One-Breasted Women, I found my voice as a writer.

I remember the moment. An officer frisked my body. Inside my boot, she found a pen and a pad of paper. "And these?" she asked. "Weapons," I replied. I had not only crossed a physical line, a political line, but a metaphorical one. There was no going back.

If my voice has changed through the years, evolved through time, I hope it has grown in empathy. I am not sure it has grown in confidence. I believe I was more confident in what I knew when I was a younger writer. Now, as I approach sixty, I am acutely aware of all I do not know, especially in these dramatic, changing times. But I trust my instincts. My questions continue to guide me. My dreams continue to instruct me. And I have fallen more passionately in love with this beautiful, broken world. Perhaps, my voice on the page has not changed as much as deepened. Humility is the word that comes to mind. Age humbles us. The Mysteries become more profound. We embrace the complexities that surround us, even as we try to embody the principles that allow us to stand upright. Conscious experience creates a path of wisdom. Listening becomes part of that path. Listening creates empathy. Love remains the base note of my voice.

SILENCE: THE OTHER SIDE

PR: In the Jeffs' school vignette in *Birds*, you describe how you learned to live within highly repressive (ridiculous?) constraints by using your maternal lineage's coping manual. You find ways to teach, to express to the children what you passionately believe in, you don't completely lose you voice, you keep your values, and you actually learn from Mrs. Jeff, who feels like a character straight out of Dickens! You learn many important lessons. But this learned strategy takes you only so far.

This is such a powerful vignette, speaking as it does about how we accommodate, how we try to live within a limited range of motion, how our lessons come in the strangest of packages. On behalf of yourself as a teacher and the children, you make deals with the Jeffs. You quote Rachel Carson, "If a child is to keep alive his inborn sense of wonder, he needs the companionship of at least one adult who can share it, rediscovering with him the joy, excitement, and mystery of the world we live in." Certainly your grandmother, Mimi, was one of those who gave you such companionship and you wished to be that one adult for the children you were teaching.

Women often justify living in repressive circumstances by saying it is just easier, they can get by, they are learning a lot, they can manage, etc.

How can we know when we have learned enough, when we should leave situations where our voice is confined, our wings clipped, our passions held in check?

TTW: What a great question. Again, I trust my instincts. Mimi always said, "The universe is energy. We are made from energy. Pay attention to what gives you energy and what takes your energy away." This has been a wonderful gauge for me throughout my life. Using my tenure at the Carden School as an example, as long as I was receiving energy from the children, I was able to give energy back to them in my classroom. When Carden stopped being a living place for me, when I started to feel as if the energy was stagnating around me and that my own energy was stagnating, I left. I also had the luxury of being able to leave and pursue graduate school. And this is no small thing. Many times, the circumstances in our lives do not allow us to leave a situation "where our voice is confined." There are bills to be paid, mouths to be fed, and we have to wait until we feel safe enough, strong enough, to walk out as the door opens. Patience may be required. But risk is also required and the trust and belief in ourselves to know that however uncertain it may feel, we will be okay. To have a voice in the world is to risk our voice, repeatedly. Fear so often gets in our way. To replace fearfulness with fearlessness is part of the process of individuation. And so is imagination. We must be able to imagine ourselves differently and in so doing, we emerge with new wings.

SILENCE: ANOTHER VARIATION

PR: You write in *Birds*, "I am afraid of silence. Silence creates a pathway to peace through pain, the pain of a distracted and frantic mind before it becomes still." Certainly anyone who has meditated, even for ten minutes, knows what you are talking about. You say, "Within silence our voice dwells."

What does it take to befriend such an enabling silence?

TTW: Silence for me is oxygen. Without it, I cannot breathe. Silence is also like water. Without it, I become thirsty and experience a withering of my spirit. And yet, silence is demanding, difficult, even terrifying at times. Silence is a force that animates my fears and dances with my demons. Distractions will protect me from the pain of silence, the truth of being alone. This I know. But I also know that I need the tonic of silence if I am to live an authentic life in contact with my highest and deepest self.

Silence becomes my healing grace.

To befriend silence is to commit to its discomfort and all it exposes and amplifies.

To befriend sustained periods of silence is to endure a period of detoxification that allows the outer noise to cease enough to hear the inner voice speak. It is not easy, but in time, an uncommon peace ensues. Silence is not simply void of sound, silence is a place of presence. Call it soul-retrieval. We are no longer running from the self, but sitting in harmony with the self: awake, alert, and alive. This is the silence that speaks to me. This is the silence I long for and would go mad without. Silence allows me to be in relationship to the world. To retreat and withdraw from community is to rejoin and rejoice with others in the return.

The nature of silence is the nature of solitude. In solitude, I find my creative pulse.

In nature, I find my universal bearings and remember the interconnectedness of all things. Through the stillness of a forest, the meanderings of a river, the rhythm of the tides, awe is awakened in me. I am listening. I am watching. Silence is both heard and felt between the intervals of thunder. Silence holds the space for loss and joy. It is where our conscience and consciousness is found. A meadowlark singing in the desert is in dialogue with silence, that ringing silence, my beloved paradox.

SOVEREIGNTY

PR: We have inherited various psychological theories, master-narratives that describe the self in terms of unity, totality, wholeness, the union of opposites, etc., the same meta-notions inherent in all monotheistic systems. You seldom use the word "self," or even the word "autonomy," which theoretically urges and implies a separation from the maternal bond. You use the word "sovereignty." In your *Fifty-four Variations on Voice*, the many voices, like Cixous' 1,000 tongues, are far from total or unified, or univocal. Like the birdsongs you learned from your grandmother, the sovereign voice has variation and range: melodic, shrill, a whisper, sociable, raucous, used to call a mate, voice alarm, raise a mobbing. You ask, "What is birdsong, but truth in rehearsal?"

Can you open that word, "sovereignty," for us, and the reasons you choose to use it?

TTW: Sovereignty can be defined as a "self-governing state." Its origins are found in the Middle English "soverain," an alteration of "reign." I would define sovereignty as self-rule, a reclaiming and a restoration of our own power, our own authority.

In America, tribal sovereignty is the inherent authority for indigenous tribes to govern themselves. I think of Ada Deer and her leadership in pushing for the Menominee Restoration Act signed into law by President Richard M. Nixon on December 22, 1973. Ada Deer's vision was not to restore things as they once were, but to forge a new relationship: federal protection of their lands without the federal Bureau of Indian Affairs' domination. "By expressing our tribal values, we changed our history," she said.

This is instructive for all of us. We can forge a new relationship with society and ourselves through our own sovereignty. The freedom to govern myself—this is a core value. By expressing our inherent values, we can change our own personal histories and not be dominated by or dependent upon the oppressor, in my case, a patriarchal religion. I was told repeatedly that a woman's place is in the home. I was told that my value and voice were contingent upon being a mother. I didn't believe that was my only choice. Sovereignty implies choice, the choice to govern myself. I chose a different path.

I choose to use the word sovereignty because the word holds dignity. Dignity is how we conduct ourselves in relationship to others. To use the word "autonomy" implies we are separate. This is an illusion. Sovereignty is deeper than separatism. Sovereignty has dignity. It is about self-respect. I am my own sovereign, not separate from the women who gave me birth, but individual, unique, determined. The women in my family had dignity. They respected themselves and they respected each other. Sovereigns. This, too, is my legacy.

SEPARATION

PR: You write, "At the heart of my emerging voice was the belief that nature held the secret to harmony and unity, not just outside us, but inside us, no separation." And later you quote your grandmother saying to you, "We are nature." So much of your writing is about the kind of deep listening that dissolves the boundaries between a woman's body and nature. But thinning the membrane between ourselves and the sensate world we inhabit is not done without consequences.

In *Birds*, you tell of a radicalizing moment when you saw a living coyote taking in the view on Gannett Peak mountaintop. You write, "Any boundaries I felt as a human being toward other creatures dissolved. We, too, were partaking of the view." Later that day you came upon another coyote, this one dead, skinned, hanging by its neck on a crossbar. Lynched. I can't help but think of Matthew Shepard, the victim of a similar hate crime.* Your companion cut the coyote down with his buck knife, the same kind of weapon used to skin the animal. At that moment, you made a vow to the coyote, "I would not remain silent." Once a vow is made, it is indelible to the soul.

You wrote of this to your grandmother, Mimi, who responded: "However hard it must have been for you to see this act of cruelty, view it as an insight into those who wielded a knife." She was telling you, in effect, do not separate yourself from any part of what you encountered. Use it all.

In what ways has your vow and your grandmother's instruction challenged you?

---

*In 1998, Matthew Shepard, a University of Wyoming student, was beaten, tortured, and left to die while tied to a fence near Laramie, Wyoming. Targeted because he was gay, the murder resulted in the 2009 Matthew Shepard Act, a Hate Crimes Prevention legislation.

TTW: In my grandmother's turquoise study, a large portrait of the Buddha's face hung above the bed where we slept. Its eyes were slits, half opened, half closed. Below the Buddha's chin were a man and woman dancing. They were naked. Mimi introduced them to us as "the anima and animus." She was a Jungian scholar. She taught us that we house both the masculine and feminine inside each of us. It is a dance. Various figures danced around the Buddha, angels and murderers, alike. Mimi spoke to us about "the collective unconscious," introducing us to a humanity interconnected and interrelated. The world was not something outside us, but inside us. We were not "the chosen people" as our religious upbringing would have us believe. We were one with the world.

So when Mimi wrote back to me saying that the hand that skinned the coyote was also the hand that freed it, she was amplifying her belief that we as human beings are capable of great cruelties and great kindnesses. The question becomes how do we bring these two hands together in prayer?

This was the sobering realization I faced in Rwanda. The genocide was not something outside of me, but inside me. If a human being raised a machete to kill his neighbor, I, too, was capable of such an atrocity. If a human being hid a family of Tutsis from Hutu extremists, I, too, was capable of that kind of courage and compassion. We are not separate from any human act, large or small, heinous or helpful. We are the full expression of the human experience. To be human is to own our shadow, both personal and collective. There is little room for judgment, perhaps the most difficult lesson of all. "The Buddha is the Divine Self," Mimi would tell us as children, "who does not judge or avenge but holds the open heart of compassion."

Try to imagine how radical this was to Mormon children growing up in Salt Lake City, Utah. Mimi was a transformational figure in our lives with Roger Tory Peterson's *Field Guide to Western Birds* in one hand and Carl Jung's *Man and His Symbols* in the other.

My grandmother did not challenge our world-view as much as expand it. In truth, Carl Jung and Joseph Campbell were so much a part of our upbringing they might as well have been Mormons! In fact, Mimi and I went to hear Joseph Campbell speak at Brigham Young University. We made a special pilgrimage to hear him. I was working on my thesis which would become "Pieces of White Shell: A Journey to Navajoland."

It must have been 1981. After his lecture, we approached him. I asked him what role he thought story played in our relationship to the Earth.

"Story is how we perceive the world around us," I remember him saying. "We need new stories to forge a new relationship with the Earth. Find them."

Mimi and I talked about this all the way home, what stories we tell to evoke a sense of place, what myths inspire us and what myths diminish us. We were always probing the depths. I miss her terribly. After she died, I didn't dream for several years because without her to interpret them with me, they weren't worth remembering.

Today, however, twenty-five years after her death, I am greatly challenged by her intellect, how much she read, how conscious she was, and the psychological courage she had to break set with her Mormon conditioning. Mimi spared us from the stranglehold of orthodoxy by infusing our spiritual education with Marie-Louise von Franz's "The Way of the Dream," J. Krishnamurti's concept of a "choiceless awareness of the moment," and the power of active imagination. She went to Ojai and Esalen to study with Krishnamurti. She went to lectures by Alan Watts. And she contemplated taking LSD under the supervision of a doctor to see how it might open up her own awareness. Of course, my grandfather put his foot down on that one. Nevertheless, she challenged us to believe that if Joseph Smith had visions, our visions were no less valid. She played with the Tarot and read *Suicide and the Soul* by James Hillman, believing each person had the right to live and die by their own will. The world is just now beginning to catch up with her.

SECRETS

PR: In *Birds*, you quote the poet, Muriel Rukeyeser: "What would happen if one woman told the truth about her life? The world would split open." The poet implies that a woman's truth is also the source of her power and that the act of telling can change the world.

As women, we hold secrets for as many reasons as there are secrets to be held: from shame, from being silenced, from fear, for our safety, from being told not to tell, and hardly ever from a sense of empowerment. In confronting your mother's blank journals, you write, "What my mother wanted to do and what she was able to do remains her secret." You also write, "We all have secrets. I hold mine," a sentence implying choice—in both cases—your mother's and yours. Further on in *Birds*, you write, "If my marriage is a secret, it is also large enough to hold secrets that I have learned not to tell. This is the nature of intimacy; discretion."

Can you talk about the various moral imperatives involved in speaking the truth and holding secrets?

TTW: I believe in the paradoxical relationship between truth-telling and secret-keeping: both involve choice; both engage power; both involve risks. Awareness of their medicine is key. As I write this sentence, a small spider is crawling across my fingers, so I will use the word web in my next sentence. As women, we spin a web of stories around us for protection. It is what feeds us and sustains us. It is also what threatens to kill us. The silk strands of our stories are created from our own bodies. Again, not outside us, but within us. Sometimes our stories are true. Sometimes our stories are false. Sometimes, the stories we tell are told without knowing what we reveal until they are reflected back to us, violently. The web breaks. We are vulnerable. This is why discernment is necessary. This is why discretion is essential. It is also why we must reflect and begin to understand what is behind our actions and why.

As women, we must learn when to speak and when to house our truth inside. Neither is easy. We pay a personal price whether we speak truth to power or withhold it. Our task is to understand what is required in order for us to thrive. Loyalty, fidelity, and integrity are most often worn as loose clothing. Honesty to the self is a tightly worn garment.

Spider teaches us to respect our calling as weavers, honoring the strength of the narratives we create. I am not talking about deceit. I am talking about the right to choose what we tell and what we do not. A woman's heart is attentive to the Mysteries. It is our practice to live with insecurity and uncertainty. We know what it means to exist with fear. Courage rises out of that fear. Too often we live for everyone else. Too often we worry what others may think. What matters to me is how I interpret my own behavior making my own map using my own moral compass to navigate. Each of us makes myths of our lives.

John Berger writes about "the secret of visibility." This intrigues me because the very idea of a secret is that something remains hidden. But what if our visible self, the light we reflect out into the world, finds its source in what we choose to keep to ourselves and for ourselves? Our secrets become our points of illumination, the candles we keep lit to see through the dark.

Holding our own counsel is nothing to be ashamed of, but something to honor. What remains unsaid becomes a private prayer, the place within us that remains humble. We can act from the center of our creation or we can hide when necessary. Spider is adept at both. A woman is feared when she opens her mouth. And she can be terrifying when her mouth is closed.

My mother left me her journals and all her journals were blank. In these empty pages, she told her truth and she kept her secrets. Power resides in choice. Every choice is both a blessing and a burden. When the burden becomes too great, and the cost too high, we must release the truth as a secret shared, a silence broken, a story freed.

A secret shared by two is a trusted conversation.

Secret Codes and the Unspeakable

PR: At the end of *Refuge*, after your beloved grandmother, Mimi, died of cancer, you write: "Mimi and I shared a clandestine vision of things. I could afford to dream because she could interpret the story. We spoke through the shorthand of symbols: an egg, an owl. And most of what we shared was secret, much like the migrations of birds."

In *Birds*, you talk about *nushu*, the secret written language developed by women living in Imperial Japan, and how the women who lacked formal education wrote for themselves and to each other in this way. There are only two photographs in your book; one is of *nushu* script that resembles bird tracks on sand. You remember, too, how you mother showed you how to write in "invisible ink" with lemon juice where only a flame held against parchment would reveal the message. As a young girl, you wrote in a secret code in your journal. You say, "I learned early how to cover myself as a writer, should the lock be picked and my words read."

For me, the best example of a secret code is when you describe how you learned to find your true voice by writing a line, then writing over it and over it—so no one, not even you, can ever decipher it. This makes me think of Emily Dickinson's poem "Tell all the Truth /but tell it slant" that closes with the lines, "The Truth must dazzle gradually/Or every man be blind."

You say that you "buried" the memory of your mother's blank journals and only when you were fifty-four, the age she was when she died, did it come back to you. Do you think that over time, through courage or for other reasons, some things we once thought unspeakable rise to the surface and demand a hearing?

TTW: Yes.

SPIRITUAL SURVIVAL

PR: You write in *Birds*, "Leaving one orthodoxy means leaving all orthodoxies." I found it striking how you manage to stay connected to your Mormon family despite vast differences in views and beliefs; you don't evade or deny your religious and social history, or the bonds with the people you came from. Love, friendship, care, loyalty, even devotion are evident in your writing. The bonds may be stretched, frayed, but are not broken.

These relationships are also the crucible for establishing your sovereignty as the vignette of lunch with your father-in-law reveals. You approach him personally, drawing on kinship bonds, and ask him to use his influence to raise money for a cause that you care passionately about, something that would benefit the wider world, something that would be consistent with his beliefs—and he asks something of you in exchange, something deeply personal: that you bring your husband, Brooke, back to the Church. Instinctively you know this would compromise not only your personal ethics but would altogether taint the enterprise you want to support.

Emily Dickinson is quoted as saying, "No, is the wildest word we consign to language." In saying "No" to your father-in-law's terms, you risked your sense of belonging, of being embedded in networks that offer social protections and rewards, for the sake of sovereignty. Traditionally, women have been expected to make the preservation of relationships their highest concern, regardless of the cost to themselves. You were not willing to make the bargain or pay the cost.

No longer willing to accept the terms of religious and cultural conditioning, what are the ways you have learned to spiritually survive?

TTW: My spiritual health is directly tied to beauty, the beauty of solitude, the beauty inherent in wild nature, the beauty of art, and the depth of my relations are all a conveyance of beauty. Beauty translates to peace. And I find my peace in writing. Writing is my spiritual practice. Paying attention, being curious, courting the questions all contribute to a spiritually rich life. I believe in being spontaneous. I believe in the power of synchronicity where the outer and inner worlds converge in moments of magic. It's the pattern that connects that allows us to celebrate the interrelatedness of all things.

Mimi would always say, "Follow the golden thread…." And I have. Each day is a creative act. Each morning, I listen from the dreamtime to what is speaking to me, what is required of me, and I make plans accordingly. I prefer to keep my days open. In fact, I schedule open days as fiercely as when I schedule my travels.

Creativity is my soul's path. If I am creatively engaged—be it in my writing, my teaching, or drinking a cup of tea on my front porch with a friend—I am present. And in presence, god dwells, however we choose to define that force, that energy. To be present is to be transformed.

You ask how I survive. It's not so much that I have learned how to spiritually survive as I have learned how to live with pain. I have learned that to embrace our pain is easier than avoiding it because when we avoid pain, it stalks us. If I can look death in the face, or not turn away from a pelican drenched in oil, I can be of use to the one suffering, even if it means just holding that space together. A grief shared is a grief endured. This has been one of the gifts of being with many of my family members throughout their dying process. It has allowed me to trust that what is hard and sad and difficult is also, tender, true, and revelatory. And often, very funny. The full range of emotions is available to us when we are broken open. To not avert our gaze is to dare to be touched by life.

What are we afraid of?

I am afraid of being numb.

I have learned that to be alive is to dance with my intuition, including not succumbing to someone else's dogma or religion. I have learned free agency nurtures my soul. I like making my own decisions, which includes making my own mistakes. Freedom is at the core of my beating heart. Perhaps it is at the core of all of our hearts. When freedom is diminished, our souls shrink.

My marriage to Brooke Williams for close to forty years has been the most immediate and enduring site of my spiritual evolution, the place where my soul has been cared for, loved, and supported. It has also been my greatest challenge to live with another sovereign. To love each other, to forgive each other, to wake each morning anew. I think it is fair to say we have been protectors of one another's solitudes and encouraged each other's growth. Our marriage has been very free. It had to be in order for us to survive and individuate, not always at the same time or interval, not always easy, but so worth "the vitality of the struggle."

Our marriage has been an ongoing transformation from taking our vows in the Salt Lake City Temple to making new vows before the wide-eyed gods of the Great Barrier Canyon mural, the pictographs and petroglyphs located in Canyonlands National Park. In a very real sense, we are Mormon refugees. Our relationship has been a sanctuary. We have given birth to each another.

I want to be of use. I want to help create community. And I need to be in the service of something larger than myself. To be of service is a deeply spiritual act. What am I in the service of? Finding beauty in a broken world is creating beauty in the world we find. This is my spiritual work.

SUBVERSIVE

PR: One of the funniest and most subversive moments in *Birds* is your description of how the word "Fuck" arose spontaneously in your mind during a sacred rite of passage in your marriage ceremony. It feels like the word was also sacred, but in an irreverent coyote way. "Fuck," an unbidden, sacrilegious mantra, created an opening, an exit, a foot in the door, so to speak, so your mind and imagination would always be wild and free.

In writing about Eve and the apple, you say, "She, (Eve) exposed the truth of what every woman knows: to find our sovereign voice often requires betrayal." This brings you to write movingly in both *Refuge* and *Birds* about your choice not to bear children, one of the Mormon's two major expectations for its women, that and the injunction to keep a journal. You say simply, "Birth control gave me my voice." I am struck by how choice and voice are inseparably linked.

You go on to write about abortion and the "conversation we are not having," the conversation arising out of the deepest womanly knowledge of what it means to have a man enter her—the milk and blood mysteries. And you say, "If a man knew what a woman never forgets, he would love her differently." I imagine by "man" you mean something more than the personal, something that includes our religious, medical, governmental institutions. In writing about these "unspeakables," you purposely break taboos. As you say, "Transgression is transmission."

I suspect there is a price you pay for your subversiveness, your willingness to transgress, to live according to rules you consider morally binding, that betrays the ones you have been given. Have you ever felt like the price is too high?

TTW: No.

SPEAKING UP

PR: There is a story in *Birds* that made me hold my breath, while my heart raced and my legs twitched from a need to run. This is the story of when you lost your voice in the Sawtooth Wilderness in Idaho; your inability to tell anyone about a terrifying predator-prey encounter with the delusional man, Joseph, even when he reappeared again, even when your team was out in the field and came upon all the evidence of madness, even when Brooke, whom you did tell, urged you to tell the police, you still did not speak out. This loss of voice, and the million reasons for not speaking (your own complicity being merely one of them), is one I am sure many women can identify with. I think of the poet Marge Piercy's poem, "Unlearning to not speak." What is striking in your account is identifying your withheld voice as "the violence of your silence." You seem to imply that silence can act as an internalized perpetrator.

Can you bring this hard-won lesson to bear on other more everyday events we might encounter where not speaking up becomes an act of violence?

TTW: When one woman remains silent, other women get hurt. I have had to live with the violence of my own silence in not confronting this man, this event. And I am not alone. I have been so struck by the conversation that has emerged in response to Elliot Rogers' misogynous video prior to his killing six individuals in Santa Barbara, California, on May 24, 2013. Almost instantaneously, women began sharing their stories of misogyny on twitter using the hashtag #yesallwomen, and it has become an open forum voicing freely, honestly, what each woman has had to endure daily, privately and publicly. The tweeter feed has been endless, a sign of the epidemic of violence, be it verbal abuse, sexual abuse, assault, intimidation, or rape.

The Atlantic Monthly said, "The Twitter conversation around #YesallWomen is a sobering reminder of how commonly women are robbed of a sense of dignity and full personhood."

The most widely shared tweet has been this:

> "#yesallwomen She's someone's sister/mother/daughter/wife."

And here is another:

> "Every single woman you know has been harassed. And just as importantly, every single woman you don't know has been harassed. #YesAllWomen"

And this tweet posted by the writer Margaret Atwood:

> "Men are afraid that women will laugh at them. Women are afraid that men will kill them. #NotAllMen #YesAllWomen"

I followed with the sentence I led this answer with:

> "#yesallwomen Because when one woman remains silent, other women get hurt."

It was met with this response, among countless other hostile attacks not fit for publication:

> Al Fresco: "Because when one woman remains silent, other women get hurt." HA! Since when does a woman remain silent???

The question must be asked why this spontaneous action taken by women on social media has provoked such violent responses from men. What is so threatening about half of humanity simply asking for respect and kindness?

We are finally having these conversations on our college campuses and within our own families and communities. As a Provostial Scholar at Dartmouth College, I have witnessed women coeds finally demanding that actions of accountability be taken by the administration. The women are calling for an end to abusive behavior sanctioned in many fraternities and the creation of a safer environment. With sexual assault occurring at an alarming frequency at this Ivy League school, President Phil Hanlan has been quoted as saying, "Enough is enough."

The culture of violence in America and the underreporting of incidents such as my own is a violence internalized by women. We must come forward. We must shine a light on the darkness. It's why I shared my own story in *When Women Were Birds*. As harrowing as it was for me to write, sharing my experience has been a healing. It is a perfect example of how a secret becomes a burning shame. I had to speak out of my grief for the harm I may have caused to other victims by remaining silent. Who knows how many other women Joseph may have hurt? And even as I write this sentence, I still question myself, "Did this really happen?"

It happened.

Why do we keep doubting our own experience? And who benefits?

SPEAKING TRUTH TO POWER

PR: In *Birds* you write, "Democracy demands we speak and act outrageously." Your work in Washington as part of the governing board of the Wilderness Society was personally depressing and depleting and helped you realize your activism needed to be local.

Your descriptions of speaking out at public hearings on Utah Wilderness bills on behalf of the land you know and love are crushing. You are told, "I am sorry, Mrs. Williams, there is something about your voice I cannot hear." Your experience speaks to the loneliness of the solitary resister, the single voice.

Later, when testifying on behalf of America's Red Rock Wilderness Act, you and a group of other distinguished writers quickly mobilize to produce *Testimony: Writers of the West Speak on Behalf of Utah*

Wilderness. Senators read from it during a filibuster and *Testimony* became part of the Congressional Record. Bill Clinton said, "This little book made a difference." And from this, "one could believe in the collective power of a chorus of voices."

What forms do your activism take today? How do you discern when, where, and how to speak out?

TTW: My activism remains on the page and in community. I write a monthly column for *The Progressive.* Topics may range from tar sands development in Utah to fracking in Wyoming to a review of the Broadway play, *The Book of Mormon.* I love having an outlet in real time, where I can engage with an audience on a more informal basis.

A book is a slow and arduous process that withstands contemporary currents. An article or an opinion piece speak to the urgency of now.

I also write for *Orion Magazine.* In 2010, I wrote a long essay on the BP oil spill in the Gulf of Mexico. It was an act of witness. And I have learned as a writer that to bear witness is not a passive act but an act of conscience and consequence. "The Gulf Between Us" was one of the most difficult and rigorous stories I have ever written. In so many ways, it broke my heart. It wasn't the damage of what the oil spill wrought that undid me; it was the beauty that remained: the courage of the people who survived, their lost jobs, their ongoing illnesses from dispersants, and the white-beaded islands of birds, the rafts of golden rays, the pods of dolphins who watched from the edge of burning waters. This is what shattered me. And the lies, the ongoing lies of our government alongside British Petroleum and the complicity of both, is an exercise in the abuses of power.

In terms of political activism, the climate change movement is a dynamic one. I have participated in several actions in Washington, D.C. and the Interior West. This fall, on September 20 and 21, there will be a large demonstration in New York City in response to world leaders gathering at the United Nations to confront climate change, yet again. Citizens will gather to demand governments act responsibly on behalf of the planet. I am willing to commit civil disobedience if the opportunity arises. It is time to lay our bodies down.

Hope has little to do with where we find ourselves now. Faith is helpful, faith and stamina and joy. I take inspiration from this haiku:

> Insects on a bough
> floating downriver
> Still singing –
> —Issa

And I am still singing about wilderness. America's Redrock Wilderness Act remains a bill before Congress. We remain hopeful. Time is on our side, even as our governor in Utah is trying to figure out a way to sell off our public lands! Never mind that they belong to all Americans, never mind it is unconstitutional.

We are hoping President Obama will expand Canyonlands National Park and create a new national monument in Utah as a stay against all the oil and gas development adjacent to wilderness study areas. It would be a fitting presidential proclamation to mark Canyonlands fiftieth anniversary.

Alaska, like Utah, is an ongoing struggle with public lands protection. If Utah's political leaders want to develop every square inch of wilderness, Alaska's leaders have just threatened to "invade" the Arctic National Wildlife Refuge. You can't make these stories up. What I have learned as a wilderness advocate for close to four decades is that conservation is a generational stance. It is never over. It is an ongoing gesture of love in the name of social and environmental justice.

When I was younger, I used to wonder, "Am I an artist or an activist?" Now, I don't bother asking the question. I simply see my life as a life engaged. Each of us takes our turn in responding to an ethics of place.

Shadow and Sin

PR: You write, "My mother's sin was her secret." There is a photograph of your mother in *Birds*. It is piercing, in the same way the French theorist, Roland Barth, speaks of in *Camera Lucida: Reflections on Photography*. He, too, was obsessed with a photograph of his long dead mother and the recurrent feeling of loss he experienced whenever he looked at it. He called a certain accidental detail in a photographic image "that pricks, bruises me," the *punctum*. For me, your mother's headscarf holding back her hair is that transfixing detail. You describe the "lock of hair that has escaped confinement, creating a curl on her forehead" which brings to mind the children's rhyme, "There was a little girl, who had a little curl . . .."

Having read your descriptions of your mother's love for Nordstrom's, the make-up counter, the blue satin robe with stars, the red dress for her last Christmas, I wonder why, of all the many photographs you probably had to choose from, this was the one you decided upon?

TTW: I chose this particular photograph of my mother because it embodies her strength. She is looking directly at the camera. There is nothing posed about it. She is standing in the place she loved most, the Tetons. There is a breeze. You see her fierce beauty, raw and exposed. You feel the depth of her character in that instant captured by the Polaroid.

SURVIVAL

PR: You have said, "Beauty is not an option. It is a strategy for survival." *When Women Were Birds* is an argument for the beauty and survival of books; the size, the way it fits in the hand, the deckle-edged paper, the opening page with a signature line, "This journal belongs to ————," the blank pages, the feathery cover, make the book itself a work of art.

How much say did you have over the book's design?

TTW: The physical beauty of a book matters to me. People do judge a book by its cover. And in the hardback edition of *When Women Were Birds*, I had a great deal of input in its design. A friend of mine who is a book artist, Mary Toscano, hand painted the feathered end papers that we hoped could frame the book. Everyone at Farrar, Straus & Giroux loved the idea. This is where we began our design discussion. One of the great pleasures of working with Farrar, Straus & Giroux is that it feels like a family. My wonderful editor, Sarah Crichton, brought us all to the table. Together, we worked closely with the cover designer, Rodrigo Corral, and the interior designer of the book, Abby Kagan. We had many conversations and tried multiple cover ideas until we all agreed that we had the right one, beautiful and evocative, like my mother's journals.

The bird in the margin that becomes a bird in flight when the pages are flipped was a gift!

It should also be noted that Farrar, Straus & Giroux took a risk in placing twelve empty, white pages in the body of the book. I wanted to give the reader the same physical sensation that I had experienced when discovering all of my mother's journals were blank. This was important to me, and they honored my request.

But in terms of the paperback edition published by Picador Books in 2013 that you refer to in your question, it was all a glorious surprise. I remember seeing the design for the first time—I was stunned by its beauty and the care in which each detail was rendered from the French fold binding to the deckle-edged paper to the feather motif they used on its cover. I loved it and, honestly, it was the first time in my history of publishing fourteen books that I did not have one suggestion, only praise. And when I held the book in my hands for the first time, it felt more like a prayer book than my story. I am so grateful that the Picador team understood what the book not only could be, but had to become—an object of beauty to be cherished and shared.

PR: A final quote from Hélène Cixous: "To fly/steal is woman's gesture, to steal into language to make it fly." This is what your work feels like to me, stealing and soaring, the work of a trickster Raven that brings light to a darkened world. Thank you.

TTW: Thank you, Patricia. My gratitude to both you and Nancy. This has been an extraordinary experience to think through these soulful questions with you and the readers of *Spring Journal*. I am humbled. This is especially meaningful to me because Mimi read *Spring Journal* religiously, underlining each page with her red pen.

I have some of her worn copies. We both revered James Hillman and had the great pleasure of meeting him. His wisdom remains: "*The moment the angel enters a life it enters an environment.*" We are ecological from day one. With our hands on the Earth, may we remember.

Robin van Löben Sels, Ph. D., is a Jungian analyst trained in Zürich and New York. Presently affiliated with the Inter-Regional Society of Jungian Analysts, she lives and practices in the Albuquerque-Santa Fe area of New Mexico. She has published poetry in many journals, including *Quadrant* and *Psychological Perspectives*, as well as in the book, *Wanting a Country for this Weather* (2003). Her psychological writings include *A Dream in the World: Poetics of Soul in Two Women, Modern and Medieval* (2003) as well as several articles in *Spring*.

GENESIS

Together we begin alone.
We are the sources of our dreams.
We learn of time by living
in time's remembering stream.

Caught in long delight, we muse
over our own reflection.
When the dry bed cracks like a map, we fall,
each in her own direction.

Time is the element we shared,
time, and the luminous fantasy
of exile. Now our wandering minds
must seek love's sanctuary.

We gather scars. Somehow we grow
with loss. We root like trees.
If we can simplify our lives
then we may come to see

the winding spirit's dance with flesh,
defining metaphor.
And move again. And move as we
have never moved before.

Things are so seldom what they seem.
The mind's eye moves by night.
A desert opens onto God.
Sing light. Sing light. Sing light.

Robin van Löben Sels

In this essay, poet and nature writer Holly Hughes uses a line from Terry Tempest Williams' *When Women Were Birds: Fifty-four Variations on Voice*—"solitude is a place"—to explore memories of her own mother, how she found her voice through activism, and how those memories help sustain her own environmental writing and activism. Along the way, she shows how birds have, for her, served as bearers of messages we need to heed and that solitude is a place we need to visit often so we might better hear their quiet voices, too.

WOMEN, VOICE, BIRDS, AND PLACE

HOLLY J. HUGHES

"Solitude is a place," writes Terry Tempest Williams in *When Women Were Birds: Fifty-four Variations on Voice.*[1] I could begin with just about any line in her powerful, kaleidoscopic collection, but today I opened to this page and will trust serendipity. Trust her voice to follow, like a raven, across the blank page.

Terry Tempest Williams' mother gave her daughter her blank journals, as well as her love of birds and the natural world. My mother, too, gave me her love of words, books, birds, and place. One of my most vivid childhood memories is watching red cardinals spar for sunflower seeds at the feeder just outside the frost-etched kitchen window, the feeder my father refilled no matter how deep the snow drifts in our Minnesota yard.

Though my mother passed along her love of place—along with the need to preserve it—it's taken me much of my adult life to learn that a place for solitude is worth seeking and preserving, too. Given the fast pace of our lives, we need to visit it often, whether carving out time for writing or reflection in a chockfull day so that we can hear our own voice or spending time in the natural world where we can hear the voices of all the creatures with whom we share the earth. But all this came later. Let's return to my mother.

Holly J. Hughes, M.F.A., is the author of *Sailing by Ravens*, co-author of *The Pen and The Bell: Mindful Writing in a Busy World,* and editor of the award-winning anthology, *Beyond Forgetting: Poetry and Prose about Alzheimer's Disease.* She has taught writing at Edmonds Community College outside of Seattle, Washington for more than twenty-five years as well as at regional conferences and workshops. Her poems and essays have been published in a variety of literary magazines and anthologies and have been nominated for a Pushcart Prize. Her website is www.hollyjhughes.com.

Here's another memory: I'm looking out the living room window to where my mother is standing across the street, her arms flung out against the elm she's determined to protect. Nearby, the bulldozers wait, engines idling and the chain saws are revving up. She's wearing a red cardigan sweater and blue jeans, her figure slight before the massive elm, the bulldozers. Behind her, a line of elms extends along the boulevard. That day she won. The bulldozers left, the elms stood, only to be taken down by Dutch elm disease years later.

We grew up under that sheltering canopy of leafy boughs she saved. This was the late 50s, which makes her an early tree hugger, taking that position before the term was used. She was just doing what she knew in her heart to be right. She didn't respond to the graphs and tables charting the economic argument for development. Instead she asked, *Where will the birds go without their home?*

I was too young to carry more than this image. I didn't know the details, the long meetings she attended, the conservationist group she organized to prevent a hotel from being built in a fragile wetlands area that lined the lakefront. But I've carried this image of her for fifty years, this image that sustains me.

My mother wasn't a natural activist, the kind of person who would choose to rebel against developers in a quiet Midwestern town. She was both by temperament and fate a follower of social norms, the wife of a doctor, whose role in that decade was carefully circumscribed: raise four daughters, attend Hospital Auxiliary events, host Portia Club, volunteer in the community, take painting and piano lessons.

Looking back now, I see mostly how she didn't trust her voice. Like so many women of her generation, she didn't have outlets for her creativity, her love of nature, beauty, and the arts, other than to be the best mother and wife she could be. She poured her heart into raising her daughters, packing sack lunches and having dinner ready each night at 6 p.m. But at what price?

That stirs another memory: my mother is pounding out the notes of *Exodus* on the piano. Whenever we heard that familiar progression of bass chords we knew we had to tread lightly; mom was in "one of her moods." Who can blame her for turning to music to make her exodus from a life that, while it appeared perfect on the surface, constrained her creative spirit? Years later, after we'd all moved out, she at last studied

French and philosophy at the local state college, took gourmet cooking classes, and opened a coffee and chocolate shop. This proved to be a perfect outlet for her creativity, while we delighted in the steady supply of chocolate truffles.

She did eventually find her voice and used it, becoming the first woman to chair the board of the YMCA camp in northern Minnesota that we all attended as kids, then returned to as counselors. Here's where she'd passed on her love of nature to her four daughters. Each summer, we'd load our green barge of a station wagon with musty, flannel roll-up sleeping bags, hiking boots, binoculars, fishing poles, and bug spray and head to northern Minnesota to the shores of Little Boy Lake for family camp. There, we all fell under the spell of the scent of dry pine needles in the sun, the sight of Little Boy Lake glittering out the small-paned windows of the dining hall, the resonant singing after meals. We returned each summer until we were old enough to attend as campers, then counselors, then sailing directors or program directors. We still return whenever we can.

Here's where birds come in: I'm in the bow of a Grumman canoe with my sister, paddling through tall green reeds and cat tails as the sun sinks into Little Boy Lake, spreading streaks of rose across the late August sky. We're paddling without speaking when we come upon a great blue heron fishing in the shallows. We all freeze, and I'm close enough to see the gleam in his ball-bearing eye—his seems to peer right into mine—before he lifts his enormous wings, flaps once, twice, and rises ponderously into the mauve sky. That moment changed me. That moment of communion with another creature, that eye contact where I felt seen, witnessed, in a way I'd not yet felt in the world of humans. Jane Hirshfield ends her poem "Three Foxes by the Edge of the Field at Twilight" with these lines that describe such a moment: "And yet among the trees something has changed./ Something looks back from the trees,/and knows me for who I am."[2]

When we're so young—I might have been eight or nine—we don't yet know who we are; we can only trust that we'll eventually find out. What I knew is that I felt more alive in that moment than I'd ever felt, and I wanted to feel alive. That chance encounter with a great blue heron inspired a life-long pursuit of such moments, and a gratitude to birds for bearing the message.

For the next decade, I spent summer days roaming the oak and maple studded hills of the Mississippi River Valley with my dog for company. When I was older, I spent summer days paddling across the blue lakes of the Quetico following the haunting call of the loon, which came to epitomize all that I loved about the wild country of northern Minnesota.

But eventually, all those good instincts were lost to the baffling complexities of navigating relationships, making one's way in the world. It was years before I found them again, and it took a dying, oil-soaked loon in Alaska to remind me of the girl I'd once trusted, the girl I lost to growing up, marriage, and a fishing adventure in Alaska that veered off course.

After my marriage ended, I returned to graduate school in English, and went to work writing catalog copy for Eddie Bauer. This worked for a few years, until, on March 25, 1989, the *Exxon Valdez* fetched up on Bligh Reef, disgorging its oily black cargo into Prince William Sound, where I'd once spent a season waiting for herring to spawn, walking the beaches of Naked Island, then returned to run a charter boat the following summer. I knew this place intimately. We'd walked these rocky beaches, collected mussels for dinner, set and checked crab pots. I'd found a sleeping sea otter, tied to a strand of bull kelp, learned how to spot seals on ice floes; I'd been stunned into silence by the *whoosh* of a pod of orcas, surfacing just feet from our skiff, then followed them down the channel, their spray as iridescent as a promise.

For two months I went through the motions of graduate school and work, watched the nightly news reports, my heart shattered and lying in pieces along that rocky coastline I knew and loved. Finally, I did what I needed to do: quit my job and bought a ticket to Alaska to work on the oil spill. I didn't know what I'd do, only that I needed to be there to witness, to grieve, to do whatever I could, whether it was scrubbing oil from rocks or rescuing sea birds. Because I had a Coast Guard license to run boats up to one hundred tons, I found a job running the medic boat. We ran the medic wherever he was needed, monitoring Channel 16 for emergencies. Since emergencies were sporadic, it quickly became evident that the greater need was to pick up oiled sea otters and seabirds and run them to the Sealife Rescue Center in Seward where we hoped they might be saved.

So many images flood back, but this one sticks. We were trudging up an oil-soaked beach on Naked Island when we came upon a loon mired in the oily muck. Upon seeing us, it tried to fly but couldn't, its wings weighed down by the sludge. It staggered a few steps, collapsed again. We didn't want to cause more distress, so we let it rest, then tiptoed closer with our net. Hearing us, it turned, its red eye bright amidst the tarry black goo that coated its feathers, its lovely white throat streaked with oil. I remembered the haunting call of the loon that had come to epitomize wilderness that I'd fallen in love with so many years ago in the wild Minnesota lake country. This loon wasn't able to call or laugh, and its red eye bore right into mine. *Do something*, it said.

I've spent many years trying to heed that command. For the last twenty-five years, where I teach at a community college in Washington State, I've made natural history essays the focus of my English classes. I've taken students on field trips to old growth forests, asked them to participate in environmental restoration projects, organized my colleagues to incorporate sustainability into the mission statement, and now serve as co-chair of the Sustainability Council. I'm heartened to see the next generation responding. We now have a student-led Green Team, composting in the cafeteria, a community garden, a hive of bees, a windmill and solar panels, and are working on banning plastic water bottles from the campus.

It never feels like enough, though, given the rising rates of extinctions, the scale and pace of climate change. I do my best to make choices to live lightly—turn off lights, take short showers, ride the bus —to reduce my footprint, but most days they seem like futile gestures, like rearranging the deck chairs on the *Titanic*. Like all of us, I fail as often as I succeed, but I carry that image of my mother, thin arms flung out to protect the elm tree she loved, the elm she could not bear to see cut down. It was the specific tree, the specific birds she knew how to care about. As we face daunting, formidable challenges to the world we love, the world we depend upon, it's easy to feel dispirited, overwhelmed by the magnitude of the challenge, so I keep coming back to this image of my mother, to that single oiled loon with its heart-rending plea.

My mother may not have always trusted her own voice, but she knew to trust the trees, the birds, and the natural world she loved. It's taken me decades to learn to trust my voice and it's happened slowly, incrementally, as my poems, essays, and books take flight, make their way out into the world. For me, trusting my voice happened when I began to focus on what words could offer, how they might be of service to the people and places I care deeply about.

We're given a voice so we can speak for those who can't—this lesson I learned from my mother so many years ago. She never said this in words, but she said it with every fiber in her being. Even when she suffered from Alzheimer's disease and couldn't remember the names of her four daughters, she still felt connected to the birds and trees she loved. We could count on them to lift her out of the fog; even just for moment we'd see her blue eyes light up when she glimpsed the red flash of a cardinal at the feeder.

Yes, *solitude is a place*, a place we can and must visit often if we're to hear the quiet voices. Not only our own quiet voices—too often lost in the cacophony of our frenetic lives—but the voices of the birds and other beings with whom we're blessed to share this planet, the voices that we can't hear unless we slow down, create space and quiet for them. Let us slow down, listen hard for their voices.

Then for our mothers, for the birds, for the trees, for all who can't speak, let us raise our voices. Let us *do something*, whatever we can, while we can.

NOTES

1. Terry Tempest Williams, *When Women Were Birds: Fifty-four Variations on Voice* (New York: Picador, 2012), p. 28.

2. Jane Hirshfield, "Three Foxes by the Edge of the Field at Twilight," in *The Lives of the Heart* (New York: HarperCollins, 1997).

In the truest fairy tales, magic and beauty are entwined in a merciless embrace, giving great rewards but exacting great costs. As she explores Terry Tempest Williams' idea of how each voice belongs to place, Leigh Melander finds both belonging and longing and a deep sense of voice in her enchanted discovery of home in the dragon-breath-wrapped mountains of the Catskills.

DRAGON FIRE:
FINDING VOICE IN THE CATSKILL MOUNTAINS

LEIGH MELANDER

"They say these mountains are blue
But in the fading spring evening they
Are humming songs of Americana and majesty
To themselves (accompanied by the ever-present black birds)
Arcing purple, endlessly along the valley, farther than I can see.
They draw me as well, wanting to ride them like earthen purple waves
All the way to the heart of it
And my heart breaks, just a little, because I don't know how
So I sing my own song with them and watch them fade into blue then black
At the end of a perfectly empty Sunday
And I am content."

—Leigh Melander, unpublished, 2013

"Each voice belongs to a place."
—Terry Tempest Williams, *When Women Were Birds:
Fifty-four Variations on Voice*

O n an early summer morning, when the greens are countless and the blue sky promises to never betray me and disappear into winter gray, I think about where I have landed. I think about land itself, the word emerging out of proto-Germanic efforts to

Leigh Melander, Ph.D., works in a variety of creative disciplines and has a doctorate in Cultural Mythology with an emphasis in Depth Psychology from Pacifica Graduate Institute. She has performed internationally in theater, music, and mask and puppetry work; explored the arts as a force for creative change and conflict resolution around the country; spent twenty years helping organizations dream themselves forward and share their visions with the world, and is a member of the Joseph Campbell Foundation Board of Directors. She and her husband opened Spillian: A Place to Revel in the Catskills in October, 2013, and she is currently launching an e-book publishing company, Meandering Press.

define a definite home or territory…we still feel ownership of land, at least in Western European culture. I am home. I own this land. And am owned by it.

I have lived in several places in my life, all beautiful, ranging from my birthplace in the regular rich green mountains of Central Pennsylvania, the outer reaches of the sky-sand-sea blurred beauty at the tip of Cape Cod, the manic, black-clad self-perfection of New York City's West Village, to the sun-sculpted golden valleys of Southern California. I have loved them all, and found a bit of myself, found a bit more courage to sing my song just a bit louder, in each place.

But I have yearned, always, for something that felt beyond reach. The Welsh speak of *hireath*[1]—a concept loosely translated to a longing for home, for the past, for what came before us, intertwined with a sense of loss and desire for belonging. Mnemosyne lives in this word, of course, offering her nosegay of archetypal nostalgia, sorrow, and hope. I have lived infused with this longing since childhood, sometimes sweet, sometimes so raw it brings me to my knees in wanting. Each place I have lived has felt to be not quite enough, the *hireath* edging me onwards to the next place, the next adventure, the next voice, hoping that I would start to fill up, and feel my body resonate with voice so strong that it feels enough, and I feel as if I am enough within it. I have had big dreams, but not always the courage to dream them forward. I have sung, but never quite as loudly as I might.

Finally, fifty years in, the *hireath* I feel is not for the next landing place, hard or soft, but for the land I live in and the land that I create on. And the land that simultaneously creates me. The longing unfurls along the ridgelines around me, as in the poem above, but the here—the deep sense of here, in a reflected and so reversed echo of Gertrude Stein's "there is no there, there"[2]—the here, here is so present, so real, and so, deeply, finally right. When I am homesick, it is most often, now, when I am home, and I simply want to go further in, to feel and breathe this land more than I am. I am no longer *vagus*. I am home. It is me.

And with being home, my voice has begun to unfurl as well, deeper and richer and more powerful than I had thought possible. I am struck by the rightness of this and by the elemental dance between myself in all of my certainties and fears, pains, and joys and those alive in this landscape. This scape I own and that owns me is liminal, other, powerful, and contradictory. I dream myself in these ways and see myself in the land as I see my own power, contradictions, and liminal otherness. These have always been a part of me. For the first time, they are a source of comfort and certainty rather than fear.

I LIVE IN THE CATSKILLS.

For some people, the Catskills are a half-forgotten, flippantly racist joke of the Borscht Belt, glory days gone and just a bit suspect. Cheap. Smelling slightly of booze, matzah, and just this side of off-color. But what lies here is so much deeper, so much more real than one-liners and a rim shot.

This land is beautiful and hardscrabble. Victories are hard-won here, and loss is everywhere. What were once impenetrable ancient hemlock forests, so heavily wooded with grand trees that local legends trap great bucks in groves, their antler spans wider than the space between the trees, became open landscape when the tanners clear-cut the hemlock to turn hides into leather. The scope of this change is hard to imagine now as the forests have returned, but old growth forests fell en masse; one tannery, in its twenty-year history, devoured an estimated 400,000 trees.[3] Farmers arrived, Scotch Irish, mostly, following the cleared land, and found a place of beauty and hardship, and soil so rocky that locals here still talk of Delaware County being the place you find "two rocks for every dirt."[4]

I am "other" here in this land of otherness, at least as far as the locals are concerned. In spite of being from the mountains just a day south of these, I am a "flatlander," forever consigned to a certain distaste and distrust by many of the people who have lived this land for the last couple hundred years. This is a time-honored tradition of despising those who come from the city, the City—New York City is "the" city here, always. It is both marketplace and despot up here, in this land of mountains and water, for we are in the New York City watershed, and are reminded often, sometimes with brutal clarity, that the City, with its small-country-sized organization, can decide our fates. Water flows from the reservoir below my house into the taps of thirsty New Yorkers without filtration. Remarkable, really, to think that only a couple of hours north of Manhattan the water still runs so clear that it can arrive without interference in the homes of almost eight and a half million people.

This lurking presence of the overlord is woven into the mythologies of place here. The Scotch-Irish arrived in this wild country, escaping the brutality of British power. I am in awe of their fortitude, as this place is not easy to live in with most (if you can live without good cell phone coverage and such) of the conveniences and comforts of life in the 21st century. These farmers began to hack out a living on small farms, with poor soil, running cattle and sheep and enduring a dramatically shorter growing season than just fifty miles south of the mountain range. After fighting for independence in the Revolutionary War, they ironically found themselves trapped into living as lifetime tenant farmers on small slices of a two-million-acre land patent, granted in 1708 by Queen Anne to a group of Americans who saw this land as the birth of a new aristocratic empire.5 They had not yet escaped the overlords. In the first half of the 19th century, they erupted in rage as rents began to rise and cattle was seized and sold at auction to pay back rent, destroying lives. A little-known revolution was fought here, the Anti-Rent Wars, where farmers rose up in a guerrilla war against the landowners and their agents, writing scathing songs and poetry about them. Ultimately, calling themselves Calico Indians as they draped themselves in outlandish calico costumes with sheepskin masks, they mirrored the warfare of the disenfranchised the world over, engaging in small skirmishes with the law until the violence exploded in the death of the local sheriff. He was shot, in all likelihood accidentally, in a chaotic confrontation at a forced cattle auction on a small farm on the edge of Andes, the town where I live. Eventually, with an 11th hour sentence commutation from an incoming governor, the farmers who had been rounded up were released and the patents vacated. For a moment, the land was owned clearly, old wounds no longer festering. However, just a decade or two later, not long after the Civil War, the next set of overlords arrived, reaching, this time, for water. NewYork City was thirsty, and arrived to roll through the landscape, flooding valleys and claiming and buying land as it wished. The wounds have not healed.

So, while I am home, I am a newcomer, always a flatlander through the eyes of the next generation of Calico Indians, who live here and roll through the next generation of resentment about being perennially on the underside of any struggle. I live in a house built by a founding family of one of the drowned towns of the Pepacton Reservoir (a whisper-down-the-alley version of the pre-European Native Americans who lived here), and can look down on placid waters and feel an echo of people who were moved from the place they'd lived for two hundred years. Our farm sold at the same time, to a man who came to organize labor and save lives of men digging tunnels, a brilliant iconoclast organic farmer in the era of enchantment with chemistry. I live in the house of an outsider, but one who captured the essence of the brilliantly stubborn resistance of the people here. My neighbors, good friends all, are all flatlanders as well, choosing to come to this place of magic and pain, beauty and exacting tolls, because they are seeking something real. And I seek with them.

This contradiction, this insider/outsider and power/powerless nexus, is one that I have worked and lived within throughout my life. It is always close to the surface. I echo with the struggles in finding/losing/wielding power and finding a creative, tenacious, contrary resistance to being told I cannot own my life fully. I own my life. My life owns me. I fight the same battles with empowered, larger-than-life forces that the farmers in this land fight; mine are with societal expectations of success, of what good girls should do, of worth. I am fed by the sheer absurdity of the fight of people to keep their poor soil because it is theirs. I love the value that is given to land we own and that owns us, and this rolls outward into meaning in many facets of my life.

And I stand fairly comfortable in the dichotomies of belonging and not belonging in the community. There is a part of me that feels most comfortable when I am on the edges of things—of communities, of groups, of built-up places. I chose to land not in the bucolic hamlet of Andes, where neighbors breathe in concert with neighbors in a sometimes contentious but always self-aware world of small town life, but as far out into the mountains as I could go (and talk my husband into joining me). I told him, as we left Californian suburbia, that I wanted to live somewhere that I did not need to see, hear, taste, smell, or touch my neighbors. And then, once I had found this place, tucked into folds of the mountains, I began the hunt for the place I did want to see people, seeking the place where I could challenge people to imagine past what they thought they were bound by, bringing people together. I could craft community here—and then step out when I wished, held by the quiet of my mountainside where the noisiest neighbors are the spring peepers in the farm pond. Here in my little valley with my old farmhouse I can be real, privately. And on the mountain where the center we have bought where I am making my next generation of art, I can seek to find realness in community.

DANGEROUS BEAUTY

Realness matters here. There is no gentling of 21st century plastic ease and comfort, fluid and flexible-seeming until it unveils itself as a new kind of tyrant to our stuff, our highways, our habits. These are real mountains, forested, with narrow valleys the early Dutch settlers called cloves, some so deep and dark they rarely see sun. Water is everywhere here and shapes the lives here as starkly and powerfully as it has shaped these mountains. The Catskills are not like most mountain ranges in this country. They are not the rippling muscle of rock pushed up by weight-lifting glaciers, neatly organized, secure in their arrangement, but instead, they are what was left behind when the water literally sculpted their form like Michelangelo shaped marble. This land was once an early seabed, and the cloves were eaten away by melting glaciers, water finding the veins of silt and gravel moved more easily, and cutting quicksilver rivers deeper and deeper until they'd dug themselves down to the bottom of the mountain.

As a result, the Catskills are a chaotic mountain range, not the aligned undulating ridge and valley fingers of the mountains of my childhood, but instead a place where right becomes left and north, south in a matter of moments. I have been lost here more often in four years of living here than I have anywhere/anytime in my life. This is a moment of that contradictory magic that pleases me—I am found in the grace here that does, in fact amaze me, even as I am lost.

These mountains offer the dangerous beauty of true fairy tales, inviting you to fall in love with flower-clad hawthorn trees standing guard of stone rings that seem like they just might have been placed by some hand, rather than weather. They invite you to look more closely, and fold themselves into secrets and then, around a corner, both themselves open into huge views…miles of blue ridge lines inviting you to ride them. They also will kill you easily. There is little mercy in this death-dancing beauty, and risks are real if you are careless, even just a short couple of hours from the most citified city in the world. There are moments when the mountains themselves feel like predators, waiting for your wariness to drop so they can freeze you, flood you, lose you down a ravine. Death lives in the heavy forest, waiting, hunting.

The people here before the waves of European settlers began in the 17th century, the "men of men" Lenni Lenape lived all around these mountains, but never within. They were too unforgiving for men, even original, and instead became the land—owned by and owning—the Manitou. Again, that contradiction: the Manitou, the life force breathing through all things lived in the place that was too easily about death for the original people. It was too grand, too magical, and became the place where life itself lived, because it could balance the fierceness of the mountains with its own. The grand gray escarpment of rock slamming up from the gentle Hudson Valley is still called The Great Wall of Manitou. The life force morphed for Native-warned Europeans into a terrifying being in the forest primordial, as far from Eden as you could imagine.

HIC SUNT DRACONES.

Legend has it that early mapmakers would write this on hand-drawn maps at the end of their knowledge of the world.[6] Here are dragons. What lies beyond what we know must be monster. Other. Frightening. Fierce.

Hic sunt dracones in the Catskills. This land is alive with dragon energy, with misty breath curling between mountains along divine creeks. Washington Irving wrote of the glorious thunder-blown storms in these mountains booming with the sound of Catskill gnomes playing games of ninepins. I think, in that flash of fire against world-turned silver in rain, those are the thunder strikes of dragons. Burning. Crashing the world open in bright light, fire tongues reaching to lick the mountains clean. I walk the road from my house through the forest and stop counting when I have measured 200 red efts, young salamanders bright orange as if they were mythic tenders and beings of fire. They are, in my imagination, young dragons, and I amuse myself while walking by conjuring images of their finishing school.

Hic sunt dracones in my bedroom. One of the first moments that this land began to inhabit me happened the first winter I was here. I came with dogs and cats and horses from easy California, alone without my husband as he returned to sell our house. Within weeks, I began to dream of dragons. Fierce. Beautiful. Female. Divinely terrifying. I don't generally remember my dreams, and have an outsider's cynical superiority about the minute dissection of dreams by fellow dreamers. I don't particularly want to hear about other people's dreams. Maybe it's simply jealousy. But here, in the silent nights—so quiet that if a single car passes on the road down the hill from us, we all awaken, knowing something has moved the air and changed the night—here, I began to dream with such ferocity. One morning I woke up and laid still, eyes tightly shut, because I knew—KNEW—that if I opened my eyes too quickly, before morning had completely landed, I would look down and see scales and talons instead of skin-clad hands.

This land began almost immediately to beat on me, to fire me, heat me, tempering me into something fierce, fair, proto-woman, long before Evian guilt and despair and servitude. Daimon-gripped, I newly began to see Lilith, Kali, and my own sense of fire as right and righteous. *Hic sunt dracones.*

EXTRAORDINARY FIRE

I saw—and see, still, the process as it happens, as it is ongoing. I find myself no longer afraid to do anything—I have spent much of my life lovingly entwined with a belief that I should not be "too." I have spent years being "too." Too fast. Too loud. Too irreverent. Too intellectual. Too independent. And I ate my own fire to avoid burning those around me, to the point where my body began to turn on itself, a digestive fire burning inward, making me chronically ill and weak. I began to understand the enormity of this fire after awakening from another infrequently remembered dream two decades earlier. Cast off by a group of not-quite friends, small and meek and flicked aside until I rose up in a conscious flame not even of rage—just pure fire power— and burnt them all like a scene in a Spielberg Saturday matinee. In that moment, I began first to understand the dragon existed, but she still remained, most often, locked in and silent. She would leak out occasionally, usually at what I felt were inopportune moments (though in retrospect I am not sure if there ever would have been an opportune one), and I neither trusted her force or my ability to contain her, so I did everything I could to keep her quiet as an overly trained pet.

Here, in this place, with the mist curling around my edges as it winds around mountains, fire comes forward, opening and burning brightly. The dragon settles in me and I in her. I become the dragon, and birther of dragons. I am no longer afraid. And in that moment, I am invited to remember, almost daily, that I am a fire creator, and that fire begets fire. So I have finally found the audacity to create a place where I can play with others and burn open paths in their psyches and synapses to imagine big, fierce, fair.

This fire enabled me to burn my way through seemingly impossible barriers to get the first part done—finding, and coming to own and be owned by the land and building where we could make this. I revel in this place and what it brings me, a connection to my mother and her love of history in a house that is storied remnant of the Belle Epoque. The builders themselves, Jewish industrial age barons, were an extraordinary set of contradictory insider/outsider and powerful/ powerless. They landed here in this unlikely place because they chose to create their own world rather than slap up against the brittle stupidity of anti-Semitic bigotry that was rolling through the United States at the end of the 19th century. They created a wooded empire, gracious, creative, looking outwards and inwards, savoring the deep summer of these mountains even as they brought art, life, and intellectual sophistication to their rusticating.

Here, singing in these mountains, helping others to find their singing voices, I am finding my own. My dragons breathe musically, and I find that there are not enough hours in the day, enough fingers on my hands, enough moments to share words to get everything that is burbling up in me, clamoring to be shared. And as I walk back out into the larger world, I am repeatedly surprised by how I am seen— for the first time in my life, walking with gravitas, carrying with me the weightiness and worth of making this place, owning this land, and being owned by it. I am, suddenly, seen as having substance. The fire burns deep now, and is no longer just a bright, quick flame easy to miss in brilliant sunlight.

It has not come without costs. I am not sure that anything of real value ever does. In my tempering, I can be hard, flashing like a jewel, but able to cut glass. I do not own the dragon, she is not tame, and she can burn when I least expect it, sometimes me, sometimes the people around me. For the first time in my life, I must reach to be kind first. I am learning, though, that mercy without mercilessness is off balance, that this dance of contradictions between creating and destroying, owning and being owned, belonging and not belonging is what my life force is made of, and my desires for a comfortable existence fade in the exquisite burning delight of casting off fear and simply making.

This is the *genius loci* here. Making does not come from ease. It comes from an unexpected alliance of beauty and struggle, it sits in the liminal places of our interiors, as well as a wild landscape that calls us forth. And I am grateful.

NOTES

1. Pamela Petro, "Dreaming in Welsh," *The Paris Review*, September 28, 2012. Accessed May 15, 2014 at http://www.theparisreview.org/blog/2012/09/18/dreaming-in-welsh/.

2. Gertrude Stein, *Everybody's Autobiography* (New York: Cooper Square Publishers, 1971), p. 289.

3. Hugh O. Canham, "Hemlock and Hide: The Tanbark History in Old New York," Summer 2011. Accessed May 26, 2014 at http://northernwoodlands.org/articles/article/hemlock-and-hide-the-tanbark-industry-in-old-new-york.

4. Julia Reischel, "Farming Stamford in 1950: These Hills are Not Barren," *The Watershed Post*, March 11, 2011. Accessed on May 28, 2014 at http://www.watershedpost.com/2011/farming-stamford-1950-these-hills-are-not-barren.

5. Alf Evers, "The Livingston Presence in the Great or Hardenburgh Patent," *The Hudson Valley Regional Review*, March 1988, Volume 5, Number 1 Accessed May 29 at http://www.hudsonrivervalley.org/review/pdfs/hvrr_5pt1_evers.pdf.

6. Erin C. Blake, "Where Be *'Here be Dragons?,'*" MapHist: The Forum on the History of Maps, April, 1999. Accessed May 17, 2014 at http://www.maphist.nl/extra/herebedragons.html.

In her essay, Marlene Schiwy invokes the 15th century Spanish tradition of *deep song* to explore her maternal legacy. She endeavors to *sing* the untold depths of sorrow and longing in her motherline throughout generations of war, emigration, and ill health, thereby restor[y]ing and envoicing these beloved liminal presences. Woven into the account of her mothers and grandmothers lives are the larger silence of the feminine voice in culture, and Marlene's own lifelong quest to come into voice.

Deep Song:
Envoicing the Motherline

MARLENE A. SCHIWY

For Lilli, Pauline, and Olga

"One need not write in order to have a voice.
A mother speaks to her children through the generations."
—Terry Tempest Williams, *When Women Were Birds:*
Fifty-four Variations on Voice

"In the language I speak, the mother tongue resonates, tongue
of my mother, less language than music, less syntax than song of
words…. My German mother in my mouth, in my larynx,
rhythms me."
—Hélène Cixous, *"Coming to Writing" and Other Essays*

I.

While reading about the history of the Roma people several
years ago, I discovered the age-old Spanish tradition of *cante
jondo,* or *deep song.* With roots in the ancient musical
traditions of India, deep song began among persecuted peoples who
fled into the mountains during the Spanish Inquisition in the 15th
century, blending elements of Arabic, Sephardic, Byzantine, and Gypsy

Marlene A. Schiwy, Ph.D., is a Body Soul Writing instructor and Jungian counselor
in Vancouver, Canada. A former professor of literature and women's studies at the City
University of New York, she is the author of *A Voice of Her Own* (1996) and *Simple Days*
(2002). Her series of filmed interviews, *Marion Woodman and the Conscious Feminine,*
was recently released and her current work-in-progress focuses on her lifelong relationship
with the archetype of the gypsy. Marlene studied at the International School of Analytical
Psychology in Zürich (ISAPZURICH) and conducts Jungian-oriented workshops and
retreats, as well as an expressive arts program for women called *Body Soul Sundays.* Her
website is www.marleneschiwy.com.

music with the native folk songs of the region. Federico García Lorca described it as "imbued with the mysterious color of primordial ages," as "a stammer, a wavering emission of the voice that makes the tightly closed flowers of the semi-tones blossom into a thousand petals."[1]

Deep song is archetypal music, a timeless, lyrical channel for the expression of sorrow, loss, and love. Though there are countless styles, each with its own mood, theme, and form, they all share a primal power and emotiveness that evoke both the personal dimension and our collective human condition, and as Lorca writes, "The true poems of deep song belong to no one—they float in the wind like golden thistledown, and each generation dresses them in a different color and passes them on to the next."[2]

The first time I came across a reference to deep song I was riveted, as if it had come to me in a dream. For weeks I spun fantasies of an unknown, mysterious music that encompassed the depths of human experience and invoked the souls of the ancestors. I wondered what my own deep song would be. Would it echo the dark suffering of past generations forced to flee across the ever-shifting borders of Central Europe in search of menial work and food, of families ravaged by endless wars, and parents who had lost one child after another to starvation and disease? Would its cadence and melody carry the stifled weeping of my grandmothers, and their mothers and grandmothers?

DEEP SONG, IN THREE STANZAS

Persephone, dark sister of my soul. You, whom I love and fear, who come to me as wise woman and witch, and show me my own endarkenment more clearly than I dare to know it. Are you the beginning, or the end? The end, or the beginning?

Gladly would I roam and dance with Kore all my days, blessed sunlight on my animal body, merry laughter of my maiden companions ringing through the air as we run through fields filled with flowers, never doubting that spring is everlasting.

But the narcissus calls me to another realm. A nether realm.

What is this fall from Motherlove into dark depths of unknown, alien Otherness? All lightness fled from my limbs, I sink into the Underworld. Gravity pulls me, compels me down into my own dark weight, where I find—not sunlight—but the merest glimpse of lunar rays reflecting off the face of water I have never seen before. The deepest, stillest pool of water I have ever known. What is this water? How deep is it, and what is hidden there? Will I drown in its fearsome depths, or be baptized into new life?

A never-ending span of timeless time flows through me.

Who am I here? A daughter lost to earth above, but perhaps not only that. The Otherness so strange at first comes into me, and I am shocked to find that Here is also Home.

* * *

I was born in Hades. The earth cracked open under my mother's feet and she plunged into bottomless despair when she lost her own mother, Pauline, unexpectedly and far too soon—not yet forty-four, and never to be my grandmother.

From 1950 to 1952, Pauline wrote letters full of love and longing to her eldest daughter, Lilli, my mother, who had been sent against her will at age nineteen to far-off Canada to earn money so that her mother, father, two younger sisters, and brother could join her there. My mother, sick with yearning for Pauline, worked as a chambermaid in a language she did not know and saved every penny for her family's passage, living only for their joyful reunion.

There would be no joyful reunion.

Pauline died in the spring of 1952, on the train carrying the family and their meager possessions to Hamburg, Germany to board the ship that was to bring them to Canada and into my mother's aching arms. They turned back to bury her instead, and it was seven more years before Lilli saw her father and younger siblings again.

I was conceived not long after Pauline's death and drank my mother's bitter tears and bottomless grief with her milk. An infant Persephone, Hades was my native land; a raging, sorrowful Demeter my mother. Ungrandmothered, I carried my mother's unanswerable loss in blood and bone, felt her terrible yearning permeate my cells and reach into my soul.

* * *

Persephone, I never wore pastels. As your handmaiden, it was richer stains of color that I sought. The mystery of indigo, purple passion, and the fiery heat of red, the emerald of green and obsidian depths of black. Magenta, burgundy, vermilion. Sienna, amber, saffron. Cerulean, lavender, scarlet. Words as sumptuous as their colors.

Your colors, Persephone. Vibrant with desire and radiant with depth, I carried You inside me all along. I know that now.

Life goes on. We dance the Dance of Ages, ceaseless flow of heartbreak and desire, abandonment and joy.

Persephone. I meet you once again—so new, and so familiar.

You, my darker, wiser Sister.

Keeper of the Mysteries. Taproot of my life.

All my life I have loved Pauline. In the handful of black and white photographs that survived, she looks much older than her years, worn out by the endless demands of caring for four children in a two-room shed with dirt floors, by illness and the grief of two stillborn baby boys, and by a difficult and abusive marriage. Years ago she came to me at night. In the dream I lay my head in her lap, threw my arms around her, and told her how sorry I was for all the suffering she'd endured during her brief lifetime. She didn't speak, but seemed serene and pleased. When I told my mother about the dream we both wept.

Not long after that my other grandmother, Olga, also came to me in a dream. "I don't know why, but every time I'm with you, I can cry," she said in German, looking relieved, even happy. Olga had lost five of her eight children, including four little girls. I'd always known about Johann, Lydia, and Emma, but when I learned about the two stillborn baby girls, I wept for my grandmother's broken heart, and for the depth and breadth of sorrow in my motherline.

There was little time for grief in the lives of my mother and grandmothers. Over the years I have felt the dark weight of their stifled rage and anguish, accepted during their lifetimes as the inscrutable will of God, and carried in their bodies as illness, depression, and killer disease. "No one is ever lost without consequence to others," writes Susan Griffin. "Loss and longing move from body to body, expressed in one place as sorrow, in another as illness, then as destruction, and everywhere as desire."[3]

I want to sing the lost lives of mothers and daughters and cherished grandmothers known only in dreams. Give voice to those precious children whose early deaths were lodged as unrelenting longing in their mothers' grieving hearts and bodies. As I sing, may the eros and creativity held captive by sorrow's leaden thrall through generations blossom into a thousand fragrant petals. Move from body to body and be expressed in one place as healing, in another as laughter, then as creation, and everywhere as joy.

* * *

We all have *deep songs* of mother loss. I know that mine belongs to a larger chorus of sorrow and resilience throughout the generations and centuries. In 2012 my mother died unexpectedly, following what was to have been a routine biopsy. Sixty years after Pauline's death, we buried Lilli on June 16th, her mother's birthday.

II.

My mother never kept a journal. She didn't even write birthday cards, leaving that task to my father instead. And although we lived thousands of miles apart for almost two decades, she rarely wrote me letters. Two or three at most, all short. Once, when I was studying in Norwich in the early 1980s and hadn't heard from my parents in several months, lonely and hurt by their seeming indifference, I wrote them a postcard in many colors of ink and signed it, in large block letters, "Remember me? Your daughter in England." My father responded quite quickly and my mother added a few lines at the bottom of his letter. "I'm sorry you felt you had to write to us like that," she wrote in German. "I guess we deserved it." I think they made more of an effort to stay in touch after that.

Nor did my mother understand my need to fill notebook after notebook with my own thoughts and feelings from the time I was eleven years old and read *The Diary of Anne Frank* in school. All these years later I'm still writing, and my journal now spans close to two hundred volumes. Is my mother's writing silence the reason I have never stopped? Whose story am I trying to capture on those thousands and thousands of pages? Whose voice is it I have been hoping to hear?

III.

My mother's journals were her cakes. Apple cakes and poppy seed cakes, German cheesecakes and Black Forest Cherry cakes, buttercream cakes and Christmas Stollen. Only rarely did she allow herself a small slice; more often she denied herself, then secretly scooped up the crumbs as she packed the remnants away.

My mother's journals were her soups. Thick, earthy soups made from vegetables and grains and bits of leftover meat. "People here are so wasteful," she often commented. "They don't know how it feels to be hungry or how lucky they are to have so much." She spoke German, I spoke English, and sometimes we spoke a mixture of both.

My mother's journals were the heavy, dark loaves of bread she baked from organic wheat and rye my father brought home in fifty-pound sacks from the prairies every autumn, and ground in the stone mill downstairs in the freezer room on baking day. Over the years, she taught my father the proper proportions of grain and yeast and salt so that he would be able to carry on after she was gone. The week after we buried her, my father baked twenty loaves of bread.

My mother's journals were her garden. That was where I saw her happiest, most radiant. "Look at that," she'd say, pointing to the lush greenery of potato, beet, and cucumber plants. "Isn't that glorious? Is there anything more beautiful than a garden?" When she could no longer plant and tend the garden, my father became her willing surrogate, subject to her crusty tutelage. "I tell him how to do it and he just goes ahead and does what he wants," she complained. It was a huge loss when she couldn't stroll through the garden anymore to check on his work because she didn't have the energy to climb up and down the stairs from the patio to the ground, and her entire body hurt. During the last years of her life, she often said with a kind of helpless despair, "*Ich bin todmüde,*" and I felt the harsh truth of it. Life had worn her out, and she was deathly tired.

My mother's journals were the quilts she knitted for me, the first one from a bag of pink and blue yarn a friend had given her, the second, from dark green and plum wool I bought with that year's Christmas gift money. "So I can always wrap myself in your favorite colors and feel your love around me," I told her.

My mother's journals were her fabrics, carefully selected through the years and stacked neatly in her chest of drawers and in the cedar chest my father had built for her shortly after they were married. Cottons and linens, polyesters and silks, rayons and velvets. The inside of the chest smelled of mothballs she'd tucked into thick bolts of wool her father brought from a textile factory in Cleveland many years earlier. I imagine every piece of fabric as a journal entry and wonder what larger story they tell.

For all her German Baptist loyalties, my mother had a rebellious streak and her hungry eyes, like mine, were drawn to anything bright and floral. Even gaudy, it could be said. Between us, we amassed mountains of fabric, a disproportionate amount of it with red, mauve, and purple flowers against a black background. She was partial to green and blue too, but in the end, purple and mauve usually won out.

Though neither of us were enthusiastic seamstresses, for years it seemed we couldn't stop buying textiles, as though their vibrant beauty could redeem the drab poverty of her childhood in wartime Germany and the many sorrowful losses that followed. As though those bright, rich colors and textures might restore her to a future with a happier trajectory, a future in which her own mother lived long enough to taste the comfort and abundance she'd never known during her brief lifetime, and which we now enjoyed. As though we could create an alternate version of the story wherein Pauline survives the fateful train journey that plunged my mother into a black hole of grief and despair from which she never really recovered.

IV.

My mother did not leave me any journals when she died. What she left behind is a slender packet of faded green airmail letters from Pauline, following my mother's reluctant immigration to Canada after the war. They're all I have of Pauline—those parchment thin, fragile letters, the handwriting as stark and angular as their lives in postwar Germany, no time or space for flourish or the gentle mercy of curves. They are written in the old Gothic German script and the few phrases that I can decipher consist mostly of godly encouragement and support. "My dear Lilli, we pray for you every day, and long to see you soon," and "Have faith that our loving heavenly Father will watch over us until we are together again."

But Pauline's longing for her daughter is thinly veiled. I imagine I can feel her love and tenderness saturating the space between the narrow lines and upright words, welling out among her frequent appeals to God's goodness and mercy. Did she kiss the letters before entrusting them to the postman in the little village in central Germany where they ended up after the war? Did she weep, and marvel to think that in a week or two the flimsy sheet of paper would arrive into the eager hands of her beloved oldest daughter, an inconceivable half-world away? Did my mother stroke those precious letters and press them gently against her cheek like a caress spanning the thousands of miles between them? Trace the outline of her name on the envelope with her fingertips, overwhelmed with longing for her "*Muttchen*"? "I was always Mama's girl," she told me. "Ella was Papa's girl."

There are letters from her sister too. Ella describes learning to type and her letters are easier to read. On February 10, 1950, she writes, "Dearest Lilli, After much longing we finally received your dear letter with great joy. Everyone in our youth group asks about you and wants to know how you are doing. Please write to me soon because I miss you terribly and I live in hopes that we will be together again before long. Please, try to make it as soon as possible. Your loving sister, Ella."

Pauline and Ella both express gratitude for the letters my mother sent them, so I know there was a time when she did write, and I am envious. What became of those letters—the only evidence that my mother ever wrote about her life—and what prompted her to stop? Was the memory of pouring her heart's longing into those letters to Germany for two long years before receiving the stark telegram announcing her mother's death so traumatic that she could never again bring herself to write? My mother did not write to me; did she fear she might lose me too?

Once she showed me a slightly beaten, dog-eared black notebook her parents had given her decades earlier. It was empty except for her name, Lilli Fender, in the top right corner of the first page, and I wondered what they'd imagined she might write in it, but she didn't know. When I asked if I could have it, she said yes and seemed surprised that I would want it. I carried that notebook with me for years but I couldn't write in it. Although it was empty it seemed to hold the unwritten story of my mother's broken heart, the weight of which forbade any lesser concerns I might have recorded there. Some years ago I gave it back to her, but now that she too is gone, I would like to have it back.

V.

"Every mother contains her daughter in herself and every daughter her mother, and every woman extends backwards into her mother and forward into her daughter," Jung wrote.

> The conscious experience of these ties produces the feeling that her life is spread out over generations [and] this leads to a restoration or *apocatastasis* of the lives of her ancestors, who now, through the bridge of the momentary individual, pass down into the generations of the future. An experience of this kind gives the individual a place and a meaning in the life of the generations, so that all unnecessary obstacles are cleared out of the way of the life-stream that is to flow through her.[4]

I was already present in my mother's unborn body inside Pauline's womb. Do men feel this passionate bodily link, this cellular connection with their mothers? Or is it passed down through the motherline in the way our bodies hold eggs within eggs, like Russian Matryoshka dolls nestled inside each other, each generation of women holding the next tightly enclosed within itself like a secret still to be disclosed?

My young grandmother's letters to my mother are a mystery to me, as her mother's empty journals were to Terry Tempest Williams. Among the prayers for God's guidance and protection in the aching uncertainties of their lives, it's everything I can't read and everything that Pauline didn't say that haunts me. I know so little of her life beyond the fact that she was always sickly and sustained six pregnancies that resulted in four living children. I am the eldest daughter of the eldest daughter of an eldest daughter, and beyond that, little is known to me about my motherline. Not one of them kept a journal as far as I know, and given the circumstances of their lives, it's surprising enough that they were literate at all. My mother had five years of sporadic grade school education in Germany during the war, and there were no English as a Second Language (ESL) programs in place after her arrival in British Columbia during the coldest January ever recorded, nor would she have had time for them in any case, desperate as she was to earn money for her family's passage to Canada.

"What would you have wanted to study if you'd had the chance, Mum?" I asked her years ago. I knew the role of homemaker left her unfulfilled, but I'd never heard her express a desire for another vocation.

"A naturopathic doctor," she said. "If I'd been smart enough." She spoke almost defiantly, as if she feared it might sound presumptuous.

"You're more than smart enough, Mum," I protested. "Smart has nothing to do with it. You just never had the opportunity to study." It hurt me that she could doubt herself like that, but I don't know if anyone other than my sister and I ever told her she was smart and creative, and if they had, she probably wouldn't have believed it, since she tended to equate intelligence with education.

She looked at me and I thought I saw skepticism in her glance. "We already have one doctor in the family, anyway," she said, half smiling, in joking reference to my Ph.D. "We don't need another one."

I never heard Pauline's voice. I have no idea whether its pitch was high or low, though I imagine its sound as soft and hushed. My mother told me Pauline was humble and quiet, and didn't talk very much. She clung to the memory of a message from her mother, delivered by her friend, Otto, when he arrived in Canada a year later, "*Grüße meine Lillilein and sag ihr daß ich sie vermisse.*" (Greet my little Lilli, and tell her that I miss her.) The faded photos we have of my young grandmother show a woman who would have been beautiful in another time and place, but whose spirit was weary and beaten and could not rise to much joy. Her husband had been brutalized by an alcoholic father and showed little tenderness to his own wife and children. In a black and white photo taken shortly before my mother was separated from her family, Pauline holds her youngest daughter, about three years old, in her lap. Her slender oval face is tilted slightly downward and to the left, as if it would have been too bold to look directly at the camera, and her eyes look sad.

I was born the year after Pauline died. Deep in shock and grief, my mother spent her 23rd birthday in terrified and lonely labor, trying to push out a reluctant earthling.

"You didn't want to be born," she told me. "They put me in a small room on my own and I pushed and pushed, but you didn't want to move down the birth canal."

"I knew where I had it good," I teased her. "Why would I want to leave?"

What remains of Pauline are the letters. About forty of them. A tablecloth that she sent my mother as an engagement present, and a few surviving pieces of a simple Bohemian coffee service that my mother's parents gave her as a wedding gift. That was what my mother had of Pauline in the new world.

Over the years that I have been facilitating women's workshops, nothing has evoked such depth of emotion or struck so close to the bone as our relationships with our mothers and their lives. Whenever the topic of mothers arises, tears begin to flow and one woman weeping frees everyone in the circle. Sometimes the sorrow in the room is so huge that I know we are mourning not only our own mothers but generations of unexpressed grief and motherloss. No matter whether we lost our mother too soon or never even knew her, felt ourselves burdened by her unlived life and expectations or carried the guilt, as I did, of living thousands of miles away for many years, felt unappreciated and alienated from her, or whether she died before we could make peace with her—it seems no one is untouched by the power of this first fierce union of bodies. Whether she was present or absent, and whether our relationship was loving or troubled or both, the story of mother and daughter is always a passionate and volatile tale.

VI.

What is unspoken in our culture is the mother tongue. The tongues of our mothers.

What is unsung in our culture is *the first music of the voice of love, which every woman keeps alive.*[5]

What is muted, silenced, suppressed, and thus unheard in our culture is the full-bodied, resonant, unapologetic voice of a woman speaking her mother tongue.

The deep feminine is the undervoice in our culture.

Women are the *cantaores* of deep song in our time.

Our mothers and grandmothers ask to be remembered, inscribed, and envoiced.

Our personal stories and the timeless feminine archetypes flow into each other like the two sides of a Möbius band. The lives of our mothers and grandmothers merge with Mother, Virgin, and Crone, and the eternal shimmers through the ephemeral present moment.

James Hillman says that Jung's great accomplishment in the *Red Book* was to open "the mouth of the dead" and hear their lament.[6] Perhaps our task is to claim the *deep song* of our lost feminine lineage and sing our mother tongue back into sound. Write our Mothers into their own story.

What happens when we attend to the undervoice, sing the deep and resonant song of the feminine—the emotion and eros, the joy and anguish of our Mothers' lives?

What is restored, and what new story might emerge?

VII.

Coming to voice has been my lifelong quest. I rarely spoke out at university, afraid of sounding ignorant and uncultured among so many offspring of doctors and lawyers and teachers. On paper I was much more daring; the essays I submitted to my revered and often beloved professors expressed the audacious curiosity I could not speak in class. The University of British Columbia's sprawling, cavernous Sedgewick Undergraduate Library was my temple; its heavy glass doors, my entry into the country of learning where all were permitted, even welcomed.

In graduate school I fell in love with the work of the East German writer, Christa Wolf, and her lifelong quest for the *living word* that could reconcile the relentless *either/or* of western patriarchy, and "greet with a smile the wrath of Achilles, the conflict of Hamlet, the false alternatives of Faust."[7] My doctoral dissertation, titled "Language and Silence: "Sprachlosigkeit" in the Work of Christa Wolf," explored the roots of silence and speechlessness, focusing on literary, psychological, and socio-political factors, including the silence of women throughout history.[8] *Sprachlosigkeit* suggests speechlessness and being without language; *sprechen* (speaking) and *Sprache/n* (language/s) are more closely related in German than their English equivalents.

At long last, I also had voice lessons in England, something I had desired for a long time. Learning to open my throat created greater depth and resonance in my voice and I gradually stopped sounding like a boy soprano, although it was another decade before my voice blossomed into its full soprano range and timbre. At thirty, I began to discover my voice as a singer.

Then, returning to my early love of journals, I started to conduct personal writing workshops for women, and wrote *A Voice of Her Own: Women and the Journal Writing Journey*, which I imagined as a great chorus of women's voices, each one expressing a unique feminine reality.[9] So, too, were my Jungian studies with Marion Woodman and at the International School for Analytical Psychology in Zürich in the service to my soul's voice, and my various vocations have all involved helping others come to voice.

Recently I have come to see this lifelong love of voice and language—whether spoken or sung, written or read—as a response to the silence of my motherline. As an attempt to reclaim and envoice what has been suppressed, to restore and re-story the lives of my mother and grandmothers; inviting, evoking, and attending what might otherwise remain lost.

"I love you so much I don't even have the words to express it," I tell my mother as we stroll slowly down Wellington Avenue, arm in arm, in the golden glow of a summer evening. I have flown in from New York after another crisis in her health.

"I know," she says quietly. "I feel it."

My sister and I say that our words of love, spoken freely and often, are what kept our mother alive beyond all medical expectations. Love of words. Words of love.

VIII.

Yearning encroaches. When I give it space, it spreads and expands, grows larger and larger, and I feel the true dimensions of my longing.

Yearning seduces. Pulls me out of the sunlit present and plunges me into memories of untold suffering and loss, and I don't know if those memories are mine or my mother's or grandmothers' or beyond, or where they belong, or where I begin and end.

> I am my mother, but I'm not.
> I am my grandmother[s], but I'm not.
> I am my great-grandmother, but I'm not.[10]

Yearning is dangerous. For my mother, torn from everything she knew and loved so soon after fleeing the Red Army's revenge, and for my grandmothers, worn out by poverty and ill health through two world wars, endless pregnancies, and the care of small children, the expression of yearning was a luxury they could not allow themselves. Once acknowledged, it could swallow them whole, paralyze and leave them unfit for the demands of daily life.

Unspoken and unwritten, their yearning imprinted itself on their bodies, inscribed itself on their flesh in symptoms like heart murmurs, irregular heartbeats, high blood pressure, heart attacks, and congestive heart failure. Their craving for sweetness in life was evident in the endless array of sweets on the table; it wasn't until I left home that I realized not everyone ate dessert twice a day.

But I felt their yearning. In my mother's underlying sadness that nothing could touch, in my grandmother Olga's gentle hand on my cheek and her distant gaze that seemed to look through and beyond me. Not that their lives were without happiness, celebration, or joy, but it always seemed as though a part of them were somewhere else. As if their attention was split between the living and the dead, and their imagination had taken refuge somewhere safe and whole in a time before their worlds were shattered by loss.

And so it falls to me, third-generation eldest daughter, to voice their yearning. I will say that throughout the horror of endless wars, they persevered, did their best to care for their families in the ways they understood, often went hungry so that their children would have food in their stomachs, and rejoiced in every tender green shoot that broke through the hard earth surrounding them. Their lives were stalwart and heartbreaking, I will say. Common and beautiful. They were not "notable women" or feminist role models, I will say, but they endured the hell of war and starvation and survived with their courage and patience and kindness intact.

I will sing their yearning. Sing my own longing to remember them and honor their humble and shining lives, to write them into their own story and sing them into their own voices. I will love the mystery of their being, and their presence that dwells inside me. I will hear the lament of my beloved dead and say who they were.

All is not lost.

NOTES

1. Federico García Lorca, "Deep Song" (A Lecture given in Granada, 22 February 1922). Accessed June 16, 2014, at http://www.poetryintranslation.com/PITBR/Spanish/DeepSong.htm.

2. *Ibid.*

3. Susan Griffin, *What Her Body Thought: A Journey into the Shadows* (New York: Harper Collins, 1999), p. 313.

4. C. G. Jung, "The Psychological Aspects of the Kore" (1951), in *The Collected Works of C. G. Jung,* ed. and trans. Gerhard Adler and R. F. C. Hull (Princeton, NJ: Princeton University Press, 1968), vol. 9i, § 316.

5. Hélène Cixous, "Sorties: Out and Out: Attacks/Ways Out/Forays," in *The Newly Born Woman,* trans. Betsy Wing (Minneapolis: University of Minnesota Press, 1986), p. 93.

6. James Hillman & Sonu Shamdasani, *Lament of the Dead: Psychology after Jung's Red Book* (New York: W. W. Norton, 2013), p. 85.

7. Christa Wolf, *Cassandra: A Novel and Four Essays*, trans. Jan van Heurck (London: Virago Press, 1984), pp. 270-71.

8. Marlene A. Schiwy, "Language and Silence: 'Sprachlosigkeit' in the Work of Christa Wolf" (Ph.D. diss., University of London, 1988).

9. Marlene Schiwy, *A Voice of Her Own: Women and the Journal Writing Journey* (New York: Simon & Schuster, 1996).

10. Terry Tempest Williams, *When Women Were Birds*, p. 50.

In her 80th year, Joyce Brady, born and raised in Harlem, reflects on her journey to retrieve her natural voice lost after her mother's mental illness and institutionalization, and the subsequent culturally imposed shame, secrecy, and silence she experienced as a result of it. She finds expression through the body in dance, poetry, and the arts, which become symbolic carriers of that original loss and the future unveiling of Spirit.

SHAME, SECRECY, AND SILENCE:
THE TANGLED ROOTS OF CHILDHOOD AND THE SUPPRESSION OF VOICE

JOYCE BRADY

What is it that I need to say?
Why is it so hard to find my voice
hidden in these catacombs of silence?
It seems I'm forever groping for what I know is there
but do not trust I can retrieve it.
When I do, will I even recognize it as a valuable piece of me?
Oh, Mama, don't you know that I who heard no voices
Find it difficult to sing?

—Joyce Brady, "Mama"

At six years old, I lost my mother's voice. I no longer heard her singing or dancing around the house while she cooked and cleaned. My mother had dressed me and my sister like the child actress, Shirley Temple, twisting our thick hair into springy curls topped with a large ribbon bow. We had play-acted in musical adaptations of Shirley Temple movies. Whenever my sister and I sang "On the Good Ship Lollypop," Mama always yelled for an encore.[1] She sprung from her place at the ironing board, kitchen table, or washing board to smother us with her wet kisses.

We were happy until one night when everything changed. On that fateful night Mama's voice was silenced. My sister and I were awakened in the middle of the night by Daddy, who took us from our Bronx home to Harlem where the family council of paternal grandparents,

---

Joyce Brady, M.S., R.N., is a retired college instructor who has also worked as nurse, art gallery director, photographer, and symbolic consultant. She has facilitated "circles of wise women," using poetry and symbolism to cultivate the authentic voice.

aunts, and uncles lived. In my great-grandmother's house, all voices were hushed, barely audible through the closed kitchen door where I strained to hear their secret conversations.

Afterward, Mama's name was quarantined like a contagious disease from our ears, except for the perfunctory "your mother" statements from Daddy. Eventually, Daddy took us on secret trips to upstate New York to visit Mama in a mental hospital. I was forbidden to reveal our Sunday trips to anyone outside of the family. It was confusing to see Mama in wrinkled clothing and with her hair uncombed. It was frightening to hear cries, screams, and shouts piercing through the barred windows of Rockland State Hospital as we approached and when we left the complex of tall buildings, near the bus depot. It was like the sounds from the large animal house in a zoo; cries of deep guttural outrage at being caged. Those caged human voices accompanied me for days after these Sunday visits.

A woman who leaves her husband, becomes independent, and sings her own songs will eventually lose the right to dance, sing, and play with her daughters: She will be exiled to a high tower of imprisonment. That personal event of silent loss became a universal truth when Mama's voice was silenced. I never knew my mother's people except as characters in stories she told about the South. Mama had run away from home when she was sixteen years old to live in New York City with her godmother.

On Mother's Day in Harlem, it was the custom for children to wear either a red or white carnation on their dress or jacket lapel. My grandmother pinned a white carnation on me, signifying Mama's death, in order to quell questions from neighbors about her whereabouts. My sister and I lied when questioned about Mama's "death" and felt pity beaming from the eyes of everyone—neighbors, strangers, and church members. When I heard the gospel hymn, "Sometimes I Feel Like A Motherless Child," I cried openly because that white carnation gave permission to miss Mama.[2] I no longer had a mirror, Mama, in which to see a reflection of myself. I conformed to my grandmother's common reminder that children should be seen and not heard.

I became semi-aphasic, not from the usual stroke, infection, or brain trauma, but as a consequence of that early maternal loss and subsequent shame about her exile. Aphasia is an impairment of language affecting the production or comprehension of speech and the ability to read and write. I had to stop talking or even thinking about Mama within the menacing silence. Maya Angelou made a conscious decision to stop talking after she was raped.[3] I stopped talking to help erase any impressions, good or bad, Mama had left on me: her talkativeness, singing, and spontaneity now caged in memory. My silence was activated at home and with family members but less so at school or with playmates. It was the conspiracy of silence at home I feared the most, those unseen, unheard, but felt stirrings that prompted a similar response within me. I became a co-conspirator with the silence. My family members were all active talkers about everything except Mama. The silence grew within me like a weed; the silence I had adapted to survive was both protective and harmful. I developed a keen sense of the other as a way to begin communicating. I questioned what others were thinking but not saying. I questioned what I needed to say based on my assumptions. I said whatever I thought the other wanted to hear, an objective other I saw but did not really know.

My first known others were my hairdressers and teachers. Going to the hairdresser was never a luxury for me. It was a necessity; it shaped my life, not just my hair. It was in that place of beauty where I was taught a woman's way of living. It was in that place where women were cared for that I was able to recall memories and retrieve parts of myself.[4] Daddy had difficulty making two or three braids out of my thick head of hair, and his final results were horizontal braid tails flying across each shoulder rather than down the middle of my back. For holidays and special occasions, Daddy sent me around the corner to a beauty parlor on Amsterdam Avenue. There, I was in the midst of a community of women whose voices I could hear, as they freely laughed, sang, and told stories of their lives. The hairdresser spoke to me through a wall mirror. I loved looking into her eyes while having a conversation through the mirror as she worked on my hair. It was in beauty parlors that I gathered from women what I needed and made it into my own mark of beauty.[5]

My school teachers were also known others, and I voiced back whatever they taught and received their personal recognition through praise and good grades. Many of my teachers served as mentors. In music appreciation class, Ms. X played classical music records on a turn table and instead of having the class be quiet and listen, she taught us to sing the words of each title while listening to the music. She sensed the importance of rhythm and song within the Black culture, and found a way to lead her students to instrumental classical music through song. Those daily half-hour classes when I was eight years old remained a blood memory for the rest of my life. As an adult, I was catapulted back to my classroom seat whenever I heard either *The Swan* or *The Tales of Hoffman*.[6] During the music test, I listened to each record, sang softly to myself as I wrote down the answer. I grew to love classical music. Parker Palmer, an educator, wrote:

> Looking back, I realized I was blessed with mentors at every crucial stage of my young life, at every point where my identity needed to grow: in adolescence, in college, in graduate school and early in my professional career.[7]

I began to separate one general other from another general other, thereby being released from a nameless crowd. Many of my teachers saw me as different from, but still connected to the rest of the class. That felt distinction was crucial because I now felt separated from Mama's mental illness and returned to the ordinary world of childhood. I no longer had to spin off in diffusion or lose pieces of myself. But I could not sense my feelings or even name them, a form of dissociation. In dissociation, that which is unbearable is closed off and isolated from the rest of the self. The person has to go on, but to do so he or she has to turn away from trauma, compartmentalizing it to keep it out of view.[8] The voice I had lost at six years old remained hidden from me and others. Paradoxically, I hadn't wanted to be different from everyone, but at the same time I wanted room to grow and become visible to myself.

During one summer school program, the girls were taught chorus line steps to a popular calypso song. Dance steps had come easily to me since I was a toddler. I was happy and unrestrained on stage, as if I was dancing at home with my sister. The guest teacher wanted me and some of the other girls to return the following morning. I did not go back. I felt exposed, ashamed, and thought I would eventually be found out. I needed to stay hidden to protect the family secret. Years later, I learned that the invitation extended to me to return the following day was referred to as a "call back." I had something special the guest director wanted to see again. But I never wanted to stand out in a crowd of strangers; I was more comfortable blending in with the familiar. That calypso song, played during rehearsal, has remained within the archive of my blood memories, along with classical music.

Once while walking 125th Street in Harlem, I heard tap dancing coming from an open second floor window, and I saw a line of tap dancing feet—black patent leather shoes with shining metal taps. The top of the dancers' bodies were hidden behind the upper window. I leaned against a street mail box for support, while my feet copied the tap routine like I had done as a child when watching Shirley Temple movies. There was no way my body could be still, walk away, or ignore the rhythmic taps on the wooden floors. My body responded with a voice of its own that I also felt. When I was ten years old, I asked Daddy for tap dancing classes. His short reply was "No, you are not going to grow up to be a hussy." My body had a voice and wanted to speak, but had to remain silent until adolescence. Dance was the main form of communication among teens on my block and I easily fit in; I learned the new dance steps and taught them to other friends. We practiced on the roof after I had hung out the wash on the clothes lines. I had hidden a portable turn-table and forty-five rpm records in the washing tub. My friends and I danced among wind-blown sheets and towels on the tar-covered roof tops. We danced until the clothes were dried by the sun and breeze. Later, I rushed to be among the first ones on the dance floor. I never tired of dancing, and dance became the primary form of socializing between my teen and young adult years. Dancing was also an essential part of my three-year nursing training; I danced in dormitory hallways and outside roller skating rinks. What I wasn't able to feel, I could dance; those unnamed and vague feelings were translated into symbolic movements in dance.

I witnessed a sacred sense of voice and dance at church with my Aunt Bunny. Aunt Bunny was the more reserved of my four paternal aunts; she never married, spoke softly, wore no makeup, and taught bible school. I was surprised whenever she left her seat in her "Sanctified" church to shout, dance, and chant. Aunt Bunny's stout body glided effortlessly in front of the congregation during the church service—gospel hymns or sermon. After church service ended, Aunt Bunny never mentioned her experience of shouting; it was as if she had just merely sneezed or coughed. Often, I saw large groups of the congregation shouting in front of the pulpit and up and down the aisles. Their bodies seemed to express some deep feelings. I could sense when

Aunt Bunny was about to rise from her seat; her eyes closed, her light skin became slightly flushed, and she swayed from side by side to the music or biblical verse. Her feeling was unleashed through her body's natural expression of voice and dance.

Poetry gave me another way to break the silence. On Christmas and Easter at my Baptist church, each child was required to recite a biblical verse, a poem, or sing a song in celebration of the birth or resurrection of the Lord. The youngest children, sometimes less than two years old, recited the shortest verse in the bible that showed the humanity of Jesus as he shed tears (John 11:13). Mothers sat in the first rows encouraging and prompting their little ones to recite the two simple words of this verse: "Jesus wept." I recited, at ten years old, like a toddler: fidgety, head down, and talking fast. Once, I recited a long poem, *The Creation,* and my body automatically moved in sync with the stanzas.[9] I lost my shyness and nervousness when speaking in public and was no longer concerned about the congregation, as my body responded to the spoken words of the poet. I acted out the words of the poem. My body had found another outlet besides dancing for its expression. Poetry became the doorway to express what had been hidden, fearful, or ignored. Gregory Orr believes poetry is a way of surviving the emotional chaos, spiritual confusion, and traumatic events that come with being alive.[10] For me, poetry was a tunnel to consciousness—a way to shift, reshape, and sustain the song I was meant to sing. Poetry allowed me to safely view what was painful within a protective shield of metaphors. The poet Tagore reflected metaphorically what was also personal:

> The song I came to sing remains unsung to this day.
> I have spent my days in stringing and unstringing my instrument.
> The time has not come true, the words have not been rightly set;
> only there is the agony of wishing in my heart.
> The blossom has not opened; only the wind is sighing by.[11]

Poetry was a pathway to an underground stream of stifled screams and a way to channel their meanings for expression. Poetry helped clear weeds, tangled roots, and brambles in my life so I could plant seeds of my new awareness.

It was the journal where my voice found a permanent springboard to the unknown. I had something I wanted to say and a safe place in which to speak. The journal was the place to mine that something; there I faced the confusion, uncertainties, and challenges in my life and found a place to pause in a sacred cocoon of possibilities. Surprisingly, I received inner guidance, *spiritual bumper stickers*, emerging from the pages of the journal, like a phoenix bird rising from the ashes. A spiritual bumper sticker was a brief statement or question from an unknown part of me that required a conscious contemplative action: I am now worthy of my own attention. How could I attend to my own needs and what might those needs be? Needs not based on the other, real or perceived, but on what I needed to thrive. Why am I here? I read many volumes of Anais Nin's journals and many of her essays. Reading Nin's words placed me in a safety net that supported a woman's need for attention and advocated for women to refuse to despair. Nin proposed that whatever the individual does for herself and by herself is something that ultimately flows back again like a river into the collective unconscious.[12]

So what could I do for just me alone? I wrote in a journal all the named and vague feelings present at any given moment. Journal writing was for the me I had ignored, deemed insignificant, and never knew. The journal became a mirror for rehearsal in the real world. Sometimes an actor rehearses her lines before a mirror to hear her voice as well as to get an audience's perspective of her presence on stage. The journal made me visible to myself. I became the only image in the mirror while others slowly faded away. At the start, I kept the journal hidden from view—under my pillow or in the trunk of my car. Eventually I was able to have it near, at arm's length, even while my youngest kids were still at home. I was no longer in hiding.

I took Intensive Journal Workshops to broaden the concept of journal writing.[13] The first workshop was a sanctuary, a neutral place to mine myself within a dedicated span of time, to chisel away the shame, secrecy, and silence while attending to the needs of the Self. The Intensive Journal process showed where I had negated myself, and the process gave my life meaning. The structured Intensive Journal was divided into myriad aspects of my life, and I was given space to fully engage with each specific area: dreams, events, and twilight imagery. I received feedback from and between the various sections of journal. I resuscitated parts of memory and captured emerging aspects. I realized I was an artist without an art form. My three grown children were artists,

and I had always supported their choice of art. At midlife, at age fifty-
two, I left a secure health administration position to explore art, and
although that decision was wrought with fear, I had to follow my
feelings that emerged in my journal in the form of a haiku:

> Sacred Intention
> Be like the eagle
> Fly where your dreams are!

I learned to move through fear, not get rid of it. Even a mouse
confronts fear to get the cheese. I had to leave my self-imposed isolation
and risk the unknown. Without tension in the oyster, the pearl would
never form. Fear was a form of tension I had to embrace in order to
make art; I had to risk moving through fear. Poetry was still a major
part of the journal; not just the poems I had copied from books, but
also poems arising from the shame, secrecy, and silence in my life.

In my early sixties, a woman friend coaxed me to read a poem
during an open mike session. I read the poem, "Mama," and could
barely get through it. My body trembled and I felt ashamed, although
my friend gave me lots of encouragement. The poem was selected for
publication in a women's journal. The editor had been in the audience
and contacted me. I was terrified but willing to be an eagle instead of
remaining a mouse. I viewed the proposed publication as validation of
my experience, not as a shaming device. I was no longer a child but a
grown woman harboring an inner child. The woman said yes to
publication. The child remained huddled in fear. I secretly anticipated
the arrival of the journal in the mail. I also felt brave that I had exposed
a personal secret to a general other. The day the journal appeared in
my mailbox, I tore off the brown wrapping and waves of shame engulfed
me like a tsunami when I saw my poem was in the section entitled
"Daughters of Mad Women." There it was, all before me in black and
white: the joy of being published, mixed up with Mama's mental illness.
I poured my feelings into my journal to stop the bleeding. I felt as if I
were being sucked dry by a vampire and was terrified. I saw new
glimpses of myself embracing the demons of shame in the open as
compost for the making of art. The poem had a bloodline of its own
and its voice released me into the collective other.

> I want to be her voice
> and the voice for generations
> of black women silenced by
> booze, poverty, depression, and that ultimate
>   escape; Schizophrenia.[14]

I had created a poem out of my fears: shame, secrecy, and silence. I wrote in my journal until the frantic shifting from shame to the happiness of being published had steadied; the needle was in the middle. It was time to let the demons out of the shadows into the light. I told friends and family and bought each a copy. I left a copy in the beauty parlor. Sometimes I read journal entries to women friends, and surprisingly I cried, even though I had written the entry without a conscious emotion. Reading aloud was a catalytic force that excavated unexpressed emotions lying beneath the words, as it has been when reciting poetry.

I had thirty-eight years of journals in stacked plastic boxes, which I seldom read again except to verify a date or place. A woman friend suggested that I leave the journals to a women's research center in New Orleans, but the idea of handing over my innermost thoughts, struggles, mistakes, and joys to a general other was too painful to consider. I needed to let them go, in order to have space and also to simplify my environment in old age. I had to wait to know what to do. Journal writing was a form of attention to the Self. It was once again not about the other. I wrote in the sweet territory of silence where I can visit myself.[15] That simple phrase reflected my path to me and a return back with new awareness. The silence was no longer menacing but healing. On the new moon, March 2014, I let all the journals go to recycling, even though I had previously thought of conducting a ritual or sacred burning. That March morning, I just let go of remnants of the past. I let go of the journals as I hope to let go of my body, effortlessly and without fanfare: My body, container of my expressed and unexpressed voices, must be released back to the earth as prayer.

> There is comfort in keeping what is sacred inside us not as a secret
> but as a prayer.[16]

Women writers, authors, and poets continue to be primary voice teachers and healers. Their creative voices have given me courage to break out of the shroud of shame, secrecy, and silence in my life. There was always a journal, in process, to mine the deeper Self. As Anais Nin reminded us:

> Creativity is a constant interaction between our life and the struggle with the larger issues such as history, whose victim we can become. And in order not to be victimized by it we also have to learn to live apart from it. It is not escape, it's having a place that we can return to regain our strength, in order to regain our values, in order not to be shattered by events.[17]

Over the years, in my journal I collected quotes and statements from my voice teachers that cultivated the feminine sensibilities that were lacking in my early life. At midlife, my youngest son was a hit-and-run victim and sustained brain trauma resulting in a subdural hematoma and emergency brain surgery. After his recovery, I resigned from an administrative position in order to be, to explore, to heal, and to follow my dreams. Although I hadn't realized it at the time, my life had been about doing and getting ahead, and where I had finally arrived was now meaningless. My son's accident created a long space for self-reflection in the midst a traumatic event. I had to step out of the controller's position and sink into softness, silence, and simplicity. Helen M. Luke taught,

> If we do not give validity to the dark, the Yin, the feminine and the receptive, if we do not consent to do nothing, to allow time for dreaming, for listening to the voice of the unconscious then we shall be in far worse case than if we waste time during the day for our excessive activity will lead us backwards, and all will be to do again.[18]

I explored art and enrolled in a community college. My three grown children were artists and I loved museums and collected art. Of course the skills I had developed in my career were useless in this new environment; I struggled to see form, lines, color, and negative space. I was without a paycheck, no longer in a hurry, and committed to the slow process of retrieving the child's voice of wonder and curiosity. I knew that art, like the journal, was also a way of giving attention to myself, though eventually I would have to work again. But for a year I played and healed. It wasn't a choice between the journal and art because the journal was an art form; my task was to make my life a work of art. Becoming who one is meant to be is not a process of becoming perfect; rather, it means becoming aware of one's sharp edges, of moving closer to the unknown and the potential in us.[19] That mid-life pause has extended into my old age. I no longer dedicate year-long pauses, just small spaces in the day to write in my journal and compose short stories, letters, and poems. The pen is the bridge between the inner and outer parts of my life.

> I cannot think without a pen in my hand, if I don't write it down, it doesn't exist.[20]

I have a voice and with a pen in my hand am able to find a place where my voice belongs, no longer trying to belong where I have no voice. With an ongoing practice of writing and reflection, I continue to mine truth as prayer.

> That which belongs to me
> Let me embrace.
> That which gives me pain
> Let me feel.
> That which makes me ashamed
> Let me expose.
> That which is imperfect
> Let me love.[21]

NOTES

1. Shirley Temple, child actress, signature song in the film, *Bright Eyes*, directed by David Bueller, 1934.

2. James Weldon Johnson and J. Rosamond Johnson, *The Books of American Negro Spirituals* (Cambridge, MA: Da Capo Press, 2002), B.II, p. 80.

3. Maya Angelou, *I Know Why the Caged Bird Sings* (New York: Random House, 2009), p. 86.

4. Joyce Brady, "Beauty Marks," in J. Duerk, *The Circle Continues: Women Respond to Circle of Stones* (Philadelphia, PA: Innisfree Press, Inc., 2001), p. 90.

5. Brady, "Beauty Marks," p. 93.

6. Camille Saint Saens, *The Best of Saint-Saens*, Phillips Classics, CD; Jacques Offenbach, *The Tales of Hoffman: The Complete Opera*, Original Recording, re-mastered with Beverly Sills, 2002.

7. Palmer Parker, *The Courage to Teach* (San Francisco, California: Jossey-Bass, 2007), p. 25.

8. Mark Epstein, *The Trauma of Everyday Life* (New York: Penguin Press, 2013), p. 66.

9. James Weldon Johnson, "The Creation: A Negro Sermon," in *The Poetry of Black America: Anthology of the 20th Century,* Arnold Adoff, ed. (New York: Harper and Row, 1975), pp. 3-5.

10. "Interview with Gregory Orr," on *This I Believe*, NPR radio, New York, 2006.

11. Rabindranath Tagore, *A Tagore Reader*, ed. Amiya Chakravarty (Boston: Beacon Press, 1961), p. 296.

12. Anais Nin, *A Woman Speaks: The Lectures, Seminars, and Interviews of Anais Nin* (Chicago: Swallow Press, 1973), p. 7.

13. Ira Progoff, *At a Journal Workshop* (New York: Dialogue House Library, 1980).

14. Joyce Brady, "Mama," *Writing for Our Lives*, Vol. 7, no. 1, p. 48.

15. Angeles Arrien, cultural anthropologist and creator of the Four-Fold Way, began each of her teachings in a circle by ringing a bell welcoming us into the sweet territory of silence. Sausilito, California, 1990-2014.

16. Terry Tempest Williams, *When Women Were Birds: Fifty-four Variations on Voice* (New York: Farrar, Straus, and Giroux, 2012).

17. Nin, *Woman Speaks,* p. 6-7.

18. Helen M. Luke, *Dark Wood to White Rose: Journey and Transformation in Dante's Divine Comedy* (New York: Parabola Books, 1995), p. 53.

19. Irene Gad, *Tarot and Individuation: Correspondences with Cabala and Alchemy* (York Beach, ME: Nicolas-Hayes, Inc.,1994), p. 116.

20. Williams, *When Women Were Birds*, p. 45.

21. Joyce Brady, an excerpt from her poem, "Reflection."

Charlene Spretnak explores the difficulties women tend to encounter when trying to express their inner perception of the dynamic interrelatedness in the gestalt of any situation yet having to work in an Indo-European language system, in which nominalization (naming things), rather than process and interrelatedness, is central. She discusses the pioneering insights of two French feminist theorists, Claudine Herrmann and Luce Irigaray, into the ways in which female subjectivity is curtailed and how it might be cultivated. Even with the obstacles in a "manstream" culture, Spretnak notes, many exemplary women artists in literature and other arts have brilliantly succeeded in creating from a matrix of female subjectivity.

In the Absence
of a Mother Tongue

CHARLENE SPRETNAK

hat was exhilarating about the bursting forth of feminism in the 1970s was the *naming* of all that had been unarticulated—or noted only sporadically, or considered an isolated incident rather than a widespread pattern. The most obvious injustices were easy to name: the widespread practice of unequal pay for equal work; the refusal of banks and stores to issue credit to married women in their own name; the banning of women, or league sports for women, by universities that received federal aid; and many more. Then there was the entire complex of prejudicial attitudes that blocked women from admission to graduate schools, fellowships, jobs, promotions, leadership or management positions, and appointment to public office. These too were easy to name as the feminist momentum built. Very soon, though, many of us came to realize that there was an even more vast and complex *cultural context* underlying all these injustices, a foundation on which they rested securely: the language, premises, systems of knowledge, and societal norms in our culture had evolved as a comfortable fit with the general preferences of the male psyche.

"Reason," for instance, was seen to be abundant in men and lacking in women, as it was characterized by the ability to separate out a few pertinent facts from the gestalt of a situation as the only elements worth considering and then to pass judgment on them by employing values

Charlene Spretnak is the author of seven books, including *Lost Goddesses of Early Greece*, *States of Grace*, *The Resurgence of the Real*, *Missing Mary*, *Relational Reality*, and *The Spiritual Dynamic in Modern Art*. She also edited an anthology, *The Politics of Women's Spirituality*. In 2012 she received the Demeter Award for lifetime achievement as "one of the premier visionary feminist thinkers of our time" from the Association for the Study of Women and Mythology. She lives in Ojai, California.

derived from a hierarchical, abstract belief structure and by stiff-arming any inklings of empathy or care, regarded as a weakness that damages the rational thought process. We began to see that the legal system, religion, and the academic fields of Western philosophy, psychology and the other social sciences, history, and analyses of literature were built on an infrastructure of male-oriented premises and practices that were presented as the natural, competent, and accomplished way for humans to think. In every direction we looked, we saw that the male and his druthers were the norm. We increasingly perceived that numerous concepts taken for granted were actually loaded expressions of patriarchal culture—that is, an orientation in which men are regarded as the cultural grown-ups and, therefore, are seen as superior to and properly dominant over the cultural minors: women and children. Some articles in grassroots cultural feminist journals featured quotation marks around nearly every phrase, term, and noun to signal the freighted meaning of those supposedly neutral linguistic components. Collectively, we mounted an exposé of the extensive and surprisingly deep ways in which our very language was supporting a profoundly rigged system.

Insights from the *Sororité*

In France a number of feminist authors exposed the patriarchal biases in various fields and suggested ways to cultivate modes of being that were not molded by patriarchal socialization. Two theorists in particular illuminated the ways in which language and thought are shaped in a patriarchal culture, providing an analysis that we cultural feminists in the United States found relevant.

The first, Claudine Herrmann, earned two law degrees and practiced law in Paris for many years. In 1976 she wrote *Les Voleuses de Langue* (*The Female Thieves of Language*, translated in 1991 as *The Tongue Snatchers*), in which she analyzes the ways in which men tend to operate linguistically within the public systems they have created. This orientation she calls "the virile system" (not intended as a complimentary label, she notes) and illustrates its operation in the French Civil Code as well as in numerous examples from French literature. Herrmann's book was introduced to me by Terry Tempest Williams when we met at a conference in 1995, and I have since shared it with others.

Here are a few of Herrmann's observations. Every word has a different meaning for men and women. Man generally prefers himself to what surrounds him, to the extent that he places his mental categories before those of objective reality. His structures of thinking are external to him (and are entirely foreign to women); he is, therefore, stunned by everything and seeks to impose control over it. Man is profoundly syntactic. He acts only as a function of his spatial, temporal, social, and economic position. If a word bothers him, he replaces it immediately with a synonym. Moreover, every man has a tendency to organize the world according to a system in which he is the center. Men's space is a space of domination and hierarchy, of conquest and expansion.

Herrmann further observed that education [in the virile system] often represses language in women, dooming them to silence and idle chatter. If woman remains herself and continues to think in terms of harmony and not struggle, of gift and not exchange, she will get herself pitilessly crushed in the virile system. In her role as lover and mate, any individuality and self-reflection in a woman appears to be in excess of what the role requires. Deprived of emotional and social identity, women spend their lives looking for themselves. All women are deceived [that the virile system acknowledges the fullness of their being], and most of them perpetually and obstinately reconstruct the self-image whose reality they are always refused by the virile system. Allowing women to participate in society is nothing if it consists of plundering what makes them different—and men cannot even imagine, without contempt, what is not like themselves. Therefore, woman must maintain a distance between herself and the men she has not chosen. She must lay out a preserve for herself in relation to them that constitutes precisely that part of her that men do not understand and often attribute to stupidity. In this virile and pitiful world, a woman who refuses to alienate herself in virile values is often considered mentally ill.

Herrmann, then, sought to name the ways in which most men she observed tend to think, which is far different from what women usually assume. After all, male behavior is associated with reason, a premise that serves well to mask prejudicial and self-absorbed motivation.

Another French feminist theorist whose work was particularly illuminating for those American feminists pondering the male-oriented conceptual character of the entire public sphere is the philosopher and psychologist Luce Irigaray. After dismantling the virile premises underlying Lacanian psychology and much of Western philosophy, Irigaray wrote *This Sex Which Is Not One* (1977); *An Ethics of Sexual Difference* (1984); and numerous other books, including her summation, *Luce Irigaray: Key Writings* (2004). She envisions a societal model she calls a Culture of Intersubjectivity in which male subjectivity and female subjectivity would be in dynamic dialogue—*if only* the female half of the dynamic were present, *if only* female subjectivity were cultivated, articulated, and respected as necessary for the full unfolding of every area of a culture's development. Irigaray sees the role of the women's movement as correcting injustices and creating new possibilities in every sphere *while thinking, speaking, and acting from an orientation of authentic female subjectivity.* Clearly, we are presently very far from such a model and can barely imagine it, though she makes many pragmatic suggestions in several areas of modern life. Regarding a language of female subjectivity, though, Irigaray, like Herrmann, only alludes to what could be.

THE DISAPPEARING WOMAN

The insights and observations that Herrmann and Irigaray began to articulate in the mid-1970s have subsequently been placed in a category called *difference feminism*, which holds that there are significant differences between the male and female sexes. In 2014, however, nothing could be further out of vogue. The long arm of social constructionism, which dominated American academia in the 1980s and 1990s, now reaches into the culture (especially via many people under 45 or so) with the premise that the social or cultural construction of identity, language, knowledge, and beliefs is far more important than mere physicality. Consequently, the freedom to express gender fluidity is considered far more significant than the presence of any material sex differences. In fact, the very mention of sex differences is dismissed in many feminist circles as "essentialist," a charge derived from a strawman argument mounted by social-constructionist feminists in the 1980s: they accused difference feminists of believing that all females share some sort of fixed, essential personality structure. In fact, our point was simply that passing through life in a male or female body (cognitive structure, endocrine system, nervous system, etc.) strongly affects the ways in which one perceives and experiences life. We hold that every individual is unique but that the dynamics of embodiment influence perception and cognition. Today that observation is widely considered pathetically benighted—to the extent that even using the word *woman* is disallowed by some feminists on the grounds that it oppressively curtails total freedom of gender fluidity.[1]

In addition, calling attention to power dynamics by using such labels as "patriarchal culture" or "the virile system" has long since been eased aside in favor of the more neutral term "the gender system," which is more acceptable to male ears in academia and elsewhere. After all, who would hire or promote an aspiring assistant professor who wrote analyses of patriarchal dynamics in various fields? In studies of gender-linked patterns in language usage, the same progression can be seen over the years. In *Language and Women's Place* (1975), Robin Lakoff identified a "women's register," or socialized speech habits, that reflected a social position more insecure and inferior than that enjoyed by men. Other feminist linguists continued this "dominance approach" to reveal the power dynamics in language usage that are inherent to our patriarchal culture. This approach, however, was followed by the "difference" approach, which shifts the focus from cultural patterns of dominance to a neutral observation that the genders use language differently, such as Deborah Tannen's *You Just Don't Understand* (1980). As she put it—with no mention of power dynamics—men simply tend to interrupt women a lot, to set the topic of conversation in a mixed group, and to use a "report style" in conversation, while women tend to use a "rapport style." Today the hippest approach in the linguistics of gender difference is known as the "dynamic," or social-constructionist, approach, which rejects the notion of any categories in favor of the recognition that negotiating multiple dynamic factors to express a socially appropriate gender construction is merely a matter of "doing gender." *All the world's a stage.*

For these reasons, many young women today are further from exploring the insights of Herrmann, Irigaray, and other cultural feminist theorists of the 1970s on female voice and subjectivity than we were forty years ago. As young people were inculcated in college courses with the notion that "it's all just social construction," and as the female preferences for intimacy and relationship were devalued as mere gender posturing, the male preference for a hook-up culture came to dominate, and a growing rape culture found a protective home on many university campuses. At the time of this writing, young women are speaking out about the extreme situation on campuses where the worst elements of virile values have been allowed to become the norm. Perhaps the decades-long drift into "this virile and pitiful world" will be halted as more women find their voice. They are not theorizing about donning and doffing gender roles as a fluid societal game: they are *naming* brutal domination and sexual assault.

Embodiment, Again

Bodies do matter. At the same time that extreme social constructionism has captured the hearts and minds of many young feminists, evidence challenging that ideology has appeared in the numerous discoveries about sex differences that are being made in physiology. Unless one is aware of the recent emergence of the new field called female physiology, though, it is difficult to escape the ubiquitous conceptual premises of extreme social constructionism and to be able to appreciate the wisdom of the feminist authors on women's voices whom we will consider presently. It is now clear that—at every organizational level of the human body, from genes and cells to organs to the whole organism—sex differences shape our reality appreciably.

In physiological and medical research, as in the culture at large, the male has been considered the norm, which has caused research findings and drug testing to reflect the functioning solely of male bodies and to be significantly incorrect with regard to female bodies. Thanks to a group intervention by nearly all the women in Congress in the early 1990s, researchers receiving grants from the National Institutes of Health have been required to include adequate numbers of women in their studies. Also, for the first time grants were given to study more of the female body than the reproductive organs. Within the first decade of this new research, sex differences were identified at every level of structure and functioning within the human body. The first wave of these findings in female physiology and medicine was delineated by Marianne Legato, M.D., in *Eve's Rib* (2001).

Women remained underrepresented, however, in clinical trials carried out by pharmaceutical corporations and medical device makers. Consequently, women experience more severe side-effects from new treatments, and many drugs—from aspirin to anesthesia—are not as effective in women. To address this situation, the National Institutes of Health released a new policy in May 2014 requiring all researchers to alter long-standing basic research methods such that an equal amount of testing is done on female and male cells, tissue samples, lab rats, and human participants; also required is that the sex-specific testing be separated so that the respective results can be studied. As Janine A. Clayton, director of N.I.H.'s Office of Research on Women's Health, explained, "Each cell is either male or female, and that genetic difference results in different biochemical processes within that cell."[2]

Our species, like others, is dimorphic down to the cellular level, regardless of what sort of gender identity one decides to adopt and maintain. Not surprisingly, then, sex differences are apparent in brain structure. In December 2013 the *Proceedings of the National Academy of Sciences* published maps of the brain's so-called connectome, showing that women have stronger left-to-right links between the hemispheres and between areas of reasoning and intuition, while men have stronger back-to-front circuits and links between perception and action.[3] In tests, women did better at attention, word and face memory, and *cognition*, while men did better at spatial processing, motor skills, and sensorimotor speed. Women also have stronger connections among "modules," or subregions, while men have stronger connections within such modules. In addition, women also have more interconnections across the frontal lobes. These findings bring to mind the widely replicated tests of perception conducted initially in 1954 by Herman Witkin, which find cross-culturally that women tend to instantly perceive the interconnected whole, or gestalt, of a design flashed on a screen, while men tend to see the foreground figure rather than the gestalt in which it is embedded.[4]

As should be apparent, women have nothing to fear from these scientific discoveries about sex differences in mental tendencies. Although neither sex should ever be limited in opportunity because of interpretations of such statistical findings, it is simply not true that acknowledging these discoveries leads straight to a biological determinism that would remove women from the public sphere and limit them to the domestic sphere. On the contrary, women's talent for grasping the gestalt, or big picture, in any situation, as well as for perceiving an awareness of the dynamic interrelatedness that is involved, makes us logical candidates for any position in which such skills are crucial, such as presidents, directors, managers, lawmakers, judges, and diplomats.

The fact that women tend to experience a more palpable sense of dynamic interrelatedness than do men does not mean that they live in a fantasy world of imagined idyllic relationships. To have a relational orientation is to perceive the quality of the relational gestalt of a situation, whatever that might be—harmonious and pleasant, infused with wariness and distrust, or wrenchingly shattered. It is simply a matter of having acute powers of perception and awareness. For instance, when subjects in a test of perception are shown a series of projected photographs of human faces, each for a very brief amount of time, women have far greater success in identifying the particular emotional state being expressed. Most male subjects just can't see it.

"Frenchwomen, stop trying!"

That is the delightful title of an essay by Luce Irigaray. With the realization that sex differences strongly influence female or male perceptions of the world, one can better grasp the insistence by both Irigaray and Herrmann that women damage themselves, repeatedly, if they attempt to hew closely to the premises and expectations of the virile system, or manstream culture, which is an extension of male subjectivity but is passed off as being neutral. One could analyze this dynamic in every sphere of life and every field of endeavor. Here we will consider the difficulties it causes in the areas of language, style, and received concepts.

First, English, like all other languages in the Indo-European group, is characterized by nominalization. That is, the main focus is on nouns, or the naming of things, rather than on process, or stages of becoming, or subtle aspects of interrelatedness. It is a language group that evolved in the early Indo-European nomadic cultures on the Eurasian steppes, which had a patriarchal social structure, a chieftain system (reflected in their burial patterns), and glorification of warriors and weaponry. Second, the concepts and phrases in which we are socialized in school and elsewhere are built on premises that felt natural to the dominant group: men. For instance, in Aristotle's foundational philosophy of nature, naming and categorization are central, rather than attention to the complex dynamics of process or interrelatedness. Third, the style of expression, both orally and in print, that has long been the admired norm is, in general, reductionist in its logic: it ignores the whole of a gestalt other than those elements deemed noteworthy by virile values. In the logical progression A, B, C, *ergo* D, for instance, an underlying premise at the stage of A guides the identification of what is to be considered and what ignored, such that the subsequent steps follow neatly—and *Voilà!* The supposedly sole rational outcome is attained.

How tiresome it is. I suspect that the silences observed in many female lives follow not only from the futility of trying to fit a relational mentality into a system designed by and for hierarchical, competitive mentalities but also from the chasm that exists between our nominalized language and the female inner perception of a richly complex gestalt of dynamic interrelatedness. What we perceive and know cannot be articulated without significant diminution. Even the interior monologue in our minds is curtailed by the nominalized language system into which we were born.

There are no doubt many reasons for women's silences, but perhaps some of the women who opt for silence are not merely exhausted mentally and emotionally by the gap between their inner life and the way the outer world is structured and functions in a patriarchal culture. Perhaps they are Linguistic Lysistratas performing a principled act of non-cooperation with the dominant situation. Perhaps they reached a point at which their personal integrity demanded of them that they *stop trying*. I do not know if this was a possible motivation in the mystery on which Terry Tempest Williams reflects in *When Women Were Birds*. She tells the reader that her mother purchased many blank journals, as Mormon women are expected to do so that they can record information about their lives and family for posterity. Her mother kept them together in an orderly fashion on shelf in a closet. Shortly before she died of cancer, she told her daughter that she was leaving the journals to her. A few weeks after her mother's death, Terry Tempest Williams opened the journals and found that every one of them was blank. Has any woman reading this account felt that such a silence, although surprising, is entirely unfathomable? Not likely. Silence is our refuge, our very private preserve.

What would language and expressive forms be like that were an extension of the female mind's tendency to experience the world as a dynamic gestalt of interrelatedness and process? That rich complexity and fullness might first bring to mind the nonverbal possibilities—music, dance, and the visual arts. The catalogue of an extraordinary exhibition titled *In Wonderland: The Surrealist Adventures of Women Artists in Mexico and the United States* (2012), for example, presents scores of intriguing works by celebrated artists who were particularly interested in expressing the female psyche. (Hardly any of them applied the label *Surrealist* to their work, though others sometimes did.) In music, Lisa Gerard not only composes hauntingly powerful songs but creates and sings her own language of lyrics on CDs including *Mirror Pool* and all those by the Dead Can Dance duo.

Even when limited to box-car linear constructions of a nominalized language marching across the printed page in orderly rows, women of great talent have found ways to break through. In *Mrs. Dalloway* (1925), Virginia Woolf created complex characters who vibrate in fields of resonant embeddedness, whether painful or sustaining. *What a lark! What a plunge!* In the years shortly before World War I, Gertrude Stein thwarted linguistic expectations and composed playful romps delivering expositions that are never frivolous. Then, too, there are poets among us who can place a few words on a page and instantly manifest the unbounded relational gestalt we feel within—Elizabeth Bishop, Rosanna Warren, Annie Finch, Mary Szybist, and many others. Such works engage with a reality that we know experientially but do not otherwise see reflected in the culture.

To draw us out of the received constrictions and stretch our options, we might well consider the creative language-building in *Websters' First New Intergalactic Wickedary of the English Language* (1987) by Mary Daly with Jane Caputi. Luce Irigaray's groundbreaking and poetic essay on voice and female subjectivity, "When Our Two Lips Speak Together" (1976), also remains inspiring. Finally, to see a searching, uncompromising female literary mind on the page, swim into "Notes of a Lyric Artist Working in Prose: A Lifelong Conversation with Myself Entered Midway" (1994) by the novelist Carole Maso. At one point, she cites Virginia Woolf's declared intention "to saturate every atom. . . to give the moment whole; whatever it includes. . . . It must include nonsense; fact; sordidity; but made transparent."[5]

To give the moment whole—this is the aim of a writer who possesses an acute awareness of the embeddedness of every atom in every moment in a complex of dynamic relationships, a writer who would never even consider writing as if she were a person who perceives the world as composed of separative, isolate elements bumping into one another now and then, in need of a hierarchical ordering for coherence. The *world* is coherent. *Every moment* is coherent with interrelatedness. This we know as women. To find ways to give voice to our experience is an existential imperative: authentic lives require authentic voice. Sadly, the pioneering efforts mentioned above were all created long ago, after which further developments have been modest in comparison. Most of us have been on drift, having largely settled, with regard to our linguistic choices and creativity. Perhaps we will regain our momentum, though. Perhaps we will yet bring forth our mother tongues.

NOTES

1. Social constructionists who reject categories of male and female as the only two sexes point out that a small number of people are born with indeterminate genitals. This is true, and not only in our species; environmental toxins are suspected of disrupting the delicate process of conception and gestation. What is not clear is whether the brain and all other organ systems, cells, and genes also have indeterminate structure in such cases.

2. Roni Caryn Rabin, "N.I.H. Tells Researchers to End Sex Bias in Early Studies," *New York Times*, May 14, 2014.

3. Geoffrey Mohan, "Brains of women and men show strong hard-wired differences," *Los Angeles Times*, Dec. 3, 2013.

4. See the discussion in Charlene Spretnak, *Relational Reality: New Discoveries of Interrelatedness That Are Transforming the Modern World* (Topsham, ME: Green Horizon Books, 2011), pp. 189-193.

5. Virginia Woolf, cited in Carole Maso, "Notes of a Lyric Artist Working in Prose," *Break Every Rule* (Washington, DC: Counterpoint Press, 2000), p. 23.

A child stutterer chooses silence to regain her autonomy and observes a world that had been drowned out by words. But once this child becomes a young woman, she is unable to imagine a space for herself within a smooth-talking community, and so she devises a private self-help method that takes her through agonizing pain to final control of her speech. Now a lecturer in English literature, Carolyn Butcher acknowledges that, even though there are residual wounds, her journey to establish her voice was also a pathway to creativity and perception.

SPEECH DEFECTOR:
A CHILD STUTTERER FINDS HER VOICE

CAROLYN BUTCHER

"Silence creates a pathway to peace through pain, the pain of a distracted and frantic mind before it becomes still."
—Terry Tempest Williams, *When Women Were Birds: Fifty-four Variations on Voice*

Out of deference to those around me, especially the adults, I chose silence when I was eleven years old. While I saw my decision to stop talking as an act of kindness to those whose faces reflected embarrassment and confusion when presented with a child stutterer, I see now that it was also an act that restored my sovereignty. After all, since the adults around me referred to my stutter as a "speech defect," I saw myself as a flawed person. But if I did not speak, I would not stutter. If I did not stutter, I was no longer defective. My choice took control of a body that had let me down, and my silence meant release from the exhausting and frustrating effort it took to force words from my brain out into the world. I had found a space of ease and peace when I decided to shut up.

My stutter started when I was in kindergarten at a girls' Catholic school in Norwich, England. The principal was an insensitive nun, Sister Julie, who used to refer to me as "the beer man's daughter"

Carolyn Butcher is a writer living in Santa Barbara, California, where she teaches Critical Thinking Through Literature at Santa Barbara City College. She has a Ph.D. in English from the University of California, Santa Barbara, where her area of interest was the works of James Joyce. She has presented academic papers at many Joyce conferences in Europe and the United States and her doctoral dissertation examined the experience of reading Joyce's "unreadable text," *Finnegans Wake.* It is entitled, "Waking the Reader: Reading Finnegans Wake." "Speech Defector: A Child Stutterer Finds Her Voice" is excerpted from Carolyn's memoir-in-progress, *The Posterity Box,* www.theposteritybox.com.

because my father worked for Guinness. I thought that she disliked children, especially those who, like me, were not Catholic. Half the student body was Anglican, and I remember her telling us that she could not forgive "our" King Henry VIII because 500 years earlier he had established his own Church of England in order to divorce Catherine of Aragon.

I am sure that the stutter was partly hereditary—my father stuttered—but looking back I can see that it was exacerbated by mistreatment, if not downright cruelty and abuse, by Sister Julie. The memory is more a physical response than a narrative; a certain tightening in my jaw when I try to remember. The only scene I can recall with any certainty is the day Sister Julie visited my classroom and asked me a direct question in front of all the other girls. In attempting to answer her, my facial muscles went into a spasm and I could not make my mouth and tongue form the words I wanted to say, and the more I struggled and tried to force my diaphragm to push air through my teeth, the more my jaw became locked. Sister Julie giggled and mimicked my convulsions until the entire class roared with laughter. Perhaps they were laughing at her, but I was seven years old and I knew that, even if they were laughing at her in that moment, the next time I stuttered they would be laughing at me. And they did. Every time. I began to stutter more and more until the day I had had enough and stopped talking.

Silence put me in control and created a place of peace and solitude. Rather than cutting me off from the world, silence allowed me to see the world expansively. I did not lose words when I ceased speaking, they just got out of my way. I became an observer, a people reader, and I liked being out in the world and figuring out alternative ways of communicating. I smiled at people a lot, I nodded "yes" or shook my head for "no," and I was a great bearer of notes.

Whenever we stayed with my grandparents, who lived in a country town in Suffolk, it was my job to go and buy vegetables from a greengrocer whom we all referred to as "the cobweb man." This was in the days when shopkeepers reigned behind wooden counters and customers asked for the items they wanted to purchase one by one. I loved the store's musty smell. I loved the soft sound my shoes made on the bare wooden floorboards and I was fascinated to watch potatoes being poured from a barrel onto the scale that had separate round weights. My grandmother had one just like it at home, and I spent hours playing "shop" and figuring out how much different things weighed. While I awaited my turn, clutching the note my grandmother had given me to pass to the cobweb man, I checked out the spiderwebs in the corners of the roof. It was there, in the cobweb man's store, where I felt comfortable in a space where speech was not necessary and where the walls, floor, and shelves seemed as much a part of the land as the produce that was sold. A smile and a nod was all that I needed to complement the magic of the words listed, one below the other on the back of a used envelope, in my grandmother's handwriting with the curly upstrokes: *Potatoes, 3 lb.; Onions, 2 lb.; Cabbage, 2; Carrots, 1 lb*. I would like to think that the adults in my family thought this through, planned ways they could make sure I would not be cut off from the world. But, I don't think this was the case. Of course my parents arranged for me to see a speech therapist but, after several sessions, she fired me. She told my mother and me that she thought I stuttered more with her than with anyone else and that therefore the therapy sessions were only making things worse. After that, I think the adults decided to ignore my stutter. Like nose-picking, the best thing to do with bad habits in children is not to draw attention to them.

As puberty threatened, I saw no future for myself. It was Britain of the 1960s, and my life as an adult was ordained to be someone's wife. But, I wondered, what boy would want to be on a date with a girl whose body betrayed her with facial spasms and cessation of breath in order to force.....out....words? As a pre-teen, skipping past the unsolvable dating problem, I would lay in bed at night trying to figure out what words, what substitutes for those beginning with "m" and "w" like *married* and *wife*, I could persuade the priest to let me use in my wedding ceremony.

A few months after my resolution to stop talking, we moved to Newcastle-upon-Tyne because my father had been asked to manage the Guinness office there. We spent the summer in a rented fisherman's cottage on the coast while my mother looked for a house in the town. I loved the wild pebble beach and swam in the North Sea that was so cold that the downy hairs on my body felt as if they were tying themselves in knots when I rubbed myself dry with a towel. Amongst the famously warm, friendly, and self-effacing Geordies, I felt happier than I had ever been. In shops, or on the bus, complete strangers would call me "pet," "love," "hen," or "hinny," and, living in this city of unconditional acceptance, I decided that I could figure out ways around stuttering for myself.

I started by not using words that began with an *M, W, B,* or *L,* but of course there were times when flipping through my mental thesaurus did not work. At my new school, it seemed as though we were constantly having to take turns reading; and, while reading aloud was torture for me, it was also unbearable for the rest of the class. As the girls took turns, beginning at one back corner and gradually working one by one through the rows of desks towards me, I could feel the tension in the room increase. My heart would beat faster and faster until I was quite certain it was going to explode out of my chest—which would be a good thing because then I wouldn't have to read and the other girls wouldn't look at me with pity or contempt. Now that I am a teacher I can empathize with the helplessness my own teachers must have felt. But they were the grown-ups, dammit, and I do not remember one of them ever taking me aside to say, "We need to talk; what would you like me to do when you stutter?"

Avoiding certain consonants turned me into a living thesaurus and my vocabulary expanded greatly. To any adult who did not know me, I must have been the little girl with the arcane syntax. Recently, I heard David Sedaris reading a section of his book, *Me Talk Pretty One Day,* which is about his living in Paris and learning to speak French. He was unable to figure out the gender of nouns and, since logic didn't work, he solved the problem by speaking about everything in the plural. It made shopping a nightmare. His refrigerator overflowed with kilos of food and his apartment had duplicates of things he and his partner would never need, such as blenders. So, like the Sedaris apartment and its embarrassment of objects that he could not use, my brain had an embarrassment of words that I could not speak.

Since consonant avoidance was only successful when I could choose my own words, by the time I was about thirteen years old I realized I had to consider other tactics. First, I analyzed my physical situation. I took an upper body inventory. I had all the equipment I needed to speak because my tongue, lips, and teeth were all in good working order. Therefore, the breakdown in the system had to be in my brain, which I knew was the command center. After all, if I wanted a leg or an arm to move in a specific way (and I would lie in bed demonstrating this to myself), all I had to do was to command it and it would obey. If I could do that with my limbs, then I could do that with my diaphragm, lips, tongue, and jaw. I just had to think my way into speaking without a stutter.

Mind over Matter—that was the mantra of my childhood. It was given to me by my mother who would use it, not in situations where she had control, but at moments when she did not. She would quote that phrase whenever any of us needed to regain control. Car sick? Mind over Matter: just decide you are not going to vomit and you won't. The doctor is about to give you an injection? Just think about something else: Mind over Matter. I remember her telling me about a report she had heard on the radio by a woman who had been tortured by the Japanese in the Second World War. As they pulled out her fingernails one by one, the woman would think to herself: I can stand just one more. Who tells their child a terrifying story like that? A woman who wants to assert the power of Mind over Matter; a woman who used to refuse novocaine when having her teeth drilled at the dentist because she didn't like her mouth feeling numb afterwards; a woman who felt that much of her life was not in her control. My mother.

Of course the drawback to this philosophy in life is that it sets you up for failure. If you throw up in the car, it is because you did not succeed in privileging Mind over Matter.

Although my mother and I never discussed my speech impediment, her attitude and outlook taught me that I could think my way into speaking without a stutter. All I needed was a strategy and so began the daily debriefings that I conducted for the next few years of my life. Each night, as soon as I was in my bed, I reminded myself how comfortable and safe I felt as I lay beneath the pictures of Mrs. Peel from *The Avengers* that decorated the walls of my room. I wanted an all-in-one catsuit like Mrs. Peel's; I wanted my hair to have that perfect flip like Mrs. Peel; but most of all, I wanted to be able to control my body and my world just like Mrs. Peel. It wasn't the actress, Diana Rigg, on whom I had a crush but the character she played: the beautiful, smart woman who could get herself out of impossible situations using her judo skills and her quick wit. Every show ended with a few minutes of banter between Emma Peel and John Steed, and although now I can recognize the underlying sexual tension between them, back then I liked the way that Mrs. Peel always delivered the perfect retort that would leave an appreciative grin on Steed's face before the credits rolled. Mrs. Peel always had the last word.

My nightly evaluation began with a replay of all the vocal interactions of the day. I made myself relive the occasions when I had stuttered—not just remembering, but re-experiencing those mortifying moments again. I imagined how my face must have looked to the person trying to have a conversation with me, and I allowed my jaw to recreate its tension. I did everything I could to acknowledge and accept the distress of the day. Sometimes I cried. Then, I talked aloud to myself. I would say: "Well, today was bloody awful. I felt so embarrassed and humiliated that I wanted to disappear, and the worst part is that the words I wanted to say stayed in my head. But, what happened today wasn't quite as bad as what happened yesterday, and there were not as many stuttering moments as there had been the day before that. I will stutter again tomorrow, but it won't be as bad as it was today, and the day after that will be even better."

I convinced myself that all this was really true, that my mind could make it true, and this became my secret nightly routine for years and years. Mind over Matter. I never told anyone, especially my father, because, even though he never said anything to me, I sensed that the way I spoke caused him pain. A few years later, the depth of his agony was revealed to me in a setting where I least expected it—a party. Despite his own stutter, my father loved being around people and they loved being with him. He was warm and gregarious in social situations and his job was in sales where he was so successful that he eventually became Sales Administration Manager for Guinness. When I was about seventeen years old, I was standing beside my father at a cocktail party when one of my brother's teachers approached us and said he was concerned because Martin had started stuttering. Before my father had a chance to respond, I said flippantly, "Oh, it's a family trait. I stutter. Dad stutters. We all stutter." "Yes," agreed my father, "it is the curse I have passed onto my children." I was stunned. I looked at his face as he fought back tears, and realized for the first time that throughout my childhood he had blamed himself for my speech defect.

In the meantime, I had stumbled onto something wonderful. I could be funny. As long as I said something quickly, before my brain had time to think about how I was going to say it, the remark would come out clearly and stutter-less. At school I became the class clown. Unlike the years in the convent in Norwich, the girls and the teachers were now laughing at what I said, not at how I was saying it. The only exception to this was when I was the narrator of our senior year drama, *I'm Henry the Eighth I Am,* and they all laughed at my Texas accent.

The late 1960s were the height of academic satire in Britain and soon *Monty Python's Flying Circus* would be the must-watch TV program for everyone of my generation. But, pre-Python, my friends and I were cult followers of *I'm Sorry I'll Read That Again*, an intellectually silly radio show that was the genesis for our sketch. *I'm Henry the Eighth I Am* spoofed the story of King Henry VIII and four of his six wives, and I was involved in writing the script from the beginning. One day, my three co-writers and I were tired, over-stressed, and stuck for inspiration, and so I read the narration with an American accent to make them laugh. Later, when we performed the completed piece for the rest of the senior girls for their approval, we toned down some of the silliness, and I read without the accent. And I stuttered. What I remember most about that day is that I did not have my old, familiar feeling of mortification. I really, really, wanted to narrate the skit that I had put so much of myself into. And so, while many of the girls looked uncomfortable, my mind was already in analysis mode trying to figure out why I had not stuttered when I did the initial reading.

It was the accent.

I asked to try it again. And I did. With the accent. Without a stutter. Smiling from the sidelines, my three friends knew I had turned a corner. That day, I had discovered the pleasure of performance, and I am certain that the high I felt then, and the high that I still feel when I speak in front of a group of people, is in inverse proportion to the low I used to feel when I was the little girl whose face contorted whenever she tried to speak in class. Now that I am a parent, I feel the agony of my father's sense of responsibility for passing on what he thought was the curse of the family stutter. Remembering his face in the audience on the night of our performance as he yelled "Bravo!" when I took my bow as the narrator, I understand why he looked so elated. Although he never said anything to me about my speaking on stage, that night he was shouting because, in his mind, the curse had run its course.

It would be naive of me to suggest that there are not lifelong wounds. I am a lecturer in literature at a junior college and I worry that I might develop a sympathy stutter if I ever have a student with a speech difference in my class. In 2011, when *The King's Speech* was released, I contemplated avoiding seeing the film. I knew that I would not only identify with the king whom my family had held up to me as a role model when I was a child, but I also knew that I would somatically feel his pain. (A note to adults here: no child cares who else has, or had, a speech defect. I did not want to be in the Stutterers' Club, no matter who else was a member.) But I did see the movie and, while I spent much of the time with flooded eyes and my diaphragm threatening spasm, I also realized that Colin Firth's portrayal gave the world an understanding of what it is like to live as a stutterer in a smooth-talking world.

A few weeks later I met the writer of *The King's Speech* after he was on a panel of scriptwriters at the 2011 Santa Barbara International Film Festival. David Seidler, himself a child stutterer, was asked by the moderator why it took him more than twenty years to write the screenplay. Seidler said that Valentine Logue, the son of King George's speech therapist, would only agree to hand over his father's notebooks if Seidler had permission from Queen Elizabeth The Queen Mother to make the movie. Writing from her home at Clarence House, the Queen Mother gave her consent with the proviso: "Please, Mr. Seidler, not during my lifetime. The memory of these events is still too painful." This last statement remains at the forefront of my memory because the longterm suffering she expresses, more than forty years after her husband's death, shows how widespread is the trauma of stuttering within families and communities—without regard for wealth or social position.

While on that panel, Seidler said something else to the audience that instantly reawakened the little girl within me as she lay in bed under the pictures of Mrs. Peel. He said, "the royal stutter is an embarrassment. You must understand that stuttering was called, until very recently, a speech defect. So, if you had a speech defect then you were *ipso facto* a defective person. You couldn't have the king of England being called a defective person, so you don't talk about the stutter."

Seidler had stuttered from the ages of three to sixteen and so he too had been, *ipso facto*, a defective person. It was in that moment that I recognized that shame had also been ever-present for me throughout my stuttering childhood and, having never had the courage to go up and speak to anyone remotely famous before, I wanted to meet David Seidler. At first, I left the theatre too full of emotion to face him, but a friend of mine saw what was happening within me and took me back in. Almost thirty years after I had found my voice within a phony Texas accent behind a microphone, I was once again silent—filled to the brim with everything BUT words. Seeing me, Seidler squatted at the edge of the stage and held out his hand. For a very long time, he held my left hand tightly (my right was clutching a wad of kleenex) and, as we looked into each other's face, he just nodded, once, very slowly. Neither of us said a word.

In the preoccupation about obesity culminating in the current so-called War on Obesity, one voice is notably missing—that of the fat person. They are not included on panels determining policy or treatment or legislation concerning them because fat people are not deemed credible. Given this sorry state of affairs, Cheryl Fuller believes now is the time for the fat lady to sing and give voice to the lived experience of being fat in a world which fears and reviles the fat body.

THE FAT
LADY SINGS

CHERYL FULLER

"What are the consequences when we go against our instincts?
What are the consequences of not speaking out? What are the
consequences of guilt, shame, and doubt?"
  —Terry Tempest Williams, *When Women Were Birds:*
Fifty-four Variations on Voice

I first came to Maine in 1963 on vacation with my brother and his
family. I remember driving on the turnpike past Waterville and
seeing a large sign advertising a restaurant called The Silent
Woman. The sign depicted a decapitated woman serving refreshments
on a tray. Both sign and restaurant are long gone. In 1963, though I
knew nothing about feminism, I viscerally understood what a horrible
image that was—a headless woman performing her service function
with the implication that this is perhaps the highest and best form of
woman, woman without a voice.

Polly Young-Eisendrath in *Jung, Gender and Subjectivity* reminds
us "we have no narrative, no plot, no paradigm for the life of a strong,
adventurous woman."[1] She also says: "in order for us to develop fully,
we must claim the legitimacy of our own experience...Even the most
accomplished women among us must practice knowing the categories
of their own experiences because these are largely unrecorded."[2]

Cheryl Fuller, M.A., Ph.D., is a Jungian psychotherapist and writer in private practice
in Belfast, Maine. She has written and taught about Medea and feminism. For the last
seven years, she has written a blog, Jung-At-Heart.com. Her current academic research
lies at the intersection of fat studies and analytical psychology. She is currently working
on a book exploring stigma and anti-fat bias and their effects on the lived experience of
fat women in and out of the consulting room.

The Silent Woman, 2013—You have seen her, or others like her, many times, the "headless fatty," a term coined by Charlotte Cooper in 2007.[3] When journalists run stories on television and in print about the evils of obesity, there she is, a fat, usually a very fat woman on the street or the beach or some other public place. In such stories fat people are almost without exception shown without heads. Why are they headless? Because the images are used without permission of the person photographed? Indeed, that is usually the case but permission is not required for photographs of people in public. Because anyone who looks like this would/should be ashamed to have her face show? Because it allows the viewer to see her as an object and not a person?

Curious about this phenomenon, I contacted a photographer, Gabor Degre, who had taken headless fatty photos used in a statewide newspaper in Maine. I asked him about this practice of omitting heads of fat people in news stories. He replied that it is a "sensitivity thing...Not showing heads gives the generic overweight person's look but is not showing that Xxx Yyy, specifically, is a fat person. If there was a story about one specific person being fat, that would be different." (personal communication, February 3, 2014) Who really is this sensitivity for? The fat person in the photo, who is deprived of her individuality by removing her head? She already knows she is fat as she lives with that reality every day. Or is it to allow the viewer to see that person as an object rather than a human being? As C.S. Lewis wrote, "How can they meet us face to face till we have faces?"[4] Judith Moore, author of *Fat Girl*, writes: "The most shameful fat facts, and those facts most avoided when the fat or formerly fat write about fatness, are facts about the fat body...What people do want to write about is weight loss and how to lose it. They want to write about self-esteem and how to gain it."[5]

For nearly all of my life thin people have been telling me what I should do to become thin like them. It gets old fast, having someone who has no idea what I have already tried, how many times I have tried, and no idea what it is like to be fat telling me what I should do to be thin, to be normal, to fit in, as if I hadn't already tried to do just that more times than I could count. For much of my life, I mutely tried hard, very hard, to do what they said. We fat people are rarely consulted about what it is like to be fat, about how we eat and move and live our lives because we are not seen as credible. Because we are not seen as reliable witnesses to our own experiences and lives. To paraphrase Young-Eisendrath, we have no narrative of a fat woman who lives a full life, much less a life free of shame. Now it is my turn to do the telling. Now is the time for the fat lady to sing.

I am a fat woman. I have been fat since I was five years old. As a young child, I used to hide from my uncle who would poke me and call me "Fatty" while singing "The Too Fat Polka" and laugh. Too many times my mother told me I was "as big as the side of a house." From early on I felt the sting and shame of being too big, too much. The humiliation of being weighed in gym class. The blind date who told his friend, within earshot, that I was a "dog." Knowing I was different and feeling shame for not being slender like other girls, like my mother.

An introvert, I am also shy, always a bit ill at ease in large groups or with strangers. Being fat only magnified that shyness. In my early thirties after years of dieting and battling against my weight, I tired of it all. I could not do one more diet, spend one more day obsessing about what I could and could not eat, one more night going to bed feeling an utter failure because I was hungry, because I was losing so slowly or not at all. There was only one thing left—the hard work to stop hating my body, to become able to look at and feel myself without cringing or eviscerating myself with insults and criticism. The work I did to learn not to loathe my fat body enabled me to go places, to meet people without constantly worrying about how they saw me. I learned a cheery, warm, and pleasant persona for public spaces, because somewhere inside I believed that if I made myself easy to be around, then at least I could avoid hearing the negative judgments about my body. I was careful to dress nicely, to try to act like I felt pretty. And as long as I didn't think about it, didn't start looking at myself from outside myself, I was all right and I could be out and about and forget about the shame I wear in my flesh. I learned to pull myself way inside my body, away from my skin, away from the surface where I could be hurt, and I could become this sparkling personality and be unaware of my physical self. I could be like Echo, the voice without a body. I could wrap myself in my invisibility cloak of charm and move through the world insulated from the judgments and scrutiny of others. In order to move around in the world, I had to protect myself this way or risk being crushed by the weight and sharpness of looks and judgments I encountered and the shame I pushed down inside.

For almost all of my adult life, I have wanted desperately to find a reason for this fat I carry, some explanation that I could rest on. At times I told myself it is all about biology and genetics, an inevitable outcome of being my father's daughter, as the Fuller women were all fat women who lived long lives. There is comfort in that explanation because if the reason for my fat is biological, then it is not my fault any more than my eye color or height is my fault; it is just the way I was made.

Other times I would fall to the other side of the coin and believe the cause lay in my troubled relationship with my mother. I read Hilda Bruch, Marion Woodman, Geneen Roth, Kim Chernin, and all those others who led me to believe that if I could just work my way through those issues, then everything would change and I would be normal, I would become thin and stay that way. So I talked and wrote endlessly about my mother and my relationship with her. I told the stories of my childhood with her so many times that they almost seemed no longer mine.

Then I read Susie Orbach's *Fat is a Feminist Issue* and once more it all became muddled, this time in feminist politics and the tyranny of the patriarchy. I began to consider again that maybe this fat body is my normal, maybe this is the body I am meant to have and that trying to beat it into submission, trying to make it smaller is to be in a state of war with myself. Without realizing it, I became part of the fat acceptance movement. Identity politics gave me a new way to experience myself and my fat. I could think about this body, my fat body, being the right one for me. I could connect myself with a primal, round, earthy feminine, an earlier and more generous version of beauty and fertility and womanliness. If I did not press too hard nor look too deeply, I could see that. I dreamed of a fat woman with colored ribbons for hair who danced naked with delight in her own fleshy abundance. I painted her. There were even moments when I felt her.

On the internet, where anyone can hide behind a pseudonym, trolls feel free to vent their fat hatred as in the following, left in anonymous comments on various blogs:

> But fat really is gross and ugly. It's a sign of indulgence, lack of exercise, poor life choices. Yuck. I wouldn't date a fat person if we were the last two people on earth.

> The last thing we need is another whining class of victims. Most of the time, fat people are victims of only one thing: their own appetites.

> Fat people are ugly and they stink. I don't like looking at them. I like looking at athletic bodies, both male and female. They are works of art (and whoever defiles the body, defiles the soul). I like the beauty of such a bio-machine in motion. It is ART. I like the shadows cast by the muscles; I like when I see the tendons push out the skin. When I see this, I want to go up to that person and strum the tendons like a violin. I don't see any of that with fat people. But I smell fat people when they spill over into my seat.

There seems to be no barrier to expressing such bigotry. And though it is usually unspoken, nearly every fat person has seen or heard enough similar judgment to be aware that any time she walks down the street, someone is thinking or saying things like that. Fat people swim in a sea of toxic prejudice.[6]

It is a battle on multiple fronts, this trying to come to terms with, to understand and be conscious about fat. First is the battle with the prejudice and condemnation of the culture, the hatred and disgust directed at fat people. How do I make my way in a world in which my very body is seen as too much, as emblematic of appetite run amok? A world in which even strangers feel it is helpful to me to call my attention to my size and/or to offer "helpful" suggestions on what I should do to become smaller, to take up less of their precious space? A world in which any time I enter an airplane, I know that there are passengers already there praying I won't have the seat next to them because I might encroach upon their space, because I might somehow touch them with the curse of my fat.

Then there is the battle within, the struggle to discern the meaning of my fat without taking on blame. How do I not feel crushed by the weight of blame for my own body, the blame that comes with the belief that all I had to do to be "normal" was to eat less and move more? The struggle is to find my way through the judgment and shame that blame brings with it.

Finally is the battle with the introjected judgments that surround me, that voice that echoes the judgments around me and attacks me viciously for being out of bounds. Telling me, in every kind of entertainment I seek out, every advertisement to which I am exposed, every newspaper or magazine I read, every form of media I consume that bodies like mine are bad, take up too much space. That I am undisciplined, lazy, stupid, gluttonous.

Lester Spence, a African-American political scientist, writes about the freedom of being in "black space" where he can be fully himself, where he knows the people there have visceral understanding of what it is to be a black man, where there is a shared cultural background and where "I can, in those spaces, breathe."[7] Contrast this with what he calls "white spaces" where he must "consciously be aware of what I am saying, of who is around me, of what I am wearing, of what I am doing, of what others are saying and doing. In critical ways, I cannot let my guard down for a moment."[8]

There is nothing like Spence's black space for most of us who are fat except perhaps at gatherings of fat acceptance activists. There are few places where I can just breathe, not have to explain myself or watch myself or work to ignore the looks of disapproval, where I fit in, where I can be and do and move without being subject to scrutiny and silent, or usually silent judgment. It is only when I am at home, with the people who love me, or with my friends or family that I can approximate that kind of space, where I feel no need to excuse or pretend to agree with the general attitude about fat. Every place else is like Spence's "white space," space where my fat reveals what must be my shame, my laziness, my self-indulgence, my gluttony, my too-muchness. When my friend, my very fat friend died, I heard people attributing her death to her weight, and during the long days before her death, as she lay in ICU on a respirator, friends of hers said that maybe now, when she recovered, she would lose weight, as if she were choosing to be fat. I imagine that morbid obesity is listed on her death certificate as a cause of her death. The truth is that she died of a virulent infection she acquired in the hospital, a hospital with a not very good infection rate.

It's not much space, fat space. It is a few rooms in the whole of my world where I can be, like Lester Spence in black space, fully myself. With a few people that I trust don't judge me or find me disgusting or believe my body is an indicator of my character or my health. When I am in thin space and I enter a room where there are other people, without thinking, I scan the room to see if there are other fat people there. To be the only fat person is to stand out in an uncomfortable way. I find relief when there is someone as fat or fatter than I am.

If I am in thin space and I go out to eat with others, say for lunch during a workshop, I am aware of what everyone eats. Women apologize to each other for eating— "I didn't eat breakfast so I need a big lunch." or "I should just have a salad." There seems to be an unwritten rule that it is gauche to enjoy eating, to eat whatever and as much as one wants. So I am careful to eat sparingly and never have dessert. I know if I have french fries with my sandwich, there will be little mental cluckings over that.[9]

I don't go shopping with other women. We can't shop in the same stores. There is no store in my town where I can buy clothes. I can't exchange clothes with other women. None of my friends wears my size.

In thin space I am always on guard. Even as I work to maintain my cloak of invisibility, I am hyper-aware of my behavior—my voice, how I move. I made myself learn to walk lightly. I am vigilant. Always aware of the others. In thin space, I am thin-skinned.

Sometimes, I am very physically self-conscious. At those times it is harder for me to not look at me from outside myself. I "see" myself when I think about going someplace new and outside of my fat space, and I can be flooded with an uncomfortable sense of self-consciousness. I feel inhibited and reluctant to go. I make myself go, but it is an act of brute force and I am unable to "forget" about the judgments and looks that I am usually able to make myself oblivious to. At those times I can't find my invisibility cloak. I feel naked and exposed. How to be in thin space without being thin-skinned, without being angry, without my invisibility cloak? I cling to my tiny fat space. And try to breathe.

If I want to be perceived as compliant, I know how to present myself as the Good Fat Person. All I have to do is talk about trying to lose weight, about my desire to be thin. I can say I have lost ten or fifteen or thirty pounds and I will be praised for my efforts, even if it is a lie. Because the Good Fat Person is apologetic for being fat and is in a perpetual state of trying to become thin. The Good Fat Person doesn't threaten thin people because she tells them she is engaged in the same struggle to subdue her body as they are. The Good Fat Person is apologetic for her fat, as if she must ask forgiveness for committing an aesthetic crime with her too-muchness or must do penance for taking up too much space. She doesn't complain about the relative lack of variety in clothing available to her and accepts that she should wear shapeless cover-ups, preferably in dark colors. She accepts as just that she pays more for her clothing, health care, seats on airplanes. Because she knows she deserves it. She accepts without protest the "helpful" advice and criticism she receives from others because she is trying to become better, to become thin.

No matter where I go or what I do, I am almost always surrounded by messages about the unacceptability of my body. The constant examination of the fat body by doctors, social workers and psychiatrists, teachers, lay people, comedians, journalists, even First Lady Michelle Obama, are in effect attempts to exert a societal discipline to make "docile bodies."[10] We fat people are meant to feel shame, to feel we are responsible for our weight. We internalize the judgments and endless indictments for our failure to have become slender, for being too lazy or hungry or weak to bring our wayward bodies under control.

Every time I have hidden my eating from others, or felt too self-conscious to eat in public something that I want, like dessert, or have avoided eating altogether, I have eaten the disgust others feel for my body. I eat their disgust and it becomes part of me. Every time I buy my clothes from designated retailers, ones who deign to carry clothing in my size and I accept that I should pay more for clothing generally of lower quality than is available in so-called normal stores, I am buying and wearing the revulsion designers of clothing feel for my folds of flesh and billowing hips and thighs. I work at making myself be less self-conscious. I can use the word "fat" with ease. I am able to talk about the assaults, large and small, to my dignity that I encounter every time I leave my house. I can do all of these things. But I can never escape the panopticon.[11] I am always under scrutiny. Underneath it all, underneath the work I did to stop hating myself, underneath the pleasant persona, way down under there where I look at myself from outside and see myself with others' eyes, in that place I judge myself as severely as they do. And feel furious with myself for being fat. And with them for their disgust. Furious for being furious. I am furious. Underneath all of that I am furious. Which I dare not show. Fury. That I do not express. That I swallow. Maybe my fat is made up of all my swallowed fury. Maybe if I let it all out, I would shrink, deflate like a punctured balloon.

Someone once said that the rage of all the fat women in the world is enough to destroy the world if let loose. I believe that.

> I fear silence because it leads me to myself, a self I may not wish to confront. It asks that I listen. And in listening, I am taken to an unknown place. Silence leaves me alone in a place of feeling. It is not necessarily a place of comfort.[12]

Breaking the silence, claiming my voice requires that I, that fat women, come out as fat. That I am fat is visible to anyone who sees me. It is not something I can hide. No cleverly designed "slimming" garment can change my body from fat to thin. It is a little strange to think about coming out as fat when anyone who sees me knows. So what does it mean to come out as a fat person?

Coming out as fat means letting go of being the Good Fat Person, the one who accepts that she must keep working to beat her body into submission. Just by calling myself fat, using that word unselfconsciously and without shame or apology, is movement away from being the Good Fat Person. Just by calling myself fat, I break the silence. But there is more to coming out fat than that. While I made the decision thirty-five years ago to stop dieting, that was not something I talked about with friends. Nor did I speak up when conversation turned to talk of diets and dieting. As LeBesco has put it, "fat activists regularly describe the experience of coming out as fat as choosing to no longer pass as on-the-way-to thin."[13] It may not seem as if a fat person could "pass," since after all our bodies are visible, but being the Good Fat Person is a way of passing by acting as if by embracing body hatred, dieting, guilt, and shame, we can then claim membership in the "normal" world by always trying to be on the way to thin.

When I was a Good Fat Person, I would delay buying major clothing items like a winter coat because of the hope, the belief, the desire that next year I would be smaller. In my closet, as in the closets of many fat women, I had things that I could no longer wear, but which I kept in the hope that next year, someday I could again wear those skinny jeans or that now-too-tight skirt. Because that is the way to be good. Always be on the way to thin, no matter how distant thin may be. No matter how long or how many unsuccessful attempts there are between now and that ever elusive goal weight.

As a Good Fat Person I did everything I could through my behavior to apologize for being fat, for taking up too much space in the world. I mutely accepted that I should have to go to special stores for clothing, deal with rude remarks on the street, comments from "helpful" friends and family about how much they worried for me and fervently wished I would lose weight, that I would stop "letting myself go." I hid my anger at the insults disguised as concerns for my well-being, the endless suggestions for what I should do to lose weight. When a waiter once told me that I did not need dessert, I did not protest. Because as a fat person, I tacitly accepted that I needed policing to keep myself in check.

In my life, I have been on just about every kind of diet you can imagine, starting when I was nine years old. Counting calories, low fat, low carb, Weight Watchers, Diet Workshop, Metrecal (remember that stuff?), diet pills, I've tried them all. I wanted with all my heart to believe that all I had to do was find the right plan and somehow magically I would be normal, I would become thin.

I did lose weight. Losing weight is actually fairly easy and any of those methods produce weight loss. But inevitably every single time the weight would slowly come back and I would end up where I was before, but in a perverse twist, a little heavier than when I started. I only stopped gaining weight when I stopped trying to lose weight. But stopping dieting is not coming out. It is an act of rebellion, to be sure, but the rebel is always defined by that against which she rebels. Coming out means letting go of the fantasy of the thin person inside waiting to get out. Coming out is to stop pretending to be trying to lose weight when I am not. Coming out is letting go of shame and embracing the body I have. Coming out is accepting myself, all of myself, fat and all.

Coming out means going in, inside myself and wrestling with the both/and-ness of it all. That yes, I come by this body honestly, but that doesn't mean it is all due to my biology. It means accepting that no matter how much I wrestle, the end of the match does not mean I will get thin. It means knowing that, yes, anger and my mother complex and all those other complexes Marion Woodman wrote about have played a role in the development of the body I have now. And in a sense, now I wear the results of having had those struggles for so long. Like the scars from any battle on those who have fought one, my body carries my scars, in the form of fat that won't go away.

Marion Woodman said of one of the patients she discusses in *Addiction to Perfection,*

> Rather than deal with the fat as fact, Ruth was trapped in unconscious identification with her large body. She had no ego with which to separate herself from whatever myth was being lived out through the fat. The reason she weighed 325 pounds was that she refused to accept the existential reality that her body was forced louder and louder to proclaim.[14]

The reason Ruth weighs 325 pounds is because she is heir to a complex brew of genes and exposure to bacteria and viruses and hormones and who knows what else, all interacting in a way we cannot yet define with how she feels, how she has been treated in her family and in the world, what she does with her anger. And no amount of analysis with even the very best analyst can give her the thin body she, and it seems Marion Woodman, would like for her to have.

And that is perhaps the hardest thing, the most difficult part of coming out as fat. To identify with, really inhabit and love my fat body. Unconditionally.

Fat acceptance and fat activism—and for many, they are one and the same—generally follow principles articulated by Marilyn Wann, author of the book, *Fat! So?* The assumption is that by claiming the word "fat" and embracing our fat bodies, somehow everything changes. This very closely resembles the principles of cognitive behavioral therapy, i.e., all one has to do to change feelings is to change thoughts. There is a degree of truth in that. Certainly working to stop hating my body was worthwhile. And choosing to use "fat" unselfconsciously defangs that word and it becomes just a descriptor, not an indictment. But just as cognitive behavioral therapy can only go so deep, so too with fat acceptance. That I accept my body as it is, that I accept and embrace my fatness does not in any way change the world around me. While accepting myself and my body is an essential first step, it is only a first step. It does nothing to detoxify the sea of judgment and prejudice I swim in.

Embracing fat acceptance gives a measure of dignity and a refuge from self-loathing, but every day I confront the assumption that fat people have lost their self-control. And frighten others because there is such a premium placed on being thin, to the point of being a public obsession. Ask them and most people say they want to be slender, but this physical perfection is difficult to attain, harder to hold on to, and they fear losing control of it. Women and men can be on diets their whole lives. A fat person, particularly a fat person who seems at home with herself and her body, is threatening. She of the jiggling flesh, the billowy hips, the soft folds of fat, flies in the face of the washboard abs, botoxed faces, lean hard size zero of the supermodels held up to us all as icons of the ideal. Fear and unhappiness get projected onto people who are bigger, and that too often translates into abuse and attacks. In attacking fat people, the person terrified of the security of her grip on her own body disassociates herself from what she fears the most— getting fat. In this time of war on obesity, the fat person is the enemy and wears, obvious for all to see, the very thing that many fear will befall them if rigid control is not maintained. The fat person becomes the example of what no one should be. Many believe fat people are really thin people who have let themselves go, have fallen for the seduction of food. We are failed citizens.[15] No matter what I do, no matter how I am able to be with myself, the reality is that there is more going on than simply how I feel in and about my body. In other words, when I leave the comfort of my home I have to deal with not only my own feelings but also my feelings in response to how others respond and react to me and to my body. As Samantha Murray puts it, "I AM my body, and this understanding is always informed by cultural imaginings about bodies. My body and fat and myself are inextricably bound up in producing and reproducing my identity, which is always already corporeal."[16]

Coming out as fat is a process, not an event. Marion Woodman is wrong about some things, but she is right about this: "if we are to find our own truth, we have to go into our darkness alone and stay with our inner process until we find our own healing archetypal pattern...It takes great courage to break with one's past history and stand alone."[17]

Each of us must find her own way through all of what fat represents in our lives, both psychically and physically, and face into its complexity to find that healing space. And perhaps most importantly, break our silence and tell our stories.

NOTES

1. Polly Young-Eisendrath, *Jung, Gender and Subjectivity in Psycho-analysis* (London: Taylor and Francis, Kindle Edition), p. 92.

2. *Ibid.*, p. 98.

3. Charlotte Cooper, "Headless Fatties" (2007) [Online]. http://charlottecooper.net/publishing/digital/headless-fatties-01-07. Accessed Jan. 30, 2014.

4. C.S. Lewis, *Till We Have Faces* (New York: Harcourt Brace Jovanovich, 1985), p. 294.

5. Judith Moore, *Fat Girl: A True Story* (New York: Plume, 2005), p. 174.

6. Em Farrell, "Obesity: How Can We Understand It?" Accessed March 2, 2010 at http://www.psychoanalysis-and-therapy.com/human_nature/free-associations/farrellob.dwt.

> "Fat is not only hated, but also seen as doing physical damage to the individual. Frantz Fanon talked of the internalised racist where the ideology of whites was internalised by Blacks. So that Blacks too associated being Black with failing, being lazy, being less, being stupid and being white meant having power, being successful and being pure! The black man or woman idealised the system of white hierarchy and held it in their own mind as a model. The same is true for people who believe themselves to be fat. They believe the propaganda that thin is better, not only in terms of health, but that it will make them a better and happier person with a higher status and so they hate who they are."

7. Lester Spence, "White Space, Black Space." Accessed Dec. 28, 2013 at www.busboysandpoets.com/blog/white-space-black-space.

8. *Ibid.*

9. Diane Zdrodowski, "Eating out: The experience of eating in public for the 'overweight'woman," *Women's Studies International Forum*, 6 (1996), 655-664. Zrdodowski interviews a number of fat women regarding this issue, and includes these excerpts from the interviews:

> Rose: I always choose healthy meals with plenty of veg . . . it depends on if people can see me when I am eating as to whether I have a sweet.

> Ella: I don't mind having fattening food such as pastry but I couldn't be seen to be eating cake or fried foods such as chips.

> Val: I have vegetarian meals because they look healthier . . . I'd rather have steak or chicken, etc. but often they come with chips and I feel as if everyone is looking at me.

10. Michel Foucault, *Discipline and Punish: The Birth of the Prison*, trans., A.M. Sheridan Smith (New York: Vintage Books, Inc., 1995), p. 136. A docile body is "one that may be subjected, used, transformed, and improved" and "this docile body can only be achieved through strict regiment of disciplinary acts."

11. In the panopticon, as Foucault writes, "there is no need for arms, physical violence, material constraints. Just a gaze. An inspecting gaze, a gaze which each individual under its weight will end by interiorizing to the point that he is his own overseer, each individual thus exercising this surveillance over and against himself." Michel Foucault, "The eye of power," in C. Gordon (ed.) *Power/Knowledge: Selected Interviews and Other Writings 1972-1977 by Michel Foucault* (Sussex: Harvester Press, 1980), p. 155.

12. Terry Tempest Williams, *When Women Were Birds: Fifty-four Essays on Voice* (Kindle Location 541-544).

13. Kathleen LeBesco, *Revolting Bodies: The Struggle to Redefine Fat Identity* (Boston: University of Massachusetts Press, 2004), p. 95.

14. Marion Woodman, *Addiction To Perfection* (Toronto: Inner City Books, 1982), p. 55.

15. LeBesco, *Revolting Bodies*, p. 58.

16. Samantha Murray, "Doing Politics or Selling Out?: Living the Fat Body," *Women's Studies: An Interdisciplinary Journal* 34:3-4, 2005, p. 271.

17. Woodman, *Addiction to Perfection*, p. 28.

"Sleeping Beauty" traces the personal and collective history of American women in the last forty years to understand how—forty years after *Roe v. Wade*—we have ended up here, facing more pushback, more restrictions, and more institutionalized misogyny than ever. Through memoir, essay, and fairy tale, the author examines the silences that enforce—often violently—limitations on women's freedoms and makes the case for the urgent need for women to speak the truth about their lives so that real change can happen.

Sleeping Beauty Wakes Up:
Breaking the Spell of Women's Silence

JANICE GARY

1.

Light fills the hall of the old Key West Armory, streaming in from the high windows like fairy dust, soft and white and unusually strong for a winter's day in January. The house buzzes with excitement until Margaret Atwood steps onto the stage and a hushed silence fills the room. I crane my neck, hoping to get a glance of her from my seat in the very back row, but I'm too short and the woman in front of me too tall. Frustrated, I shove my purse under me to get some height and there she is—her unruly mane of wiry hair, her too-white complexion, her eyes—blue, steely. Steady.

Perched on my roost of leather and lumpy wallet, I'm not steady at all. I feel like a flighty bird unseated by an inexplicable feeling of anticipation mixed with dread. The blank pages of my journal rest in my lap, open and waiting.

Margaret takes her seat on the raised dais, like a Goddess or a Queen, which she has been to me ever since I read *The Handmaid's Tale*, a science fiction fantasy that chilled me to the bone every time I held it in my hands. Don't be silly, I'd tell myself. There was no reason to fear what kept creeping into the back of my mind while turning the pages, which was that this could happen, might happen—that our freedom, our gains

---

Janice Gary, M.F.A., is the author of *Short Leash: A Memoir of Dog Walking and Deliverance*, winner of two Silver 2014 Nautilus Awards, and a 2014 Eric Hoffer Prize for Memoir. Her work has been published in numerous national publications including the *Baltimore Review*, *Literal Latte*, and *Kaleidoscope*. She was on the faculty of the 2013 Summer Study Program at the C.G. Jung Center in New York City ("Dreams and Memoir"), presented a session on "Women's Silences" at the 2014 Associated Writing Program Conferences, and teaches memoir and creative writing at the Writer's Center in Bethesda, Maryland and at Anne Arundel Community College. Her website is www.janicegary.com.

as women in America were merely a rickety scaffold holding up a barely
built cathedral.

In 1985, when the book came out, I had just left a bruising career
as a punk rock singer and was diving into the "Dress for Success"
eighties, throwing away my spandex and stilettos for the female version
of male suits, complete with the floppy "feminine" bow ties women
were encouraged to wear as they entered into the corporate class. We
were post-liberation women, well past the messy fight for access to
contraception and abortion fought by our older sisters, moving on to
executive suites outfitted with soft carpeting and glass ceilings. Atwood's
story of fundamentalist Christians stripping women of their rights and
dividing the female population into breeders and groomers and
"Marthas" was just elaborate futurist fiction, right?

Twenty-seven years later, I have come to hear the woman whose
words have haunted me ever since I read them. Among the sea of bodies
near the front seats, someone raises her hand and asks Margaret how
she came up with the idea for *The Handmaid's Tale*. Did she think
something like this could ever happen to women? Really?

Atwood barely blinks as she gives her answer. "I didn't make any
of this up," she says. "It has happened and it is happening."

I can feel my heart sinking below the polished pine floorboards
as she speaks of the handmaiden Leah in the Bible, of the way
women are used and abused around the world, of the threat of
fundamentalism and fascism, the use of fear to coerce women and
enforce the privilege of patriarchy. "You can always tell when
authoritarian rule is on the rise. The first thing they do is attempt to
take control of women's bodies."

I scribble her words as fast as they are spoken, but after awhile the
roar inside my head is so loud that very little gets through. What I
had intuited when reading this book, what I knew in my heart and
could not allow into my head, has just been confirmed by the woman
who wrote it.

It has happened. It is happening.

And I can't pretend otherwise anymore.

2.

As a child, the tales that nurtured my young mind were of
Cinderella, Sleeping Beauty, Snow White, stories full of castles and curses

and handsome princes. Growing up in a chaotic household with a father who was both a King and an ogre and a mother who fed me on fantasy and fear, fairy tales were not make-believe, they were *must-believes*, the only way out of a world where a small girl had little control over her life and even less power in the kingdom.

"You think you're Cinderella, don't you?" my father would say when I balked at doing chores at home or tending to the small tasks he assigned me when I accompanied him to his dry-cleaning store on the weekends. Half-joke, half-rebuke, we both knew he was stating the obvious. I dusted and washed and baked at home, and then bagged clothes, took lunch orders, and cleaned the bathroom in his store. Most of the time, I didn't mind the work, even took pride in it, because it made the King favor me. What I did not see was how this affected my Mother, who had Queenly dreams of her own, and my sister, who was forced into the role of Court Jester. Like Cinderella's evil step-mother and step-sisters, both of them envied me—although there wasn't much to envy besides the attention of the King.

Then again, what else mattered? In our family, our culture, our 1960's America, where women had limited options in the outside world, the favor of the King was everything. Women, big and little, were pitted against each other in a world that hinged on access to the men who ruled. Limited resources to male privilege made enemies of sister and sister, mother and daughter, a dynamic that exists to this day in the stereotype of the catty, back-biting woman.

Surviving in a landscape of lack takes cunning. You must find ways to slip in through closed doors; be grateful for the scraps you are fed, shed clothes, shed soul, give away yourself and pretend to like it. Do not see. Do not hear. And do not speak unless it's what the powers that be want to hear.

The way I learned to survive was by following the bread crumbs of my fairy tale heroines. I was crafty. I kept my mouth shut, did what my father told me to do. I learned to flatter him and listen and not say what was on my mind. I was really, really good at this, anticipating wants, needs, moods before they erupted into rages. If something happened that felt wrong, I buried my feelings, took on the shame, and didn't say a word. It was obvious what happened to women—like my mother—who talked back. They were cursed: *Bitch. Cunt. Friggin' whore.* Blood was spilled. Bruises appeared.

As I polished the faucets and waited to be rescued, I bided my time and bit my tongue. I believed, with all my heart, that one day my prince would come.

3.

1974. The world is upside down. My father is dead, having taken his life four years before. Woodstock has come and gone. The youth counter-culture has made its mark and the war in Vietnam is finally over. Women have burned their bras and pushed back against male chauvinist pigs. *Roe v. Wade* has just passed, granting women the right to safe and legal abortion. Contraceptives have made "free love" possible. It's a good time to be young and female in America.

At nineteen, finally unfettered by my father's chains and "the man's" rules, I am a wild child. My world is weed and long-haired hippie boys, rock and roll, women's lib, and power to the people. I hang with hippies and break the rules. I call myself a feminist and claim that anatomy is no longer destiny. I can go anywhere, do anything. *I am woman. Hear me roar.*

But the truth is I am more kitten than lion. I am naïve and needy, wanting so badly to be a part of something bigger than myself that I routinely ignore the darker truths lingering on the edges of my beloved counterculture.

At a Santana concert, I dance with a hundred others in a daisy chain, our bodies facing the crowd of people who have gathered around us in a circle. Each time I pass a certain part of the circle, hands reach out and grab my breasts and crotch. A year later, walking among the crush of people in the streets of a Florida "Spring Break" town, anonymous hands again grab my ass, my tits and I keep walking, shocked and silent and untrusting of the truth my body knows. I ignore the way my beloved male rock icons write lyrics in their songs that demean and debase "chicks" like me. Ignore? Hell, I'm so clueless, I sing along.

But being voiceless for so long drives me to want to express myself. I write my own songs, sing the blues of strong women—Bessie Smith, Big Mama Thornton. After my first year of college, I run off to California to become a rock star or at the very least, to live in the land of peace and love. Heading out to a friend's house on a dark night, I am jumped on the street, choked almost to unconsciousness, and dragged into an abandoned garage where I am raped. After it's all over, the man who has assaulted me empties my pockets. He robs me of my last twenty dollars but returns my small stash of pot. "Here," he says. "I don't want to take your stuff."

Even though I'm in shock, I realize the irony of his statement. He has just taken everything, including the soul of who I might have been.

The day after the rape, I call the Berkeley Women's Center Hotline. Two women arrive in a van and take me to a Consciousness Raising session, which in a happy coincidence is being held on that very day. I do not report the rape to the authorities, nor does anyone suggest I do. In the early 1970's, police are "pigs," the enemy. There is no rape hotline, no rape kits, and not much support from law enforcement. In those days, the standard advice from the police is: "If rape is inevitable, relax and enjoy it."

In a room full of macramé plant holders and paisley prints, I become the focus of their consciousness-raising. What happened to me, they point out, has been enacted on women for centuries. I need to turn it around, use my experience to empower myself and other women. To drive their point home, they quote passages from Eldridge Cleaver's recent book, *Soul on Ice,* where he advocates raping white women to further the radical black agenda.

My mission now is to become a soldier in the sexual wars. "Remember," they say, "The personal is political."

At first, I eagerly take on this mantle of activism. Being angry feels a lot better than feeling fear and pain. But no amount of feminist raging can take away the obvious. I am fearful. I am in pain. And I'm ashamed of feeling this way, because the message is loud and clear, even from the women who claim to fight for women. *Get over it.*

The problem is I can't.

4.

For three decades, I will suffer from undiagnosed Post Traumatic Stress Disorder (PTSD), a psychological disorder that, ironically, was first identified in veterans of the war in Vietnam, the same year I was raped. Sexual assault and "domestic" trauma will not be acknowledged as triggers for PTSD until the mid 1990's and, even then, women will not get the help they need because they are ashamed and afraid of being blamed for what happened to them. The prevalent view, one that hasn't changed much over the ages, is that most women are either lying or asking for it.

As America enters the 21st century, thousands of women like me will still hide, still pretend they are "over it," limping like emotionally foot-bound Chinese courtesans through the rest of their lives.

When I walked out of that consciousness-raising session in Berkeley, it was like a blindfold had been ripped off of my eyes. I saw evidence of women's subjugation everywhere: in the working world, in academia, in the newspapers, in ads, on billboards, on television. It was overwhelming to be this clear-eyed, this awake to how woman were kept in their place and indoctrinated into submission.

Finally, I couldn't stand it anymore. Untreated and traumatized, being cognizant of the endless onslaught of female repression became too much for me. I returned home to Ohio and let go of fighting for women, instead concentrating on navigating through the world with my invisible handicap. Although I shook with fear when I walked on the streets alone, I got on with my life as best as I could. I went back to school, rode the wave of the rights that had been established for women, pretended things were not that bad, not for me, not for women in general. I took a Women's Studies course where the most strident voices in the room were those of the lesbian separatists. Although still committed to the idea of women's rights, I became unsure of exactly what being feminist meant.

I liked men. I wanted a boyfriend, a husband, a life. My problems, my own struggles took center stage. The pervasive misogyny I saw right after the rape receded into the background. To be honest, it was a lot easier just not to look.

Like my fairy tale heroine, Sleeping Beauty, the sting of reality was too much for me. I welcomed the trance of not knowing.

Meanwhile, thorn bushes began their steady climb up the castle walls.

5.

The 1980's threw kingdoms all over the globe into a panic. Religious fundamentalists in Iran dethroned a king and took Americans hostage. The Ayatollah and his followers banned women's mini-skirts and freedom, hiding them in burkas and confining them to the walls of their homes. In our own country, Ronald Reagan and his cronies ushered in an age where politicians curried favor from the religious right, asserted their voices as the "moral majority." Our economy took a dive. Gas prices went up. Manufacturing jobs began to go down.

The revolutionary fervor of the 1960's and 70's was gone. What was there to fight about, anyway? The Vietnam War was over, women had their rights, black and white America were integrated. The youth culture was no longer young. Hippies were out. Yuppies were in. Conspicuous consumption became the drug of choice. People had kids, mortgages, responsibilities.

Women, who had been college-educated in unprecedented numbers in the previous two decades, began to think about having careers, not just jobs.[1] A quiet revolution was taking place in the business world, driven not only by equal opportunity but by the need for additional income to maintain a family in an economy burdened by the soaring inflation of the 1980's. Women were no longer relegated to being nurses, teachers, or secretaries. We could be managers, bankers, even doctors and lawyers, if we got into the few allotted spaces in law or medical school. Skirted suits gave way to pantsuits, which were as much an acknowledgement of women's place in the business world as it was fashion statement.

Great strides, it seemed. But while we took on increasing responsibilities, our roles as homemakers and mothers did not change. Now we had full-time jobs in addition to kids and household tasks. We were working harder than ever, for lower wages than men in jobs that offered limited promotional opportunities, often in a workplace culture of sexual harassment. The old pattern of keeping silent to keep what little we had became the fallback position. Feminism didn't seem relevant anymore—after all, we had the ability to plan pregnancies and earn a living. Wasn't that enough?

Because women were no longer forced to depend on a man for their basic needs, they had more choices. The divorce rate skyrocketed as women who were able to support themselves left abusive and unhappy marriages. Sisters were "doing it for themselves," Aretha Franklin and Annie Lennox sang in 1985. Of course, for many women that meant leading the life of a single parent, saddled with more responsibilities than ever. Our freedom became another kind of ball and chain.

Who had time to think about what had *not* changed for women, that we were still underpaid and overworked, that we were underrepresented in Congress, the Boardroom, and the very top echelons of business? American women, including our daughters, sisters, aunts, friends, and mothers, were still victims of rape, harassment, and domestic violence. In fact, for many, domestic violence did not end with separation or divorce, but took on a new, darker edge as boyfriends, lovers, and husbands continued to threaten, stalk, beat, and murder women who had the ability and gall to say "No."

In 1976, only three years after *Roe v. Wade* granted women the right to a safe and legal abortion, The Hyde Amendment passed in Congress, which banned the use of federal funds for abortion except in cases of rape or incest and the health of the woman.[2] This was the first volley in a long and unrelenting battle of the legislative chipping away at the right of a woman to determine her fate. Abortion clinics were protested by picketers holding up pictures of fetuses in jars, then by threats and violence.

We turned our heads as we drove by those demonstrators with their bloody fetus signs. We kept re-electing male lawmakers who added clause after clause to the Hyde amendment to further erode a woman's right to choose. We went about our lives, thinking our work was done.

Were we asleep? Or just too damn busy?

5.

I was asleep.

It was a willful sleep, assisted by alcohol and drugs to keep the flood of fear from rising to the surface. The goal was not to feel. Not to know. To dream the dream of denial.

Then my fairy tale came true. I married my handsome prince. We bought a small castle and lived somewhat happily ever after.

But my prince did not rescue me.

I did.

6.

We can try to run away from our past, but it attaches to us like a shadow, waiting to be made conscious and freed. Because of the dynamics of my childhood, the too-close relationship with my father and unsteady one with my mother, I became a woman who turned to men for friendship as well as love. I longed to be "one of the boys," both for protection and the fear of acknowledging myself as a powerless woman.

Locking away my true self behind a persona of bravado, I hid the effects of the rape well, keeping silent about the terror that consumed my body when walking alone on the streets. By sheer guts and the company of my husband and canine protector—a fierce wolf-husky— I was able to navigate my way in the world.

Eventually I took steps to resuscitate my dreams. I went back to graduate school and got a degree in cable communications, a new technology which was just beginning to take hold across the country. And along with my husband, I formed a punk/new wave band.

It was the band that was my undoing.

Being the only woman in a rock and roll band is like having an all-access pass to the boy's locker room. I never knew there were so many derogatory terms for women or so many inventive ways to refer to sexual acts. At first, I tried to assert my own artistic vision, but I grew less confident among their smirking comments and grunting asides. My guitar player, a particularly messed-up misogynist, had strong and strange views about women. According to him, sex with females was supposed to be only for procreation, which might have explained his proclivity for sex with men and disgust for the many women he did fuck. He was a strong personality, charming and abusive like my father, and I fell under his spell, eventually allowing him to dictate the way I dressed (stiletto heels, push-up bras), the way I did my hair (bleached and teased), they way I sang—which he insisted should sound as "little girly" as possible.

If I ever had ideas about putting my own words into the world, my own music, the music of a strong woman singing about her life, that dream was slowly slipping away.

When the guys joked about women I knew and liked, or ended rehearsals with a call for "poon hunting," I shrugged it off, laughed at their "jokes." Why? Because, the potential reward—the fame and fortune to be had—was worth the compromising and denial. And like a lot of women who align themselves with anti-women men, I foolishly believed being in their camp made me immune to their disdain.

I felt like a traitor to myself.

7.

Hippie chicks, punk girls, we all have to grow up sometime. After the guys in the band decided they didn't need a "chick singer," I resumed my career aspirations, dressing in bland polyester suits and slowly rehabilitating my wild, bleached-out hair. Alone in my room, I wrote songs that reflected my deeper self, writing a lot at first and then a little and then very little.

I tried to make it in the corporate world, and was quite good at it, even though I felt like a fraud. Eventually, the psychic wounds I had tried to stitch shut with booze and drugs began to rip open. I dreamed of my father pulling me into the grave with him.

And I began a long process of healing myself.

8.

The night I was raped, I did not scream. I did not utter a single word. Not once. The voice I was trying to birth as a young woman in California, the voice I attempted to wrestle out of a childhood of not being heard, left me that night.

It took a very long time to get it back.

When I finally could speak again, I wrote a book. It was about a woman who needed to walk with dogs by her side for most of her life, a child who both loved and feared her father; a girl who witnessed the dismantling of her mother's voice by a man wracked by the twin furies of mental illness and a broken heart. It was about a young woman whose spirit was banished to the underworld for a very long time.

It was my story and I said so.

You cannot hide when you write a memoir. As I was writing, I had to push past the critics in my head who told me to give up, who asked "Who wants to hear about this—a decades-old rape, a woman held captive by her own thoughts, a childhood of terror and silence?" "Who?" I swatted away the voices, kept my head down and fingers on the keyboard, because I thought I knew the answer: other women who have been raped, other people who have lived in fear and shame, anyone who has been told to shut up.

And me.

I needed to hear it. Hear the sound of my own voice finally saying what it needed to say so desperately, for so long, but never could.

And as I found out, other people needed to hear it, too.

Once my words were out there for anyone to see, a strange thing happened. I discovered that my story was not just my story. It was and is the story of many people who tell me, in whispers, in phone calls, in e-mails, at book fairs—*it happened to me, too. I never told anyone.*

This, I realize, is how spells are cast.

And how they are broken.

10.

Let's talk about the spell of silence. Or not talking about the things that we cannot stand to see. Things like rape. Incest. Murder. More girls have been killed in the last fifty years, precisely because they were girls, than men were killed in all the battles of the twentieth century.[3] Yet we stay quiet. We do so to protect ourselves, to remain invisible so we will not be shunned, shamed, or annihilated. These dark truths are taboo, a violation of the social order. To utter them is to rip the veil off the lie. To invite disorder. Chaos, even. But that is the only way to create change.

Judith Herman, in the introduction to her landmark book, *Trauma and Recovery*, states, "The ordinary response to atrocities is to banish them from consciousness. Certain violations of the social compact are too terrible to utter aloud; this is the meaning of the word *unspeakable*."[4]

The price we pay in keeping silent is considerable. Around the world, women are enslaved, tortured, murdered, kept ignorant, hidden, mutilated, raped, beaten, battered, and stoned. Even worse, they are made to feel responsible for their abuse.

It is this shifting of the blame onto women that helps keep the seal of silence intact and makes the crime much more palpable—both to the one who commits it and society at large. I am thinking of what my own father would say every time he beat my mother: "She asked for it."

Who would ask to be beaten? Who would ask to be raped, to be abused, to be held against one's will? The assumption that a woman is guilty until determined innocent is the story that we, as a society, tell ourselves in order not to believe, not to hear, not to protect women. It is the story that keeps women from telling their stories. It is held in place by shame, the most potent curse of all.

Shame mutes the tongue, keeps the unspeakable unspoken, because to speak of what happens is to indict oneself. Shame says not that one *was wronged,* but that one *is wrong.* It protects the perpetrators and perpetrates a climate where the unspeakable can happen again...and again.

And again.

When the publicity phase began for my book, I found myself wrestling with using the word "rape" to describe what had happened to me. "Assault," I wrote for one publicity blurb, then "attack." Then, "sexual assault," which felt slightly more accurate and slightly more comfortable than the shame-loaded word for what actually occurred.

During a radio interview, I did the old soft sell and said the book was about the thirty years I spent enduring the effects of being "attacked" on the streets of Berkeley. The interviewer, a woman, said, "Well, yes. But...Oh, let's say what it was...You were raped."

"Yes," I said. It was a relief to have it all out in the open.

After the interview, she told me that she, too, had been raped as a young woman. "It's time we stopped skirting around the issue."

Skirting around the issue instead of addressing it head-on. Isn't that what we wearers of skirts are supposed to do?

From that time on, I worked on confronting my reluctance to speak the word. The more I said it, the more the consonants and vowels of that unspeakable word were formed, the easier it was to own it, contain it, wring the core of its meaning into being.

11.

Rape.

The origins of the word come from Middle English, where the meaning referred to the violent seizure of property. Later, it denoted the "carrying off a woman by force," which eventually became, "forcing of another person to have sexual intercourse against their will."[5]

But it is this first definition, "a violent seizure of property," that provides the key to understanding the heart of the problem for women. The fact is, underneath it all—despite voting rights and the equal opportunity and the ability to decide whether or not to have children—remains the age-old assumption that women are property.

If you are property, you can be owned, but you cannot own yourself. If you are property, laws can be made restricting your use and boundaries.

The United Nations recently underwrote an unprecedented study on violence against women. Out of 10,000 men surveyed, one half reported the use of physical and/or sexual violence against a woman and one quarter of those surveyed admitted to rape. The most common motivation that men cited for committing rape was sexual entitlement—a belief that men have a right to have sex with women regardless of consent.[6] In other words, women's bodies as public property.

As American women, we know we're one of the lucky ones. We have access to education and freedom of expression; we can work, play, vote, drive cars, fly planes, crash through glass ceilings, travel unescorted through our days. And we can own property. But ownership of the female lands—including that small but fertile acreage of womb and uterus inside us—is still very much in dispute.

That brings us back to the Handmaid's Tale, narrated by a woman who was once independent and free but now finds herself living the life of an anonymous breeder. If you think this is a fairy tale, consider this: Between 2011 and 2013, over 205 abortion restrictions have been enacted on the state level, more than in the last ten years combined.[7] Even at the federal level, women's rights are on trial. One example of this recent trend is the 2014 Supreme Court decision *Sebelius v. Hobby Lobby,* which ruled that an employer has the right to limit a female employee's means of birth control.[8] Rape, the violent seizure of a woman's body, continues to be seen not as a crime, but as a lie made up by women who regret having given in to their sexual urges. This unspoken assumption underlies the assertion by several politicians during the 2012 United States congressional election that during a "legitimate rape" a woman cannot become pregnant because her body shuts down the reproductive cycle.[9] It also speaks to the bullying of a thirteen-year-old girl who was gang-raped in 2013 by members of local football team and accused on social media of "ruining lives" when she pressed charges against her perpetrators.[10] And what happens if a pregnancy does occur as a result of rape and a woman does not or cannot obtain an abortion? In thirty-one states, the rapist is granted paternity and custody rights.[11] Think about it: there are laws on the books that grant perpetrators access to his victim for the rest of her life.

Perhaps the most alarming trend in anti-female legislation is the current enthusiasm for fetus "personhood" bills that are being floated through state legislatures. This law, which denies a woman the ability to terminate a pregnancy for any reason, grants more rights to a zygote than the adult human whose body it resides in. In essence, it reduces a woman to a version of Atwood's handmaiden.

When I first read *The Handmaid's Tale,* my psyche was still too unstable to endure the fear and outrage the story awakened in me. But writing and telling my truth has transformed me. I can speak again and I'm not going to shut up, even though it's still scary, even though coaxing the words out can be hard and difficult work, even though I know there will always be those who will try and silence me and my kind.

"Folk wisdom is filled with ghosts who refuse to rest in their graves until their story is told," Judith Herman says. "Murder will out. Remembering and telling the truth…are prerequisites both for the restoration of the social order and the healing of individual victims."[12]

Walking the malls and streets of America, I see little girls everywhere dressed as fairy princesses in crinoline tutus and pale pink tights. How I would have loved to be able to dress like that in public as a child. But I'm concerned that another generation of women may be falling for the illusion that they are powerless and that their only way out is to dream of handsome princes and magic potions. A high school teacher tells me that many of her female students say their plan for the future consists of marrying a rich man who will take care of them. The fantasy lives on.

Fairy tales were originally written in code to warn children—especially girls—how to make their way in a hostile world. The advice was subtle but clear: Be patient like Cinderella. Be passive like Snow White. Be beautiful like Sleeping Beauty. And keep silent. Magic will save you, the stories say.

I say words will save you, save all of us.

This is how it works. We tell our secrets, our shame, our suffering. We hold each other up as one story after another, one tale, then two, then more, get told. We begin to see that bravery has its own kind of beauty.

When Sleeping Beauty awoke, nothing had changed; all was as it was one hundred years ago. In fairy tale terms, that's a happy ending. In reality, it's a nightmare. Women have suffered for centuries and continue to do so. We cannot afford to re-live the past. Unleash your voice, your anger, your truth. Wake to your own story.

This is how new endings begin.

NOTES

1. J.H. Bishop, "The Explosion of Female College Attendance," *Cornell University CAHRS Working Paper Series* (11-1-1990):1.

2. Frederucj S. Jaffe, Barbara L. Lindheim, and Philip R. Lee, *Abortion Politics: Private Morality and Public Policy* (New York: McGraw Hill, 1981), p. 129.

3. Nicholas D. Kristof and Sheryl WuDunn, *Half the Sky: Turning Oppression into Opportunity for Women Worldwide* (New York: Knopf, 2009).

4. Judith Herman, *Trauma and Recovery* (New York: Basic Books, 1997), p. 1.

5. *Oxford English Dictionary* (Oxford: Oxford University Press; 2 Sub edition (December 5, 1991).

6. E. Fulu, X. Warner, S. Miederma, R. Jewkes, T. Roselli, and J. Lang, "Why Do Some Men Use Violence Against Women and How Can We Prevent It? Quantitative Findings from the United Nations Multi-country Study on Men and Violence in Asia and the Pacific"; UN Partners for Prevention (September 10, 2013), pp. 42-44.

7. Elizabeth Nash, Rachel Benson Gold, Andrea Rowan, Gwendolyn Rathbun and Yana Vierboom, "Laws Affecting Reproductive Health and Rights: 2013 State Policy Review," Guttmacher Institute, April 20, 2013. Accessed May 14, 2014 at http://www.guttmacher.org/statecenter/updates/2013/statetrends.

8. Michelle Goldberg, "Alito's Hobby Lobby Opinion is Dangerous and Discriminatory," *The Nation*, June 30, 2014. Accessed Aug. 20, 2014 at http://www.thenation.com/blog/180461/alitos-hobby-lobby-opinion-dangerous-and-discriminatory.

9. John Eligon and Michael Schwirtz, "Senate Candidate Provokes Ire with Legitimate Rape comment," *New York Times*, Aug. 19, 2012. Accessed Aug. 20, 2014 at http://www.nytimes.com/2012/08/20/us/politics/todd-akin-provokes-ire-with-legitimate-rape-comment.html.

10. Jessica Glenza, "Victim Bullied After Rape Allegations Against Torrington Football Players," *Register Citizen*, March 20, 2013. Accessed May 25, 2014 at http://www.registercitizen.com/general-news/20130320/victim-bullied-after-rape-allegations-against-torrington-football-players.

11. Shawna Prewitt, "Raped, Pregnant and Ordeal Not Over," CNN.com, Aug. 23, 2012. Accessed May 25, 2014 at http://www.cnn.com/2012/08/22/opinion/prewitt-rapist-visitation-rights/.

12. Herman, *Trauma and Recovery*, p. 1.

This article narrates transformational experiences, ranging from the author growing up poor in Southern Appalachia with crossed eyes and suffering a disfiguring accident that caused facial scarring, to her being the only family member to graduate high school and college, along with her facing discrimination in job interviews because of a country accent. She tells of continuing her journey, earning a degree in creative writing and becoming a university professor. This tale of triumph and endurance hinges on finding mentors in school, and not forgetting root connections, while building a stronger—more balanced—foundation in order to help others overcome suffering in their own lives.

FLYING BY WORDS—FROM THE FRONT PORCH TO THE PODIUM:
EDUCATIONAL INDIVIDUATION AND CREATIVE ENDURANCE

GERALDINE CANNON BECKER

"Your voice is out there. Your voice is strange."
—Anne Sexton, "Angel of Hope and Calendars"

Strange or not, I wanted to start singing after reading the following quote by Terry Tempest Williams, "Once upon a time, when women were still birds, there was the simple understanding that to sing at dawn and to sing at dusk was to heal the world through joy. The birds still remember what we have forgotten, that the world is meant to be celebrated."[1]

This morning I woke up to sirens blasting, something extremely unusual in this rural, university town on the border of Canada. Domestic violence was reported, and a woman has been shot and killed. She had two young children, who were not home at the time—so much pain and suffering for these victims, and another woman's voice has been silenced.[2] Just last week, headlines were full of news about the Santa Barbara shooting spree—a young male, killing six people and

Geraldine Cannon Becker, M.F.A., is an Associate Professor of English and Creative Writing at the University of Maine at Fort Kent (UMFK). She publishes creative writing under her maiden name, Geraldine Cannon. *Glad Wilderness* (2008) is her first book of poetry. A featured "focus on faculty" member, information on her various academic and creative presentations and her publications are hosted by Blake Library, at UMFK (https://www.umfk.edu/library/faculty/scholarship/). Formerly an "at risk" student, she has worked for over ten years with "at risk" learners in the women's literacy group, WE LEARN (Women Expanding: Literacy, Education, Action, Resource, Network), helping to empower disenfranchised women through literacy.

wounding thirteen others, targeting women in revenge for social rejection—sharing videos and a hate-filled manifesto.[3]

Also in headline news was Maya Angelou's death, at age eighty-six. She remained silent for a number of years in her own childhood because of violence endured as a rape victim. Her pioneering memoir, *I Know Why the Caged Bird Sings,* details that story, and also the birth of her love for language.[4] *Time Magazine* speaks of her "glorious human endurance" and her "relentless creativity." In telling an interviewer what she would like to have included in her own obituary, she responded: "What I'd really like to have said about me is that I dared to love. By love I mean that condition in the human spirit so profound, it encourages us to develop courage and build bridges, and then to trust those bridges and cross the bridges in attempts to reach other human beings."[5] Angelou's last tweet, posted on May 23rd, was also glorious and thought-provoking, "Listen to yourself and in that quietude you might hear the voice of God."[6]

IN THE BEGINNING WAS THE WORD...

The past is often present to me. I can still hear the sound of the church organ, and I can almost feel vibrations in my chest, when I think of marching into Bible school as a child. The first Bible verse I ever learned there was Mark 9:23, "All things are possible to him that believeth."[7] I knew while memorizing it that I would have to say it in front of the whole church, with all eyes on me. My heart was like a caged bird.

I remember the first thing I had wanted to do with the verse was to edit it. In fact, I had marked the word "him" out in order to fix it, because as a girl I also wanted to be included in the phrase. I was sad when my teacher said I could not change words of the Bible, but "him" really meant all children of God—not just boys—so I could speak up and let my own little voice be heard. I had taken that verse to heart and just knew if I only I had enough faith, then anything could be possible. It was not easy for me to be the person I thought God wanted to see, though, because I often fell short of perfection in my own eyes, if not in the eyes of others.

I had once felt perfect in the eyes of God. I had been full of wonder and curiosity, before I lost my confidence and started feeling inferior and ashamed of my own appearance. Yes, I still remember how I felt before I first realized I was different—before I heard someone say, "She would have been beautiful, if only she hadn't been born with crossed eyes."

I often heard the phrase "poor thing," when people looked at me, but this was usually only when they tried to make eye contact and that failed to happen, so I assumed it was because of my eyes. I really didn't know what "poor" meant, but I knew I was different from the ladies with nice handkerchiefs and perfumes. I had to learn not to look at people for any length of time, and I really did not like to have anyone look at me. I could only focus temporarily, and then one eye or the other would begin to move away, startling any new acquaintance.[8]

Later, I realized that although we had many poor friends and neighbors, I was probably one of the poorest people in that Southern Appalachian Bible school class. I still had great expectations for myself, and I really wanted to let my little light shine, as the words said in a favorite church song, but bad things kept happening to me. When I was in the fourth grade, for example, I was almost electrocuted while some home repairs were being made, and I ended up with severe scars on my face, especially my mouth, which gave me even more reasons to stay quiet, to try to hide my face, and to keep out of the spotlight. Having a tutor come to the house and teach me that summer because I had missed so much school was a significant turning point in my life.

Every summer, my sisters and I would play that we were at school, taking turns being the teacher, but I was not just playing school with my sisters that summer. This was the real thing. A genuine teacher came to my house, and often stayed longer than planned, because she loved working with me. She said it was a joy for her. That's when I knew, instead of just being different, that I wanted to make a meaningful difference in life—in my own life and in the lives of others. Against all odds, I knew I wanted to be a teacher.

Life did not suddenly stop being tough for me with my vocational decision, though. After that summer, I had to go back to school and face people who had questions about my scar and my new glasses, because in addition to the obvious problem of me having crossed eyes, we had discovered through vision tests that I was also near-sighted. I sported a new pair of frames—a popular,

Kool-aid-brand multi-colored style, and I actually enjoyed getting attention from my classmates, at first.

However, what I enjoyed even more was that I could finally see small details on the blackboard, and suddenly I felt so much smarter. Thick lenses that allowed me to see leaves on distant trees in ways that were not impressionistic also added another layer between me and others. Of course, the fun-makers called me four-eyes. I ignored them, immersing myself into studies, keeping nature journals, writing notes, making observations on life, and reading whatever I could get my hands on—all the while thinking maybe someday I could be a teacher. I knew nothing, then, of cost.

WHAT DID I KNOW?

I had always loved language. Words spoke to me on the page in ways that made me want to live and breathe them. I felt interconnected with words. I am sure this is in large part due to stories I grew up listening to folks tell. My own father was a great storyteller. Often, stories that were told were based upon real events; sometimes they had a moral, but more often than not, history was handed down.

As clichéd as it is now, I knew knowledge was a kind of power and it all hinged on language. I knew this early on when things would come in the mail and my father would have to ask an older child to read them aloud. My father could not read well (he only went to the second grade), but he had an excellent memory for keeping track of stories and important information. The world had opened up for me like a book when I could read, and I wanted to be able to teach him, but it was a world he could never open to himself.

Just as I had pretended to teach with my sisters, playing school on the front porch, I had also pretended that I had an audience for the words I had collected in notebooks. I would often be found reading aloud from the porch stoop when I thought no one else was around, but foolishness was what they called this when there was real work to be done.

Fast forward to career counseling week in high school, where I watched my class form into two groups, for either vocational school or college—I had friends in both camps. I was standing still when the librarian gave me a nudge toward the vocational table. I signed up for vocational school, as had been expected, but I really wanted to teach. Why not sign up for college? It was not expected of me.

GREAT EXPECTATIONS...

In school, I had some great teachers, but the ones who always gave me the most attention were my English teachers. They encouraged my writing "hobby" and one of them even hinted at the possibility of a career in writing. He took me to a young writers' conference, and helped me get my first work published. Writing was such a dream. With my confidence boosted, I worked harder just to be able to graduate from high school. I thought that would be my major accomplishment.

My future beyond that day was dim. The same day that I signed up for vocational school, my English teacher assigned a comparison paper, requiring research on a topic of our choice. I decided to compare students who signed up for vocational school to students who signed up for college. What went into the decision-making process?

When I searched the library for college brochures, to my dismay, the counselor had them. We were not on the friendliest of terms. I often found myself struggling against the grain in classrooms, sometimes pitted against teachers who had low expectations of me; sometimes trying to ignore the bullies, I tuned everything else out, too. When I asked for the brochures, he laughed, asking, "*You're* not thinking about going to college, are you?"

At that time, in that office, I made my decision. "Well, yes. Actually, *I* am," I said as confidently as possible. One thing I had discovered was the impact of words delivered with a specific tone and voice. I felt a strange sense of power. Back then, I did not know anything about archetype possession, but what C.G. Jung has called a "splinter psyche" may have started to become autonomous, taking over when my inferiority complex was triggered.[9]

With one change in my attitude and demeanor, the counselor immediately became more professional. He told me about a few scholarships and said I would have to take some college prep classes that I had not been scheduled to take. It would be a struggle, but I knew that I was up for the academic challenge. I had started a process of revising a life that had felt unbalanced—mind, body, and soul.[10]

As a teacher, I hoped to make a meaningful difference in life, and though meaning is variable from person to person, in his well-known book, *The Will to Meaning*, Viktor E. Frankl notes that each unique individual has a specific purpose, part of which is to reach beyond ourselves, to make connections with others, and in so doing, become more fully human. He states, in fact, that if a person passes up on an opportunity to fulfill a meaning in his or her life, that person will be "in no event a truly human being. For it is a characteristic constituent of human existence that it transcends itself, that it reaches out for something other than itself."[11]

WHAT IS SEEN IN THE UNSEEN?

A phenomenal event that actually helped me feel more "truly human" occurred to me right before I left home for college, and I took it as a sign that I was on the right path. I felt assured that I was doing the right thing to continue my educational journey, even though I knew that it was going to be hard for me and my parents. One day I came home from school, and I went straight to bed because I was tired from a long, stressful day. Later, I woke up and it was pitch dark, but there were two strange lights on the ceiling.

There was a bare bulb hanging in the middle of the room and it was not turned on. My eyes moved toward the wall, and two lights moved in unison to the wall. I felt queasy as my eyes moved toward the window across from my bed. The lights bounced back at me and I could see a reflection of myself. The light was coming directly from my eyes! My eyes had never moved in unison this way before. I was so afraid. I closed my eyes and felt as if I would explode with light. I felt hot and my palms were soaked.

Then, I heard a clear voice say this simple statement: "Look through the window of your own eyes." I didn't understand what was happening to me. I only knew that this power emanating from within was something "other" than myself.[12] It was more than human. I thought then that God or some Angel of God was with me. It was a fearful time, and I kept my eyes closed until I felt the powerful presence leave. Then, I ran to my parents' room. They listened to me and helped me calm down. We made an emergency appointment with my "eye doctor" the next day.

The optometrist could not explain this occurrence in medical or scientific terms. However, he told me about corrective surgical methods and mentioned a variety of ways to afford payments. My family was so poor that I did not think surgery was feasible at that time, but I did not forget about the option. In fact, I did go back to him four years later, when I had graduated from college, and he helped me make arrangements to have the corrective surgery. I was afraid of changing my vision, but as a teacher, all eyes would be on me, and I wanted my students to know where I was looking.[13]

My life was actually even more chaotic when I went to college than I had ever expected it would be. I ended up on academic probation my first semester, because nine days after I left home my father, Jesse Cannon, died of a heart attack—"the silent killer." I managed to return to college after the funeral, immersing myself in studies. The work was harder, and I could barely concentrate long enough to keep up, but people were generally understanding of mistakes and helped me get into a routine. In my first year away from home, I made some lasting friendships, and even met the man who would eventually become my husband.

In times of great stress (such as suffering in grief), introverted, "at-risk" learners may give up and disappear. I did not stop going to classes, in part, because once again I was fortunate to have some very caring teachers. "Education," as one of my first professors informed me, comes from the Latin "*educare*," which means "minding or tending with care, or drawing out knowledge." However, sometimes I felt like two different people. It was harder for me to write academic papers, and to keep up the persona of "an elevated academic."[14] It was much easier for me to be true to my own nature, "down-home/creative." I could always write narrative poems and tell stories, even if they were difficult stories. Internal motivation was my greatest strength, and my creative journal writing helped me find a needed balance in my life. I struggled, at times, but I was determined to continue.

After I graduated with certification to teach high school English, it was still difficult to find a good job in education. Interviews did not always go well for me. My Appalachian "hillbilly" accent seemed to surprise people. I could almost hear their thoughts in my mind: "*You* want to teach English?" It is true that after undergoing corrective eye surgery, I was not "magically" more confident. So much had been altered so quickly, and I still had to ignore the vision in one eye or the other, because the alignment was not completely perfect. Sometimes I would misjudge in reaching for anything handed to me in a face-to-face meeting. Yet, I didn't want to endure another "risky," not to mention costly, corrective surgery.[15]

<h2>Hope is a Winged Thing</h2>

When I was in college, my poetry teacher, Susan Ludvigson, encouraged me to apply for an advanced degree in creative writing. With an M.F.A., she assured me, I would have a better chance of teaching classes on the college level, even working with smaller classes, following my dreams of making a difference in life through education. With a background in psychology, she also mentored me in keeping a dream journal and exploring the content of my dreaming mind. She knew of my hopes and dreams, and she also knew something of my fears. She could have been addressing me in the poem "What if," from her book, *Everything Winged Must Be Dreaming*:

> What if
> when you entered your mind
> with purpose, you found not the field
> you'd told yourself to imagine, the wild
> strawberries of childhood strewn
> among the tall grass where you lay
> under apple trees, but a land flatter
> and wider than sight could take in.
> What if you forgot how to bring inside
> the music that used to begin
> in your gradual waking, and in the space
> before sleep, when rain began softly,
> and all your sweet longings loosened.
> What if traffic and telephones
> continued their commerce, so loud
> you couldn't remember how your skin felt,
> floating. There is this fear,
> stalking the hours. One day
> it might disappear, that place
> you could go at will, where your own
> voice hummed like a mother,
> a crooning that let your blood

slow, the poem of the body
riding blue murmuring crests, naming
its love, loving its life.[16]

Her words hummed to me in that "mothering" way, and I murmured, too—not drowning in the blue dreaming—nor falling, but flying—dreaming myself into a new kind of waking. Of course, I had my fears, but I took her advice on starting a dream journal—and I began making plans to continue my education. This time I would be learning more about the practice of creative writing, while seeking an M.F.A.

One of my fears from childhood was that I might die before I wrote down all the things I thought I needed to write. I didn't want to die a wordless death. I had never read John Keats, but my English teacher gave me a copy of the poem "When I Have Fears," and I connected immediately with his work.[17] I still have a fondness for the Romantic poets and their ideas of transcendence. At that point, I had wanted something in my life to transcend death—something to last forever. I thought a close examination of my life could tell me what that would be, and that I would put it down in writing for creative endurance.

I had also wanted to collect family stories, and I used to ask Moma [*sic*] to talk about the births of each of her eight children, especially the boys she had lost. Her first baby, Walter Gene, died when he was six months old. He had been a "blue baby," they said, born with a hole in his heart. I was six months old myself when my brother, DL [*sic*] Cannon died, due to leukemia, at the age of seven. The telling of stories about my birth had always been intertwined with the tale of his death. I was the first child to be born in the hospital, and he had held me in his arms on the way back home, sitting in the long front seat, between Moma and Daddy. Those details were special to me.

I can also remember Daddy telling me and my little sister about the boys and how they had been dressed on their last days when we would go put flowers on their graves. DL and Walter had beautiful little lambs and hearts on the tops of their tombstones, and I would hug them, and talk to my brothers while we were there. I called them my little brothers, because I thought of them that way, even though they both would have been older than me, if only they had lived.

Death has been a constant companion to life. Some people tell me they can clearly remember the day they learned of their mortality. I cannot remember a time in my own life when I didn't know that one day I, too, would die. Every year of our lives we live past the day we will eventually die, though there is no way to know the exact year, to date or time. This is just as poet, W. S. Merwin recognized in his poem, "For the Anniversary of My Death," which begins: "Every year without knowing it I have passed the day/ When the last fires will wave to me/ And the silence will set out/ Tireless traveler/ Like the beam of a lightless star."[18] Indeed, we may celebrate life with an extra candle on the cake each year, but death is right there with us all along. Why not acknowledge this, and talk about it?

Shared stories have creative endurance. One of the earliest Bible stories I was ever told began in a garden, and because not a day goes by that I do not think of beginnings and endings, gardening also helps me embody and become more fully aware of my connections through changing seasons to something that exists beyond myself. As C.G. Jung says, "Nature herself demands a death and a rebirth."[19] Hope remains within me for something that will transcend and endure beyond death.

It is as Jung says, "whether he understands them or not, man must remain conscious of the world of archetypes, because in it he is still a part of Nature and is connected to his own roots."[20] I know that I have been fortunate through my ongoing studies on my lifelong journey of educational individuation to have been able to connect my love for language and my love for nature together with Jungian and archetypal studies. I have also been privileged to help others through hardships in their lives.

ON BEING HUMAN

I first learned about C.G. Jung by taking some life-changing classes with Dr. John R. Locke, who was on my M.F.A. thesis committee. In fact, I have modeled some of my own classes on those I took with him. After I earned my degree, I worked as a Lecturer while my husband worked to complete his Ph.D. program in comparative literature. On August 28th, 2000, at the start of a new semester, our Jungian mentor, Dr. Locke, was shot and killed by a disgruntled student, who then took his own life.[21] Two more lives silenced too soon.

That very morning, thinking of my own hectic class schedule, I had been reminding myself: "Be Gentle with Yourself," which was something Dr. Locke had leaned down and whispered to me one day in the hallway just outside his office. I am still grateful for his lessons, and to have his quiet voice weaving through my memories.

It is never easy to move on from such tragedy. In addition to being the chair of the comparative literature program, Dr. Locke had been my husband's dissertation chair, so it took him longer to finish. I think anyone who knew Dr. Locke was numb for a while.

However, many people were moved to action. A memorial garden was spearheaded by Maeve Maddox and was built in Dr. Locke's honor on the campus. The Dr. John Locke Memorial Library was built by Dr. Virginia Krauft, to honor him and to house his collection of books, which he bequeathed to her. Dr. Krauft posted a poem that Dr. Locke once kept hanging in his office on the website:

> The world of books
> is the most remarkable creation
> of man
> Nothing else that he builds ever
> lasts
> Monuments fall
> Nations perish
> Civilizations grow old and die
> and after an era of darkness
> new races build others
> But in the world of books are
> volumes
> that have seen this happen again
> and again and yet live on
> still young
> still as fresh as the day they were
> written
> still telling men's hearts
> of the hearts of men centuries
> dead.[22]

All these years, I have been on a path of individuation, identified by C.G. Jung as a life-long journey towards wholeness. According to Daryl Sharp, "Whoever embarks on the personal path becomes to some extent estranged from collective values, but does not thereby lose those aspects of the psyche which are inherently collective. To atone for this "desertion," the individual is obliged to create something of worth for the benefit of society."[23] Even as I continue my process of educational individuation, while teaching others I am creating something of lasting value through my own life's work with words— teaching, tending, and caring for the world one class at a time—one project at a time. As I say in the dedication of my first book of poems, *Glad Wilderness*, "Step by step, we create our own ways."[24] I want to better understand myself, as I continue to seek balance, but my real purpose in life seems to be to help others on the path, too. I feel most nurtured as I nurture others.

I have experienced the light and I have been in dark places where it seems no light may ever shine. Just as my oldest daughter started her own first year of college, our family suffered through the death of my only living brother, LC [*sic*] Jesse Cannon, who was a country/ western musician. He was exactly the same age as my father had been when he died the year I first started college as an undergraduate. Ironically, the day my brother died was circled on his calendar, for it was the day his country music legend and hero, Johnny Cash, had died in 2003. At my brother's funeral, music from both Cannon and Cash were played. The preacher knew our family well, and told stories going back three generations, "May the circle be unbroken. . . ." We sisters circled around our mother for strength.

In *Ego and Archetype*, Edward F. Edinger demonstrates how little children all over the world will draw lines—crossed lines and circles— and even depict themselves as circles from an early age. He said, "All of this indicates that, symbolically speaking, the human psyche was originally round, whole, complete; in a state of oneness and self-sufficiency that is equivalent to deity itself."[25] Indeed, I have been seeking that balance in my life all along. However, I know that individuation is an ongoing process that may never be fully complete.

I have realized that even though my eyes have been corrected, I am still cross-eyed—for my eyes are often on a cross inside a circle, a well-known symbol of what Jung called "the Self," or the God-within.[26] I am looking through the window of my own eyes. I see a crossroads where work needs to be done. Jung kept asking, "Three are here, but where is the fourth?"[27] Likewise, I am four-eyed, and the window has four parts. I may not have depth perception, but I know of the depth and I have an enriched faith now. I know I am not alone.

I have now been teaching for over half my life, and I still find great joy in it. I try to help students see intricate patterns and connections across the curriculum—and in their own lives. However, there are times when it is harder than ever for me to do my job, and there are sometimes fears of disgruntled students, even though we have been provided training to deal with this. Some students seem more focused on grades than on the learning process, and when shootings are in the news, it brings back memories of my own suffering and pain. There will always be tragic events in the world. What can we do to help with the pain? That is what I keep asking. We can reach out to the other in us as well as to others. We make connections. We can love. Hope endures.

To Die and Fly…

I am working on a creative project to help school children turn some of their own memories, dreams, or reflections into a collective display of individually painted ceramic tiles. Art is healing. Art tells stories. Not too long ago, fires raged in the center of our town. Lots of things that people had hoped would endure for years were gone in a very short time. However, there was love, and hope for the future. The generous outpouring was amazing. This community came together to help victims, and good things are still coming about because of that horrible event. I have been helping plan a memorial/reflection garden that will be created as part of the Fort Kent "Phoenix" Project.

Poet James Dickey once said in *Self Interviews*, "I die and fly by words."[28] I've voiced this wish, in *Glad Wilderness*, that through words "at least/ my fingers find wings."[29] We may ask what if…what if…, but we may never know unless we try. Instead of shutting down completely or hiding away, what if we risk flying in the face of our fears? As James Hollis says, I "step into largeness" by making choices to take risks and enlarge myself as I help others enlarge themselves.[30]

I'm not just doing this on the college campus, and with my local community now. For more than ten years I have interacted with an international women's group that works to empower disenfranchised women through literacy—WE LEARN (Women Expanding: Literacy,

Education, Action, Resource, Network). I have helped edit their journal *Women's Perspectives* and helped with the newsletter, but this year I joined the Board of Directors, and even co-chaired the conference—"Women's Literacy Gardens." I'm digging in and tending deeper and wider—working with "at risk" learners, collecting stories told from gardens to publish in an edited volume, and leading what I am calling imaginative "Soul Flowering" workshops, through which it is my hope that participants will open up like large blossoms, and begin to make deep and wide connections for themselves that will go beyond the safe space of the workshop environment.[31]

Participants may need trained help from professional counselors to be able to take risks and free themselves to explore that "other"ness they will encounter. Some stories are hard to tell, but often the hardest stories to tell are the very ones that must be told. Looking back at my young self, it is hard not to see me as others must have, but I can still remember how I originally felt. That positive spark is still there in the darkness, and I can reach out to the "other" within myself, as well as in others.

On my path of educational individuation, I have sought to get to know myself better, flaws and all, which has helped me to empathize with and better understand others. I believe we have to live our own lives as fully as possible, and with our own integrity and authenticity. We have to have strength and courage to withstand times when we may falter, when we are suffering, when we may not be so brave and strong after all. We have to get through these times with an unselfish love that is not only inwardly focused, nor only outwardly focused, but one that reaches both deep and wide—with greater awareness of what really matters as the journey continues. We are not alone.

Listen, and someone is humming, a murmuring of abiding love in a life that springs eternal... The birds are singing—sometimes in harmony, though sometimes cacophony prevails. We can sing out, like the little bird in Robert Frost's "The Oven Bird,"[32] and our voices will be heard—making something of what others may have perceived as "a diminished thing," as we die and fly by words.

As twilight falls on another day, I know this community will need to hear more healing songs. There are more stories to bring to light, with courage, hope, and endurance. Possibility abounds, for anything to happen.

NOTES

1. Terry Tempest Williams, *When Women Were Birds: Fifty-four Variations on Voice* (New York: Farrar, Straus, and Giroux, 2013), Kindle edition, Loc. 2126.
2. Julia Bayly, "Police search for 'armed and dangerous' man in connection with death of woman in St. Francis," in *Bangor Daily News* (Bangor, ME), May 31, 2014, http://bangordailynews.com/2014/05/31/news/aroostook/state-police-aroostook-county-sheriffs-deputies-investigate-reported-shooting-in-st-francis/.
3. Kate Pickert, "A Murderous Spree: Death, Sorrow and Regret in Santa Barbara," in *Time Magazine* (New York: NY), June 9, 2014, p. 14.
4. Maya Angelou. *I Know Why the Caged Bird Sings* (New York: Random House, 1969).
5. "Maya Angelou, Legendary Voice," from "Milestones" in *Time Magazine* (New York: NY), June 9, 2014, p. 16.
6. Meena Hart Duerson, "Maya Angelou's guide to life in 12 tweets, 'listen to yourself,'" in *Today News*, May 28, 2014, http://www.today.com/news/maya-angelous-guide-life-12-tweets-listen-yourself-2D79725413.
7. Mark 9:23 (King James Version).
8. I had the rare X-pattern strabismus (http://www.ajo.com/article/S0002-9394(11)00067-5/abstract). Both of my eyes moved independently of one another—up or down and out. This usually takes more than one surgery to correct.
9. C.G. Jung, "A Review of the Complex Theory," in *The Structure and Dynamics of the Psyche*, vol. 8 of *The Collected Works of C.G. Jung*, trans. R.F.C. Hull (Princeton, N.J.: Princeton University Press, 1969), § 202-3. All future references to the *Collected Works* (hereinafter "*CW*") will be by volume number and paragraph number.
10. This college decision story appears as "Positive Impact," in a WE LEARN (Women Expanding: Literacy, Education, Action, Resource, Network) newsletter, April, 2006.
11. Viktor E. Frankl, *The Will to Meaning: Foundations and Applications of Logotherapy* (New York: Penguin, 1988), p. 55.
12. See notes 9 and 11 above.

13. Geraldine Cannon Becker, "Looking at You," in *Our Stories, Ourselves*, eds. Mev Miller and Kathy P. King (Charlotte, NC: Information Age Publishing, 2011), pp. 37-40.

14. Jolande Jacobi, *Complex/Archetype/Symbol in the Psychology of C.G. Jung* (New York: Routledge, 1999), p. 56.

15. See note 8.

16. Susan Ludvigson, "What If," in *Everything Winged Must Be Dreaming* (Baton Rouge, LA: Louisiana State University Press, 1993), p. 40.

17. John Keats, "When I Have Fears," in *The Essential Keats*, ed. Phillip Levine (New York: Galahad, 1993), p. 20.

18. W.S. Merwin, "For the Anniversary of My Death," in *The Second Four Books of Poems* (Port Townsend, Washington: Copper Canyon Press, 1993), p. 115.

19. C.G. Jung, *The Archetypes and the Collective Unconscious*, *CW* 9i, § 234.

20. Jung, *CW* 9i, § 174.

21. "Campus Shooting Tragedy." August 29, 2000. http://newswire.uark.edu/articles/9274/campus-shooting-tragedy.

22. Virginia Krauft, Dr. Locke Memorial Library Website. http://johnlockememoriallibrary.org/.

23. Daryl Sharp, "Individuation," in *Jung Lexicon*, http://www.nyaap.org/jung-lexicon/i.

24. Geraldine Cannon, *Glad Wilderness* (Austin, TX: Plain View Press, 2008).

25. Edward F. Edinger, *Ego and Archetype* (Boston, MA: Shambhala, 1992), p. 8-9.

26. C.G. Jung, *Aion: Researches into the Phenomenology of the Self*, *CW* 9ii, § 296.

27. Edinger, *Ego and Archetype*, p. 189.

28. James Dickey, *Self Interviews* (Baton Rouge, LA: Louisiana State University Press, 1970), p. 79.

29. Cannon, *Glad Wilderness*, p. 60.

30. James Hollis, *What Matters Most: Living a More Considered Life* (New York: Gotham Books, 2009), p. 63.

31. "Focus on Faculty: Featuring Geraldine Cannon Becker." http://www.umfk.edu/calendarcalevent.cfm?event=2014_04_23_Focuson FacultyFeaturingGeraldineCannonBecker.

32. Robert Frost, "The Oven Bird," in *Mountain Interval* (New York: Henry Holt and Company, 1916).

This essay follows one woman's journey through the silences of childhood betrayal into a mature silence of forgiveness. Using the ancient myth of Demeter and Persephone, the author postulates that the lack of a myth of the Divine Feminine hinders the full development of the power of voice in both mother and daughter.

A Legacy of Silences:
Transforming the Silence of Absence
to a Silence of Presence

MARILYN L. MATTHEWS

Whether observing my own process or mentoring others, I have noticed that speaking up and out is difficult for many women. Before the age of menarche, girls have voices; we shout, confront, are curious, tell stories, and are not afraid to talk. But at some point in our lives, we stop speaking with certainty. We begin to apologize, to discount what we know. What arrests our wonderful, curious voices? In this short essay, I explore some of the issues that cloak women's voices in silence and propose ways that silence can enhance our lives.

A conflict arises when I consider sharing my story: I am a woman in a collaborative leadership position learning from my vulnerability and mistakes to tolerate uncertainty; I am also the vulnerable inner child who is still caught in fear and rage and sorrow. I struggle constantly to bring myself to a place of balance (if I can use this term when the desolate feelings of doubt and shame arise) between old patterns—that of hiding, feeling too big, too much, and at the same time, never enough—and the newer more healthy behaviors I am currently living. I have been assaulted by shame and guilt most of my life, especially when I dare to reveal this secret—my childhood trauma—to take it seriously and reflect on its painful consequences.

Marilyn L. Matthews, M.D., is currently president of the New Mexico Society of Jungian Analysts as well as Chair of the Archetypal Exam Committee for the Inter-Regional Society of Jungian Analysts. She is a psychiatrist and a Jungian analyst with a private practice in Santa Fe, New Mexico. Publications include "Reclaiming Women's Voices from Echo's Long Silence," *Quadrant*, XXVII: 2, Summer, 1997; "Interpretation of 'The Snow Queen,'" in *Psyche's Stories, Vol. II,* 1992; "Apocalypse Now: Breakdown or Breakthrough?", *Psychological Perspectives*, vol. 52, issue 4, 2009. Her primary interest is mentoring women to find their authenticity, authority, and voice.

Expressing myself has always been a problem. I blurt out something raw and unassimilated, as often as something wise. Because my questions are often ignored or unanswered I wonder if they are unimportant or off the mark. I feel too visible and yet not visible enough—and therefore not heard. To speak or not to speak—that is the dilemma. Over time I have learned to hold my thoughts and feelings inside a cage so that they don't spring out, stirring up chaos.

Unfortunately, such restraint causes the cage to get too full. Then the angry, sad, or blunt words burst out. Such words carry power to hurt, to damage, to separate rather than connect. Out of that ensuing shame, I restrict my voice—my inner truth—and stay silent. This silence and the shame it carries is also cultural and very powerful. I want to expand the space around me by exploring silence.

My childhood was spent living in a middle class church-going, choir-singing, bike-riding neighborhood in Cleveland Heights, Ohio. On Sunday mornings in good weather, we all piled into the car; Dad drove us to the Chagrin Reservation. On those special Sundays this place was our "church." The car had to ford a stream to reach this particular site. At the top of the hill was a clearing, a large outdoor park with wooden picnic tables and iron grills, surrounded by giant trees resounding with bird calls, wind soughing through the leaves, the pine-needles thrumming with the breeze. We pretty much had the site to ourselves those early Sunday mornings. There we would unload the car, set the table, and eat an immense breakfast of eggs, bacon, and toast cooked to perfection on the iron grill. Food always tasted better in this setting. Then as our parents savored their morning coffee and leisurely read the paper, my sister and I roamed well-marked paths under the trees. We listened to the high-pitched "Wuk, Wuk" cries and loud rat-a-tat-tat pecking of Pileated woodpeckers—huge birds nearly two feet in length—flashing their red and black and white feathers high in the sunlit branches.

The backdrop for this seemingly serene upbringing was the Second World War. I remember black-out curtains and night silence, ration cards for sugar, flour, and eggs, plastic packages of a white thick substance that looked like lard. Those packets contained ersatz butter, holding a yellow button of food coloring that we had to break and then knead through the "lard" until the coloring was evenly distributed.

My parents did not talk about the war. Nevertheless, its miasma seeped into everything, lurking in the silence of things not spoken.

I remember when I was about eight years old, walking on Lee Road past Fazio's, an Italian deli, hearing a very loud low rumble of a plane. It sounded so close, so loud, I felt unexpectedly frightened. Looking up, I saw the largest plane I had ever seen. It was a B-52 bomber, flying low in the sky. The fear evoked by that sight and sound never left me. Six years later while I was wandering in the empty fields around our new home in Hudson, Ohio, I heard the sound of a large plane. This time I didn't look up—I just ran to the nearby woods, my heart pounding like a drum, my breath coming in gasps. I could not tell anyone. The War had been over for eight years by that time. But the fears and the deaths and the wounds were present in the silence, in the unspeaking—and unspeakable—silence.

Not a pleasant silence—thick with unspoken fears, covered up with nice words, ugly with lurking ghosts—it waited for the unsuspecting child to open her heart or her ears. I didn't—open either my heart or my ears. Instead, I read, opening to my imagination where so much more was possible, and at the same time creating a space that was temporarily free from misery. Back then, the stories I read were written in third person, masculine, singular. I did not read girls' stories. I read about boys and men who took action, who figured things out, who faced their fears with the help of the animals that befriended them. The characters were alive in my mind. I could live vicariously there.

It was a safe way to escape what lay beneath the war environment which I could not look at or reflect upon for many years because of repeated trauma. I was given regular enemas, which I vigorously resisted, from the ages of about three to five. These events—the war black-outs and silence and the forceful penetration of my child body—coincided. I did not really understand until I was in my 50's that enemas are considered a form of sexual abuse. Because I had some signs and symptoms of post-traumatic stress, I did wonder about the possibility of sexual abuse. I also had a hard time relating to either parent. But I just didn't—couldn't—label enemas as sexual. Too much shame, guilt, anger, and deep sadness, none of which were ever heard or acknowledged. Again that disturbing silence.

As I begin to tell the stories behind the silence—those of my inner child's broken heart—tears threaten to spill over and run down my cheeks. Although I stop them out of old habit—a desire to flee from the terror of knowing—the urge to drop into the sadness remains. What is this sadness? It takes the form of a clutching in the pit of my stomach, a gritting of my teeth, a deep heaviness in my chest from which emanate deep sighs, as I try to stay present to the experience. These symptoms carry the fear that has often prevented me from feeling this deep sadness. This sadness is not depression or despair; perhaps the old term, melancholy, suits this feeling best, and softens the terror of memory. Chogyam Trungpa's description of a spiritual warrior is when the heart opens so the tears can begin to flow. I find that happening often as I explore this secret shame.

No one in the family spoke about what was real to me as a child. Instead, that which was really happening was more present in the silences than in spoken words. Winnie the Pooh and Christopher Robin were my healers when I was sick. Which was often. As a youngster, I spent a lot of time in the hospital. The unspoken spirits which lurked in the silences dove into my gastrointestinal tract begging to be known, recognized, spoken, considered, and reflected upon. Although by that time, the enemas had stopped, their after-effects lingered. The difficult price of that silencing—no outlet for the rage, the terror, the hurt, the betrayal by both parents—was psychosomatic illness. Nausea, vomiting, diarrhea, constipation, abdominal cramping—belly pain which caused me to get on my hands and knees and rock in the bed to calm something that could not be assuaged by any amount of medications or any amount of tears.

It was, I later discovered, a pain of the deepest emotional sort—suffering that comes when a child is exposed to the agony of others—and her own—that she cannot fathom or express. I had no tools or support to stand back and witness. At that time, medicine did not acknowledge psychosomatic illness—those somatic intrusions caused by unexplained horrors revealed too early to a child's psyche. Not until recently did contemporary psychoanalytic thought validate that when a child's intense affective states are consistently invalidated by the other, she learns not to trust her own experience. The world I lived in—my family and my culture—did not discuss feelings. The emotions stirred by horrific battle scenes of World War II, and later the horrors of the Holocaust, were masked by patriotism. People did not speak about the unspeakable. Not then—barely now. Silence again. Terrible silence, full of unmentionable specters. It is probably no surprise that I began "making rounds"—that is, going to visit other patients on the adult ward—when I was eight years old as a patient under observation for an unknown illness. Later, I studied to be a physician, entering medical school at age twenty.

Reflection on the myth of Demeter and her daughter, Persephone—still a mystery thousands of years later—helps me understand the drama in my life. Myths are codes, stories of powerful archetypal energies which play out in our human lives. They call to us to decode and humanize their actions. Allowing this myth to penetrate to my core, I feel deep sadness when I consider my particular mother/ daughter bond. That depth of sadness has lurked underneath all the terrible silences of my childhood. My recent 75th birthday brought the next initiatory shock, an impetus to delve into the pain of that story.

Demeter, the Great Mother, replete with fecund power of growth and fertility, loves her daughter, wanting to protect her and keep her close—perhaps too close for this daughter who is growing into her maidenhood, still innocent but definitely moving away from her mother's watchful eye. The action begins with the innocent daughter gathering flowers in a field—a narcissus, described as having a hundred blossoms, that drew Persephone to it. In that moment of plucking the flower, Hades, the god of the underworld, of death, drives his chariot through the crack in the earth and plucks this beautiful daughter to be his wife. The mother/daughter bond is suddenly ruptured, and the daughter goes to "hell." In my life, that bond was broken by the "rape" of my child body—the enemas—by the dark god, the animus of a mother whose maternal instincts were deadened by the lack of support in her family of origin and her culture. To return from the deadness of the underworld—the forceful invasion of my body and the consistent invalidation of my feelings—has been a long process.

The daughter, Persephone, is her mother's beloved daughter. Was I ever my mother's beloved daughter? Or simply an extension of her own being, and thus a threat to her and her sense of control when I began to separate from her? I know very little about my mother. She never spoke to me about her childhood or her young adulthood. My mother, a softly pretty woman, was mostly silent—silenced before I was born. She was a first-generation American, born of English parents who emigrated in the early 20th century from London. Her eldest brother died in the 1918 flu epidemic when she was only ten years old. I do not know if she grieved. Her other brother was very nervous. Her parents—like many of that day—showered the boys with material goods but did not give their only girl child any toys. Not even a doll. Was that true for mother? I do not know. She never said a word to me— only once to my sister did she reveal this childhood lack.

What astounds me now as I reflect on the myth is that my mother never spoke of her mother. She never told any stories about her life, her upbringing, her parents. It was as if she had no mother, as if the father that guided her was the spirit in the church—a patriarchal God that ruled behavior rather strictly—an archetypal energy of perfection. Many years later, when I was helping her downsize her apartment, she told me stories about each knick-knack that I packed. By that time, I was deaf to her. I had given up trying to understand her, to talk to her.

As I continue to reflect on this myth, several moments become illuminated. In the myth, both mother and daughter have first to discover/recover who they are, as themselves. When a daughter leaves home, she often moves from one element of "darkness" to the next. Without really ever leaving "home." The myth describes Persephone taken by the dark god, forcibly breaking the mother/daughter bond; the fact that Persephone wandered far from her mother's watchful gaze is not emphasized. In my case, I never trusted mother or dad again, but acted as if I did; I suppressed my own nature so that I would not know or examine my traumatic history until much later in life. In the underworld, Persephone eats nothing; she does not assimilate her experience, does not wish to relate to the dark god. For me, that meant that over the years, my internal voices became very dark. My sovereignty and my agency remained in the underworld, undermined by those dismissive voices, both interior and exterior.

Demeter's identification with her raging sorrow is broken first by Iambe (Baubo), the old servant who lifts her skirts revealing her pudenda, and whose lewd gestures and bawdy jokes make Demeter laugh. By lightening her mood, the old nurse brings Demeter back into balance, reminding her of the power of life, death, and transformation. Another breakthrough comes with Metaneira's protest, the human mother's anguish at seeing her son in the fire. The goddess can no longer hide the truth of her being. In my own life, I have hidden my strength—and my truth—by believing that men's lives and words hold more value than my own. It is only now that I myself am a crone that I can confront my own hidden dark initiating rituals—and question my mother's behavior. As a crone I remember who I am, and live that feminine truth.

Meanwhile, Persephone, close to panic and weeping for her mother, gradually becomes intrigued by the dark god. She can do nothing else. Except that she does not eat anything there. What does it signify that the daughter doesn't eat? Is this her resistance to assimilating the experience of the underworld? Does that resistance permit the development of an inner sovereignty with which she can free herself from the mother's body and step into her own power and agency? I did not have a classic eating disorder; I did have a psychosomatic illness that repeated itself for many years with pain— nausea, vomiting, diarrhea, cramping—until I was finally able to stand with myself and ask why. Why now? To connect the dots between emotion and action.

When Hades is about to release Persephone to go to her mother, he pleads for her to remember their relationship. Before she leaves, Hades impels her to eat a seed of the pomegranate. Persephone resists but then swallows that seed from her own volition. Pomegranate: the red of blood—life, birth, death—of many seeds, of fertility—these are the qualities the daughter takes back with her to her mother. She now has her own form of power, shared with her spouse and earned from her time spent in the underworld. It is just this moment that is alive for me in the myth. No longer is she only the daughter of the Great Mother. She herself is now a queen.

Perhaps one of the mysteries of Eleusis is this moment—when a girl becomes a woman, aware of the power she has, that she can have, not as her mother's child, but of her own agency as woman who is herself—virginal, not mother's daughter. This is a powerful moment—this awareness of being not just daughter but maiden, with the possibility of learning, exploring, and living her own sovereignty. This transition can be difficult, especially if the mother and daughter have few role models or rituals of transformation. That moment in which a daughter grows beyond her mother, and dares to live more expansively than her mother could, threatens not only her own loyalty but can also stir envy and retribution from the mother.

Do myths stay the same? No. Like other parts of the psyche they evolve as we develop and are affected by our culture. Demeter stopped being the Great Mother many thousands of years ago. The dual effect of the loss of the sacred feminine in Western culture and the rise of patriarchal values—power over versus collaboration, individualism over relationship—have made mothering much harder. Our instincts about mothering are shaped by the culture in which we live. When the culture does not have models for living and valuing from a strong feminine base—maiden, mother, and crone—the destructive spirit of the collective becomes more prevalent. Women and men are then more likely to identify with and live as victims of those patriarchal judgments about the inferiority, dullness, and lack of creativity of women.

Photos I have of mother from the early 1930's show a soft, beautiful woman whose very being curved around the cat, dog, baby that she tended. Her soft gaze focused on nothing else—these photos showed me a mother whom I do not remember. I remember her face as a mask of darkness, absolute judgment, and displeasure. Her mouth would disappear into a lipless grimace; her eyes became flat; her brow furrowed. How truly frightening that gaze—a mask of judgment, all connectedness dead. The silence—so full of recriminations, judgments, hurt, anger—so many stories. What had I done wrong? Was this irreparable? Oh, I must be bad. Something is wrong with me. I am unlovable. It was a physical thing—a cold feeling in the pit of my stomach, clammy hands, breathing more and more shallow. I lived with the dread that I had already caused irreparable damage. That I done something that I didn't know about that could not be undone. Would I never know the "real" truth? I was sure that no one would ever tell me.

The familial and cultural denial of the atrocities that occurred in World War II—that deadly, silent killing energy displayed in newsreels at all the movie theaters which was part of our national heritage, was not part of what adults discussed with their children—at least not in my family of origin. The enemas disappeared into "normal" family practices, not to be discussed or questioned. What I as a child of those war years took into my little body was the premise that unless I shaped up, did it right, and did not speak about anything that might distress adults, I would disturb the fragile peace of our family complex, as well as that of my little world, and of my church. My ability to stand back and witness, to reflect, to come into mind, was not possible. Instead, I used dissociation of mind from body/psyche as a defense against the terrors of intense affect.

My parents' silent withdrawal gave me freedom to explore nature's silence. I spent hours in the field at the corner of the street where we lived, a field alive with tall grasses, weeds, flowers, trees with branches where I could disappear for hours in my imagination. The mama woodpecker making her nest in a bolt hole of a dead tree let me watch from a perch on a nearby limb as she fed her babies. The grasshoppers danced; the cicadas sang incessantly. That silence was vast; that silence was solace.

I got through both college and graduate school by memorizing, taking copious notes, and later, trying hard to make sense out of what I'd read. I always felt afraid, like an imposter—a "fact" frequently spoken by male peers especially in medical school, who felt threatened by women entering their domain—as well as by my contemptuous inner voices.

Medical school was tough, not only because there was so much to learn but also because all the teachers were men who had little experience in guiding women into the mystery of healing. There were few mentors with whom to speak about the ineffable. I had felt its presence for years but had no words to express it. This spirit drove me to work long hard hours, to give of myself to others, to study and read and assimilate as much as I could. However, no matter how much energy I put into this amazing field, I could not find words to express myself. I could not pass oral exams. I did very well on written exams and failed miserably on orals. I froze up and forgot everything I knew. Each time it was a shocking and cruel experience that continued to undermine my sense of self.

I survived medical school and fears which bordered on panic by having this dream early on:

> *I am driving down a lonely road and see a Hasidic rabbi complete with flat-brimmed hat, side curls, and beard, dressed in black*

walking on the side of the road. I stop. He tells me, after looking
deeply at me, to read the 62ⁿᵈ Psalm.

I awoke and immediately read that passage: "For God is my refuge.
He alone is my strength and salvation. I shall not be afraid." What a
gift! That lovely reading became my mantra. Repeating this phrase kept
me safe. Unfortunately, it didn't help me find my voice. As I reflect on
this pivotal dream now, I realize the importance of the Hasidic presence.
That sect, formed by Baal Shem Tov in the 18th century, was a less
academic, more emotional way of experiencing the immanent presence
of God. The dream offered me mystical support to balance the
intellectual emphasis of medical school.

My first residency—four years in Obstetrics and Gynecology—
taught me to deliver babies and do surgery, not a light field. When
our boss, Dr. B_____, asked us why we had chosen this field, I was
startled. I chose this branch because I enjoyed delivering babies, seeing
the light and love in the parents' eyes, taking care of women. Hearing
that first wail of a newborn's voice. There was excitement and tragedy,
mystery and agony in this arena. Wasn't that enough? Dr. B_____ stated
that for him people entered that field either because they didn't
understand women, or didn't like them. I realized with a sinking feeling
that there was a little bit of truth in both for me.

Dr. B___ was a good teacher and leader, although his opinions
were not always easy to hear. For example, one day after he had observed
me perform a surgical procedure, he took me aside and told me that
I'd never make a good surgeon by being timid. Be bold, he said, and
take the responsibility that I could kill. As you might guess, that
statement of fact went in deep. I had to come to terms with that
possibility of doing harm. I had to responsibly acquire surgical skills
that were quick and accurate.

For a while I performed abortions and was quite active in the
Planned Parenthood organization. I loved counseling women about
caring for themselves and their babies. I had seen too many beautiful
young women have their lives snuffed out by the tragedy of having
an unwanted pregnancy, and worse, trying to abort the child. The
stigma of being pregnant, of having no way to care for or support
another child, of getting no help from the father of this child—
who in that time and place was often a rapist who had taken away

the woman's choice. Before the decision of *Roe v. Wade*, the atmosphere was very charged. My training began in an era when gram negative septicemia, a result of a botched back alley abortion attempt, led inexorably to that woman's death. And we, the medical staff, had nothing in our toolbox that could intervene. At that time—1964-1968—there was no treatment. We watched helplessly while these girls died a terrible death. The contempt for these young women—most likely due to our powerlessness in the face of rampant infection—was difficult to bear. When abortions became legal, I did choose to help women in this difficult situation. But after several years of performing abortions, my body said "No." I was stunned by this inner certainty. Once I allowed myself to explore the verity of that voice, I knew I could no longer perform this act. Though my body opposed my surgical participation in abortion, my voice actively supported women in their choices of birth control. I continue to express my belief in the right each woman has to decide what happens to and in her body. That was, after all, the original meaning of the *Roe v. Wade* decision: a woman's right to make decisions about her body.

In the midst of this early medical practice my first husband was killed in a hit-and-run accident when our sons were eight and five and a half years old. I struggled for more than a year to hold everything together, to provide both nurturing and a livelihood, as well as manage our grief and loss. The attitude that had been a companion in my youth proved itself again—keep a stiff upper lip, don't be vulnerable, don't let anyone see your weakness. My second marriage provided ompanionship and relief from being a single parent. It also introduced a deeper measure of thinking. This man—a dear friend from my college years and I could talk; we could discuss subjects that I had never before explored. We both made the decision to become Jungian analysts. Training in this field answered a deeply felt need in me to wake up, to come to know myself on an inner level and to find my own voice. I trained to be a psychiatrist, going through a second residency which opened me to another level of mystery—the majesty of the psyche. It took ten years for me to adjust to a new way of being: that of listening to others' pain and anguish rather than trying to fix something.

Silence still had more lessons to teach me. Many years later after finishing my psychiatric residency and my analytic degree, getting a divorce, and living on my own—no spouse, no children—I had trouble sleeping. I would get up and sit in the dark, in the silence of the night overlooking Lake Michigan. That was the beginning of my sitting practice. The silence taught me to listen more deeply to myself, to wait. At first the cacophony of all the unspoken fears and doubts, judgments, and lacerating recriminations, almost deafened me. But something kept me coming back to the dark and the silence.

Formal meditation practice began when I moved to New Mexico in 1987. I started with *vipassana* meditation, eventually quitting because the intensity of focus in that method of practice disturbed the barrier of repression I had so carefully built. That barrier held behind it the reasons for all the pain and cramping and eruptions of the gastrointestinal tract which could not assimilate or digest my family's toxic nurturing.

Next, I spent a number of retreats in the early 90's with Thich Nhat Hanh, a Buddhist monk and master of mindfulness meditation. His ability to speak compassionately about suffering, both his own painful feelings of anger and betrayal as well encompassing the suffering of others, was a revelation for me. Ultimately, however, without a community or a teacher, mind and story got away from me. I was plagued by attacks from the collective unconscious. By this time the inner voices had become quite vicious, I think, because I kept busy and could not reflect on or about my childhood. Finally, I found a meditation teacher who taught me to be present to whatever came up without judgment; he invited and encouraged me to put into words my experiences when I returned from my explorations of the depths.

The first time I was able to let go of the story and just stay present to the experience, to the feeling, I was astounded by the quiet. By the silence. Quiet mind. I asked the teacher, "Where did it go?" Meaning, where did all the energy go? All that strong emotion which had threatened me for so many years with the drama—fear, murderous rage, and doubt that was near panic: Gone. He just looked at me with such softness, such compassion, and said nothing. That was the beginning of my being able to stand with myself, to not disappear into a dissociated state when strong emotions came up.

Now, when I can't sleep, or the boogie men of politics or of the media beat the drum of fear in my ears, I sit in the dark and I breathe. In spring, summer, and fall, I go out and sit under Heaven's canopy of stars and clouds and feel the vastness of the Universe above my head. Lao Tsu asks if the universe is agitated and then answers with the advice to go out at night and sit under the desert sky and feel. I pull the silence from wherever it is. And I breathe in the sounds of silence—including the voices, the TV, the cars, the birds, the rushing of blood in my ears—my life energy. Eventually I come back to now—to what is happening right now.

Diving deeper into the Eleusinian myth helps me to feel the loss: not just of Persephone, of the daughter I never had, but also of the mother, the woman whose voice was silenced before I was born. After more than thirty-five years of exploration, I think I understand at least part of my mother's silences. I think in her own way she was working hard not to open her own cage of darkness. I have had to learn to translate that darkness—both hers and my own. She could not learn that. Her sense of her feminine self was too fragile. All her heart and thoughts went to the Christian dogma that held her, made it possible for her to continue living and, especially after Dad died, to find meaning. To never question authority, to never express doubts. When she gave me enemas by force, she had learned, like many women of that time, to follow "The Doctor's Advice," even if it went against her deep maternal instincts. There was no Great Mother available—nor was her own mother in the picture.

So how to translate the darkness? My western ego-mind wants an answer—a fact, a thought, a noun—that temporarily settles the queasiness of uncertainty and doubt in my gut. That type of answer, while momentarily beneficial, allows me to leap out of the experiences. To pause and listen to the voice of bodily sensations and emotions requires a different way of knowing, that of the ancient practices of divination, like Runes, the *I Ching,* and Tarot cards. Each of these latter methods works through a phenomenon called synchronicity—defined as meaningful coincidences, not causally related, that impacts me deeply.

Recently, I celebrated my 75th birthday. In the weeks leading up to this milestone, symptoms of increasing tension and headaches alerted me that some part of my psyche needed my attention. Though I spent time with friends, saw an intense play, *Coriolanus,* listened to the band, Pink Martini, and had a massage, the internal pressure continued; I got grumpier and heavier. There was something about being alive for three quarters of a century that was more intense than any previous big birthday. It was time to throw the Runes. The first rune that I drew was the blank Rune—The Unknowable. This was the situation now—the unknowable, a time of self-transformation. In order to understand this Rune I had to stop being so busy and listen. I had to practice being present in my body, bringing all five senses to bear in this moment of uncertainty. When I do not try to name this uneasiness, a door opens to a new perception of the situation: an answer that for me often leads to another question.

The Rune Odin—the blank Rune—is both beginning and end. According to Ralph Blum's *The Book of Runes,*[1] it is a Rune of complete trust, and indicates contact with my true destiny, a process that reveals itself many times, like a phoenix rising from the ashes of fate. What I notice is restlessness, as if all the events—evidence of my path—are being scrambled. As if I am being shaken in a giant tumbler by an unknown force. As if my knowing of me, of who I am, is shifting—again—as it has at each moment of initiation into the next phase. I do not like sitting with the discomfort of not knowing what's next, the uncertainty of life. Perhaps it is the fact that seventy-five years of life bring me closer to the Great Unknowing that we name Death, an ending.

My waking life is filled with a feeling I call "grumpiness." An irritating, complaining, resisting, negating, fault-finding voice that doesn't want to change. Doesn't want to look. Doesn't want to know. Is not curious. This part feels so threatened! It is remarkable to explore this aspect now that I am allowing myself entry to its obfuscating obstructionist tactics. This part of me, the ego, has enjoyed—become so identified in fact—with a sense of control and belief in its supremacy, that now that the end [that's how it talks: THE END] is closer, it might be losing, might be closer to NOT BEING ABLE TO CONTROL. And that possibility frightens *this* ego a lot.

This issue of control—or lack thereof—has been around for most of my life. Potty trained by eleven months of age. Repeated violations of my physical body by enemas, catheterizations, sigmoidoscopies, surgical procedures, anesthesia with ether. A growing unconscious alienation from my body, or more specifically, an alienation from my power over and in and with my body. A body/psyche that did not get to say, "No." I—my ego—had been assimilated into Western culture: mind over body, noun over verb, dogma over experience, power as the only truth. Intellect/Logos over Heart/Eros.

Now the blank rune, the unknowable, is moving in me. My mind feels blank in a new way. I notice that I have been labeling this blankness as a judgment: I *don't have words*; I *don't know what to do*; I *don't know what's going to happen.* A tremendous sadness, a great grief, an unnerving restlessness, moves through me that I have called "grumpiness." That label has made me think that I am stuck. It makes me want to push, to try harder. To Make Something Happen. To Do Anything Else than just stay present.

When I can quiet the mind and all its frantic grabbing at nouns, names, and explanations to make this "blessed unrest" go away, I gradually become aware of a deeper element of silence: pleasurable awareness of the symphony of life all around me. Sitting in a busy coffee shop on a Saturday morning, with all the voices and words, the sounds of dishes-clinking, trays-slamming, life-living, difference-making, all-giving nature of being—LIFE—being, not just doing. Active silence—not NO-THING. I soak up this life energy. Suddenly I can see and feel more deeply into the grumpiness. I feel separate; seventy-five years (three quarters of a century!) have become a judgment, a stopping, a closing, an ending because this "I" doesn't know what is next. Doesn't want to examine too closely a change that wants my attention.

I start to realize that being busy is a familiar way for me to avoid the past, to elude the now. Uncertainty is in the foreground. I can no longer trust my strength, dexterity, or balance in the old way. Though I am active—walking, yoga, teaching, working—my current pace is slower, the silences longer. I have to consciously work with my impatience, my lack of compassion for self and others. I must be alert to a growing awareness of my impermanence. It's a hard thing for ego to allow—not-being. That's its fear: no longer being. Stopping. Ending. Dying. Going. No longer coming.

But wait a minute. What am I exploring? Am I not opening my heart to the restlessness, to the uncertainty of not knowing? These thoughts are reflections on my lessons of silence. My sitting practice creates space in which I am not overwhelmed by my feelings or thoughts. In other words, by "re-cognizing," I register a repeating pattern of behavior, slow it down, and am present to the physical, emotional, and spiritual aspects of the behavior. Through this slow process of intent, I can arrest the pattern—the complex with all its feelings and thoughts—and allow the archetypal core to become humanized. Silence at this time in my life is no longer deadening. It is enlivening, a time to savor what I am learning in this next phase of my life. Silence is now a valuable staple for exploring and experiencing a living center that holds, a new way of expressing "me."

NOTES

1. Ralph Blum, *The Book of Runes* (New York: St. Martin's Press, 1982), p. 118.

Despite outer accomplishments that might have amazed our grandmothers, many contemporary women still struggle inwardly to "find our voices." This is a psychological process of developing inner authority and learning to express it authentically. The myths of Echo and Cassandra, lived by contemporary women and visible in Jungian analysis, illustrate the loss and recovery of the authentic female voice.

Beyond Echo and Cassandra:
Finding the Voice of Inner Authority

KAITRYN SHEEHAN WERTZ

"When the time comes to you at which you will be forced at last
to utter the speech which has lain at the center of your soul for
years... you'll not talk about joy of words. I saw well why the
gods do not speak to us openly, nor let us answer. Till that word
can be dug out of us, why should they hear the babble that we
think we mean?"
— C. S. Lewis, *Till We Have Faces*

"Find your voice" has been a feminist mantra since the sixties.
Originally a rallying cry for the inclusion of women in public
discourse, it later morphed into a well-worn metaphor for
the expression of female authority. The phrase is loaded with emotion,
evoking the history of women's long silence and aspirations for authentic
expression. When Hillary Clinton, campaigning for President in 2008,
announced that she had found her own voice, pundits and bloggers
on both the left and the right went wild in a warring frenzy of praise
and condemnation.[1] Meanwhile a Google search for the phrase obtains
over 564,000 results for services that promise to help us find our voices
through endeavors as wide-ranging as religion, fashion, social
networking, wedding planning, and divorce.

Kaitryn Sheehan Wertz, M.Ed., L.M.H.C., is a licensed psychotherapist and Jungian
analyst practicing and teaching in Jupiter, Florida and Lafayette, Colorado. She is a
graduate of the Inter-Regional Society of Jungian Analysts (IRSJA) and a faculty member
of the Boulder and Florida Jungian Seminars. During the 1970's, Kaitryn was a founding
member of Kriplau Yoga Center of Lenox, Massachusetts, and she remains interested in
the psychological understanding of yogic and Hindu teachings and symbols. Kaitryn can
be contacted through her website www.katewertz.com or at kate@katewertz.com.

The voice that we seem so eager to find is that of inner authority. In a five-year project aimed at discovering "women's ways of knowing," a group of psychologists and educators conducted extensive interviews with American women of varied ages, socioeconomic backgrounds, and educational levels, discovering that women repeatedly use the metaphor of voice to depict their development of mind, self, and authority.[2] This tendency is at odds with the visual metaphors (for instance those equating seeing with knowing or knowledge with light) that are used most often in science and philosophy.

Metaphors involving the mind's eye encourage standing at a distance to get an objective view, an orientation more in keeping with the Logos principle of differentiation, while metaphors involving speaking and listening suggest ways of knowing through dialogue and interaction, an orientation more based in the Eros principle of relatedness. The study concludes that, for most American women, a sense of self and self-worth most commonly occurs within the context of feeling connected to oneself and others—and that it is typically understood and expressed through the metaphor of the voice.

Western history has not been kind to authoritative female voices. Socrates' wife became infamous as a shrew with too sharp and loose a tongue, even though Plato described her as a loving spouse. Aristotle wrote, "Silence is a woman's glory, but this is not equally the glory of a man."[3] Paul advocated the elimination of women's voices from the early Church, arguing that the fall of humanity had occurred due to Eve's sinful use of speech: she persuaded Adam to eat the forbidden fruit. Paul wrote, "I do not permit a woman to teach, nor to have authority over the man; she must be silent." (Timothy 2:12)

Throughout the Christian era, silence has been considered a feminine virtue and speech a feminine vice; from the middle ages into the twenty-first century, cartoons of women with their lips padlocked have remained popular. Even in contemporary life, writes linguist Deborah Tannen, speech described as articulate, committed, passionate, or fluent in men tends to be labeled as strident, shrill, or excessive in women.[4]

Against this long background of suppression, it is tempting to compensate by idealizing the female voice and turning a deaf ear to its shadow. And yet the shadow is there. Women can indeed be strident and shrill at times, perhaps especially when first struggling to discover and express personal authority. Both men and women may use their voices in service to power, drowning out other voices with the force of their own and deadening relatedness with intolerance. Some also drown out relatedness by incessant chatter devoid of meaningful content, "the babble that we think we mean."[5] Gossip, for example, is almost universally associated with women's speech and it can be a way of using one's voice to diminish, rather than enhance, other people. This is memorably depicted in the musical comedy, *The Music Man*. As the town matrons gather to gossip, they pick apart their neighbors' reputations, singing rapidly in high-pitched, bird-like voices, "Pick a little, talk a little, pick a little, talk a little, cheep cheep cheep, talk a lot, pick a little more."[6] While these uses of the voice may posture as power, they lack the deeply grounded relatedness to self and others that is the voice of true psychological authority.

This authority is the ability to experience our own thoughts, feelings, and perceptions as valid and valuable, leading to self-trust, agency, and responsibility for being the authors of our own lives. Understood psychologically, finding one's voice is a process of developing psychological authority and learning to express it authentically. Genuine inner authority, in other words, is more an internal than an external process.

My interest in this topic emerges both from my personal efforts to develop an authentic sense of inner authority and from my experience with other women—patients, friends, and colleagues—who have shared similar concerns. Early in that process, I dreamed that I was desperately trying to get a little girl to the emergency room. Her head was almost completely severed from her body, hanging by a thread. Although I regarded myself as having a strong and authoritative voice, it was a voice that spoke from the neck up. The dream set me on a journey to heal the split between mind and body/soul and to develop a deeper and more full-bodied voice.

Many of the routine accomplishments of contemporary women are unimaginable to our grandmothers, yet the inner struggle to "find our voices" continues. Beneath successful personas, we may lack a felt sense of our own deeper value. Without vital access to positive images of female authority, even success may leave us feeling empty, inferior, or fraudulent. Fearing exposure as undeserving, we may continue to seek our value through outer accomplishments, hoping that the next "seal of approval" from an external authority will finally confer what is missing.

These difficulties have a cultural underpinning. The legacy of patriarchy has profoundly colored our perceptions, attitudes, and images of authority, which have long been "genderized" through association with male figures and images. I vividly recall hearing my father tell my little brother that he could grow up to be President of the United States. "Me too!" I exclaimed. "Girls can't be President," my father replied. "But you could be First Lady...or even Miss America!" Even at six, I sensed that these aspirations were a distant second.

Based on messages like this, women raised in a patriarchal society or family culture may learn to exclude authority from their self-images as incompatible with a socially approved feminine identity, creating a double bind between feminine identity and authority.[7] Women who claim authority have often been labeled as controlling, domineering, or bitchy, while those who don't have been labeled dependent, depressed, or masochistic.

The mother is usually the first figure of authority in a child's life, and necessary psychological separation from her tends to create strong defenses against female authority in both women and men. As adults, we may continue to experience women's authority through the negative pole of the mother complex.[8] For some women, this problem is managed by projecting authority onto male figures, but this solution denies women the fuller validation that might emerge from access to an internal voice of female authority. To uncover such a voice, women may need to begin as in Marge Piercy's poem,[9]

Unlearning to Not Speak

She must learn again to speak
starting with I
starting with We
starting as the infant does
with her own true hunger
and pleasure
and rage.

Two Ways We Lose Our Voices

Echo

Diane spoke so softly that she was often ignored completely. She simmered in silent resentment whenever this happened but she never raised her voice. "Nobody cares what I think," she said repeatedly, with an air of self-pity. But the truth was even more difficult to face. After a lifetime of silent compliance and conflict avoidance, Diane had no idea what she really thought or felt. Her tentative voice was actually a faithful instrument that conveyed a vacuum of personal authority. Instead, Diane derived her sense of authority from identifications with her husband, her church, and her social group.

Married for thirty-five years to a controlling, judgmental, and uncommunicative man, Diane had spent her life trying to please others: her mother, husband, employers, and friends. But as her sixtieth birthday approached, she felt empty and depressed. She realized that she knew nothing of her own wants and needs and feared that time was running out. Initially she asked if I could administer tests to determine her interests, as she had no idea how to discover them on her own.

In the first dream she brought to our sessions, Diane chased a frantic, silent little girl around a small room, trying to stop her efforts to get out, suggesting to me that her soul was confined and silenced in too small a life. But Diane had difficulty working symbolically with this or the other dreams she occasionally brought, seemingly eager to please me. Instead, she chatted about the news of the week, reporting her own activities and her reactions to the doings of others. Beneath these narratives ran a stream of continuous anxiety: Diane wondered whether she was good enough, financially secure enough, and loved enough. She feared she would end up poor, widowed, and friendless.

From an archetypal perspective, Diane lived within the Greek myth of Echo, the nymph who assisted Zeus in his philandering by distracting his wife Hera with her stories. In punishment, the jealous Hera cursed Echo with the loss of her capacity to initiate speech, except in meaningless repetition of others. Echo fell desperately in love with the beautiful youth Narcissus but her repetitive speech only provoked his contempt. Dismissed, Echo wasted away in the wilderness until nothing remained of her but a faint and repetitive voice.

Like Echo, Diane had lost her voice through the curse of a negative mother. Her father's preferred companion and confidante from early childhood, Diane became the target of her mother's envy and narcissistic rage. Like Hera attacking Echo's ability to generate speech, Diane's mother contemptuously devalued and foreclosed any attempt Diane made at self-expression. Just as the voiceless Echo was drawn to the proud Narcissus, Diane was unconsciously attracted to self-involved people, both in marriage and in friendship, hoping always to win the approval she craved through compliance.

Because the Echo complex is grounded in the negative mother, women who operate from this pattern may be dissociated from the positive maternal ground in the form of the physical body. The mythological Echo loses her body altogether, wasting away until nothing remains but a repetitive voice. Diane could not recall any experience of being securely held or comforted by her mother and this primal disconnection manifested in adult life as excessive weight, a variety of aches and pains, and numbing of sexual desire (recall that Echo fled from Pan's lusty advances). In fact, Diane's struggle with self-expression arose from a pervasive sense of numbness that made it difficult to experience physical sensations or to access emotions, much less to recall dreams or exercise imagination.

At the heart of Diane's suffering was a depressive form of narcissism, in which she consciously identified with a self-image of shame and inferiority, while projecting value onto others. Diane lived out the pattern of Echo by partnering with people who embodied Narcissus' grandiosity; she unconsciously strove to regain her lost self-esteem through association with admired (and secretly envied) others. But just as the empty Echo became the object of Narcissus' contempt, Diane became the scapegoat for others' projected and disowned shadows.

I noticed Diane's Echo pattern through the pressure I felt to counsel her rather than trust her ability to access her own authority. This was congruent with Diane's expectation that I become another idealized partner to compensate for her lack of value. I worked to balance giving enough metaphoric "food" to allow her to form a secure attachment, while not becoming one more outer authority for her to echo. In this initial phase, she would press me for answers to her dilemmas, becoming anxious when I refrained from counseling her and relieved when I succumbed—though she seldom actually acted upon my suggestions. Instead, she attempted to fan my narcissism by chattily reporting how she had repeated my wisdom, Echo-like, to others.

In time, we were more able to use our sessions as a place where Diane could practice voicing her feelings, wants, and ideas, no matter how tentative. As we worked to identify what she really thought and felt, and to get past her fear of expressing herself, Diane's voice became stronger and more direct. She even disagreed with me when she thought I was wrong—something that would have been unimaginable at the beginning of her therapy. This led to a compensatory period of some inflation in which she attended only to her own voice, with little regard for others. As she experienced more of the grandiose pole of her narcissism, she became angry at the people who had treated her dismissively, creating tensions with those who preferred her silent compliance. It became important in the development of Diane's authority to face the ways she had colluded in her own dismissal. Behind an innocent, self-effacing persona, easily intimidated by the aggression of others, lurked a passive-aggressive, entitled shadow, accustomed to silently manipulating others through her seeming helplessness. In facing and claiming aspects of that shadow, Diane began to recognize the silent power she had wielded in relationships.

As Diane developed a capacity to identify and express what she felt, thought, and wanted, she was more able to assert herself and to risk more authentic expression. After a period of increased tension and confrontation, her marriage grew more satisfying. She spoke to her pastor about her desire to do more than stuff envelopes during her volunteer time at church. Before long, she was chairing church events and performing in the annual play, admitting that she liked being in the spotlight. The following winter, Diane was invited to join a volunteer group serving in a Haitian orphanage, her first trip without her husband in thirty-five years.

Diane's life expanded and her mood improved. She lost twenty-five extra pounds and ended a troubling relationship with a domineering female friend, now recognized as a recapitulation of her relationship with her mother. In the place of that exclusive and demanding friendship, Diane cultivated a number of new friendships with other women, coming to feel more genuinely connected and less alone. Through her effort to develop a more authoritative, genuine voice, she had become less of an Echo—more present and alive, and more able to extend care to others.

Cassandra

The Echo pattern is not the only way women can be silenced. We can also lose our voices through being vocal without the inner authority that makes communication effective. Although such women may speak profusely, they are often not taken seriously, even by themselves. Some may fall into the pattern represented by the Greek myth of Cassandra.

Cassandra was a Trojan princess who was given the gift of prophecy by Apollo in exchange for her promise to lie with him. When Cassandra reneged on fulfilling her part of the bargain, Apollo added a curse: no one would believe her prophesies. It was thus Cassandra's fate to foretell the fall of Troy, and her own murder, unable to convince others to heed her warnings. Cassandra's eventual fate was decapitation, a vivid image of profound psychic disconnection.

Laurie Layton Shapiro has written incisively about the Cassandra complex and my reflections are guided by her work.[10] The Cassandra pattern appears in extroverted, hysterically-organized women in whom there is a split between a rationalistic, judgmental animus and an intuitive, feeling shadow. Although the Cassandra woman has strong intuitive gifts, she tends to discharge anxiety by frantically blurting out unmetabolized intuitions. Like the boy who cried "wolf," she is met with disbelief on all sides.

Thirty-year-old Hannah often seemed to assume the role of a Cassandra, anxiously perseverating over possible worst case scenarios. Post-traumatic hyper-vigilance led her to present both major problems and minor inconveniences as impending disasters, drowning out her accurate intuitions about the underlying states of people and situations. Hannah was, however, anchored by her faith, and found an outlet for more thoughtful expression by composing essays for Christian magazines. She wrote about the contradictions of claiming to be both "pro-life" and pro-war and excluding gay people from the commandment to "love your neighbor." Her essays rang with authoritative passion and compassion. But she couldn't hit the "send" button. Hannah didn't fear having her articles rejected—she feared they would be accepted! Then she might be exposed to criticism, anger, or even persecutory attack. So she continued to write but she never sent. Her caring, insightful voice went unheard.

Hannah was well able to access a sense of personal authority and to express it privately, but not publicly. Her voice was silenced by a dread of hostility and aggression that had a basis in early experience. She had been a bright and extraverted child, closer to her charismatic father than to her mother. He was proud of her intelligence and he enjoyed her quick wit. But when her father was drinking, he would react unpredictably to Hannah's feisty exuberance, punishing her with brutal physical and verbal abuse. Hannah learned to constantly test both the temperature of his mood and his level of intoxication before she spoke.

Hannah's inner world reflected the split in her father, with a bright, spiritualized, Apollonic animus shadowed by a dark Dionysian brother. No matter how sunny things seemed, she knew that a devastating storm could erupt without warning, and she learned that it was better to silence her voice rather than to risk upsetting anyone. As we explored the projection of her father onto her potential readers, Hannah had a few successes in hitting the send button and she was gratified when some of her articles appeared in print.

But it was not until her newborn son was diagnosed with a congenital heart condition that Hannah found a more directly authoritative voice. From the early weeks of his life, Hannah worried about a slight rasping sound in her baby's breath. She felt that something was very wrong, but her concerns were dismissed by her pediatrician as those of an over-anxious mother and by family members as her typical tendency to be a "drama queen." Her Cassandra complex constellated as Hannah continued to urge others to take her concern seriously and they continued to dismiss her. She was torn between her intuition that something was wrong and the self-doubt evoked by others' patronizing denial. We agreed that Hannah's foreboding about her baby might or might not be valid information, and she insisted on further tests. Her baby's rasping breath was, as predicted, benign—but he also had "silent" cardiac malformations so life-threatening that emergency surgery was required.

In the years that followed, Hannah worked to trust her perception of the truth and to voice it in a more contained and measured way, even when it upset her husband, parents, and doctors. Repeatedly, she was assured that her child was "out of the woods" when he was not. Repeatedly, she had to insist on more diligent testing, more accurate explanations, and more creative treatment options. Repeatedly, she was brushed off as a hysterical mother. And repeatedly her intuitions were right. With these experiences came a new trust in the value and validity of her inner experience, a new authority. No longer recognizable as an ungrounded young woman silenced by the effects of past trauma, she found a new authoritative voice through advocacy for her son.

Isolated at home because of her son's inability to tolerate infections, she started a social networking community where she and other "heart moms" could exchange information and support. When an anonymous visitor to the site posted a venomous attack, the very type of attack she had once feared, she held her ground and expressed her truth. Her ability to advocate effectively for her son eventually led to an advocacy role for other children and parents affected by heart disease, who were less able to speak on their own behalf. Hannah helped create a foundation to support families during their children's hospitalizations, advocated for parents and children with medical staff, and spoke before state and federal legislators to raise awareness about needs for research and care. While she continued to struggle with anxiety about voicing her opinions in public and to worry about adverse reactions, her commitment to children's care was a higher calling. She had discovered her authoritative voice on her son's behalf and now used it for others.

The Cassandra pattern portrays a neglectful mother in the background. During the mythical Cassandra's birthday feast, celebrated in the temple of Apollo, her mother drinks too much, forgets about her, and stumbles home, abandoning the young Cassandra to the unmediated archetypal energies imaged as her fateful meeting with Apollo.

Hannah's mother was certainly prone to a pattern of neglect. Herself the child of an abusive, alcoholic home, she remained married to Hannah's father, ignoring his brutal abuse of Hannah, because of the financial security he provided. She was able to maintain denial of the abuse by physically leaving the house when her husband drank heavily, abandoning Hannah to her father's abuse and repeatedly dismissing or minimizing Hannah's attempts to voice the truth. Hannah's relationship with female authority thus became one of deep distrust.

Hannah's development of inner authority required a connection to a positive maternal image strong enough to contain her tendencies to anxiety and hysteria. Along with a positive transference in her analysis, Hannah found a comforting symbol of abiding maternal love in the image of Mary as the sorrowing Pieta. Through this image, Hannah could connect with the archetypal good mother, one able to remain present to her child's suffering, continuing to love and contain his tortured body even when she could not protect him. The power of Hannah's negative mother complex receded as a feeling connection to this positive image of inner value and female authority became stronger. This was the very containment she had needed from her own mother. As she did her best to give it to her son, Hannah also felt the healing comfort of a connection with the archetypal good mother. Child of a neglectful mother and an abusive father, Hannah's love for her child enabled her to redeem a family legacy of destructive parenting. Her willingness to suffer consciously, inspired by the Pieta, deepened her maturity and opened a connection to the inner authority of the Self. While the voice that emerged remained vitally connected to her strong intuition, it also became more grounded and related.

ELEPHANT VOICE

An ancient symbol system from a distant culture gives clues about the archetypal nature of the authentic voice and its development. The seven chakras of Kundalini Yoga are considered to represent centers of consciousness linking body, mind, and life energy, located at nodal points along the spine. These centers offer a model of psycho-spiritual development that has survived for thousands of years, remaining symbolically relevant today; yoga's many practices, teachings, and truths are now well-established in the western world.

Each element of imagery associated with the chakras represents the collective intuitions of countless generations of adepts, expressed in visual form. The chakras are depicted through particular geometric shapes, Sanskrit letters, animal rulers, and personified deities. Although each of the lower five chakras is symbolized by an animal, only the elephant appears twice.

In the first, or *muladhara* chakra, located at the base of the spine, a gray elephant represents the physical base of conscious life and the carrying power of psychic energy.[11] The word *muladhara* translates literally as root support. Psychologically, this chakra is related to our most rudimentary survival instincts and it holds primitive fears of annihilation and abandonment.[12] According to Jung, the first chakra consciousness is focused on maintaining one's physical existence through adaptation to the physical world and the demands of society. Psychological life is dormant and the symbolic capacity is undeveloped. Jung considered the elephant in the first chakra to represent the carrying power of the earth and the base of psychic energy, describing this as "the tremendous urge which supports human consciousness, the power that forces us to build such a conscious world."[13]

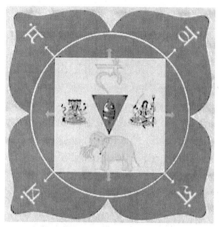

Figure 1: Traditional Presentation of the First Chakra

The elephant appears again as the presiding animal of the throat chakra. The fifth chakra, or *vishuddha*, located at the throat, is associated with the voice, sound, speech, hearing, expression, and creativity.[14] When the elephant reappears here, it is white, signifying a spiritualization of the earlier, more physical elephant energy. The symbolism of the fifth chakra depicts our potential to connect below with above, to join body and mind in the expression of authentic voice.

In the throat chakra, the white elephant is depicted along with a full moon, while a crescent moon rules overhead. A white, downward pointing

Figure 2: Traditional Presentation of the Fifth Chakra

triangle contains both the elephant and full moon. These are all cross-cultural symbols associated with the archetypal feminine principle. The masculine principle is represented in the blue color of the outer circle and in the petals of the lotus, which bear the sixteen Sanskrit vowels, considered to represent spirit. This chakra is an image of feminine soul encircled by masculine spirit, a union of opposites, taking place at the neck, where body and mind come together.

In the state of consciousness symbolized by the fifth chakra, the two opposing energy currents in the body, one considered lunar and the other solar, are thought to unite, balancing archetypal masculine and feminine energies within the psyche. Psychologically, this suggests a consciousness in which mind and body, as well as capacities for relating and differentiating, are in balance. This balance, occurring at the throat, gives rise to the authentic voice, one that integrates bodily, emotional, and intellectual knowing.

The doubled appearance of the elephant, in both the first and fifth chakras, indicates a connection between the energy centers at the base of the spine and the throat, between our "seat" and our voice. There is a world of difference between a voice that speaks from the neck up and one that arises from the depths of bodily knowing. Women who have primarily identified with the intellect may believe we have found our voices before we have found our depths. The dual elephants suggest that the true voice of authority arises from the bottom up.

There could not be a more fitting animal than the elephant to preside over the voice chakra. Living in deeply bonded matriarchal groups, elephants are prodigious communicators. They snort, scream, trumpet, and roar. Conversations among family members continue all day, with close to seventy different sounds for communication identified to date. Many of the calls occur at the level of infrasound, a low-frequency rumble below the hearing range of humans, which can be heard over at least 110 square miles.[15]

The authority of the total psyche or the Self, connected to bodily knowing through the first chakra, finds creative expression in the fifth chakra. When we connect our bodily roots with our voice, above is linked with below and spirit is connected with matter, imaged as the spiritualized white elephant of the throat linked by the spinal column to the gray elephant of the root chakra. In this state the voice arises full-bodied from the depths. This coming together of body and mind allows us to express the voice of our deepest inner authority. Rumbling just below conscious awareness like the elephant voice, it is the sound of potential wholeness.

The Speech at the Center of the Soul

Jung considered the symbolism of the fifth chakra to represent consciousness of psychological reality.[16] He described *vishuddha* consciousness as the ability to recognize the world as a reflection of the psyche, allowing the withdrawal of projections and the dissolution of identity relationships with other people. We find strikingly similar imagery in the alchemical stage known as the *albedo* (or whitening), which also uses images of whiteness and the full moon to suggest a similar development: the *albedo* has been interpreted psychologically as a stage in which shadow projections have been withdrawn and synthesis can begin.[17] By symbolizing this development with the throat, yogic tradition associates it with the development of an authentic voice.

But as we withdraw the projection of authority from others to seek an inner voice, we may discover that the voice we find is not singular. Just as the voices of collective authority can be a Babel of competing opinions, so also, when we turn within, we discover an internal Babel. Our many complexes have voices and they clamor and compete for dominance. Jung developed the method of active imagination as a way for the ego to differentiate among these voices and establish a conscious standpoint toward them. Like fairy tale heroines with their sorting tasks, we can only discover and trust an authentic inner voice through much work at differentiation. Otherwise, in the name of "finding our own voice," we can easily be seduced into replacing the tyranny of collective authority with the tyranny of a complex.

In conversation with these voices, we hear the reigning deities and devils of the psyche and they seem to hear us too. These inner voices stand outside the conscious knowing of the ego and yet they influence the ego directly. Jung did not imagine individuation as a static achievement but as a relationship, an ongoing dialogue in which these deeper voices are brought to consciousness through a "shuttling to and fro of arguments and affects (which) represents the transcendent function of opposites...a living birth that leads to a new level of being."[18] Through such experiences, the ego's sense of identity is altered and the Self, as center of the personality, is strengthened. A new voice of authority emerges from the babble, one that Jung calls "the cry for personality."[19] It is the speech at the center of the soul, our elephant voice. By consciously hearing its counsel, we build our deepest authority.

NOTES

1. Maureen Dowd, "Can Hillary Cry Her Way Back to the White House?" *The New York Times,* January 9, 2008. Accessed July 14, 2009 at http://www.nytimes.com/2008/01/09/opinion/08dowd.html.

2. Mary Field Belenky, Blythe McVicker Clinchy, Nancy Rule Goldberger and Jill Mattuck Tarule, *Women's Ways of Knowing: The Development of Self, Voice and Mind* (New York: Basic Books, 1986, repr. 1997).

3. Thomas C. Brickhouse and Nicholas D. Smith, *Routledge Philosophy Guidebook to Plato and the Trial of Socrates* (New York: Routledge, 2004), p. 22.

4. Deborah Tannen, *You Just Don't Understand: Women and Men in Conversation* (New York: Harper Paperbacks, 2001).

5. C.S. Lewis, *Till We Have Faces* (New York: Harcourt 1956, reprt. 1984), p. 294.

6. Hal Leonard Publishing Corporation and Meredith Wilson, "Pick-a-little, talk-a-little," *Songs From the Musical Comedy The Music Man* (New York: Frank Music Corp, 1954).

7. Jean Baker Miller, *Women and Power* (1981), in J. V. Jordan, A. G. Kaplan, J. B. Miller, I. P. Stiver and J. L. Surrey, eds. *Women's Growth In Connection* (New York: Guilford Press, 1991), p. 204.

8. Polly Young-Eisendrath and Frances Weidemann, *Female Authority* (New York: The Guilford Press 1987), p. 45.

9. Marge Piercy, *Circles on the Water* (New York: Alfred A. Knopf, 1985).

10. Laurie Layton Shapiro, *The Cassandra Complex: Living with Disbelief* (Toronto, Canada: Inner City Books, 1988).

11. C.G. Jung, *The Psychology of Kundalini Yoga.* ed. Sonu Shamdasani (Princeton NJ: Princeton University Press 1996), p. 51.

12. Swami Rama, Rudolph Ballentine, and Swami Ajaya, *Yoga and Psychotherapy: The Evolution of Consciousness* (Honesdale, PA: Himalayan Institute Press, 1976), p. 178.

13. Jung, *Kundalini Yoga*, p. 51.

14. Rama et al., *Yoga and Psychotherapy*, pp. 201-208.

15. PBS Online (n.d.), *Nature: Echo of the Elephants: Elephant communication.* Accessed October 11, 2009 at http://www.pbs.org/wnet/nature/echo/html/talk.html.

16. Jung, *Kundalini Yoga*, p. 47.

17. Marie-Louise von Franz, *Alchemy: An Introduction to the Symbolism and the Psychology* (Toronto, Canada: Inner City Books, 1980).

18. C.G. Jung, "The Transcendent Function" (1953), in *The Collected Works of C.G. Jung*, vol. 8, ed. and trans. Gerhard Adler and R. F. C. Hull (Princeton, NJ: Princeton University Press, 1960), § 189.

19. C.G. Jung, "The Development of Personality," CW 17, § 303.

Artemis is the archetype in women whose instincts are fiercely protective of vulnerable others—like a mother bear. Qualities such as focus, competitiveness, sisterhood, an affinity for nature and animals, brotherly-egalitarian relationships with men, plus an indomitable spirit are Artemis qualities in feminists, environmentalists, and activists. The myth of Atalanta, a mortal woman who was "under the protection of Artemis" provides insights into this archetype, as do the contemporary examples mentioned in this article. Actress and Special Envoy of the UN High Commission on Human Rights, Angelina Jolie, in her personal life and screen roles as an action star, embodies this archetype as does fictional Katniss Everdeen in the *Hunger Games* trilogy.

ARTEMIS AND BEAR MOTHERS:
FIERCELY PROTECTIVE, INDOMITABLE WOMEN

JEAN SHINODA BOLEN

"Undressing the Bear" is a chapter in Terry Tempest Williams' *An Unspoken Hunger: Stories from the Field*. In it, she tells bear stories, relates dreams of bears, and shares anecdotes that point to a connection between women and bears. She writes:

> We are creatures of paradox, women and bears, two animals that are enormously unpredictable, hence our mystery. Perhaps the fear of bears and the fear of women lies in our refusal to be tamed, the impulses we arouse, and the forces we represent.[1]

Among the stories in this particular chapter, there is a description of a bear dream from a bookseller friend of Terry's who tells of sharing it with a male customer:

> "I dreamt I was in Yellowstone. A grizzly, upright, was walking toward me. Frightened at first, I began to pull away, when suddenly a mantle of calm came over me. I walked toward the bear and we embraced." The man across the counter listened, and then said matter-of-factly, "Get over it."[2]

Jean Shinoda Bolen, M.D., a member of the C.G. Jung Institute of San Francisco, is the author of *The Tao of Psychology, Goddesses in Everywoman, Gods in Everyman, Ring of Power, Crossing to Avalon, Goddesses in Older Women, The Millionth Circle, Like a Tree, Crones Don't Whine, Close to the Bone, Urgent Message From Mother, Moving Toward the Millionth Circle*, and most recently, *Artemis: The Indomitable Spirit in Everywoman*. She is a Distinguished Life Fellow of the American Psychiatric Association and a former clinical professor of psychiatry at the University of California at San Francisco. She maintains a private practice in Mill Valley, California. Her website is www.jeanbolen.com.

** This article is composed in part of selected excerpts from Jean Bolen's new book, *Artemis: The Indomitable Spirit in Everywoman*, especially the chapter entitled "Atalanta, Artemis, Mother Bear." This book was released on September 1, 2014 by Conari Press, San Francisco, and the excerpts published from it herein are printed with the publisher's permission.

Terry mused: "Why? Why should we give up the dream of embracing the bear? For me, it has everything to do with undressing, exposing, and embracing the Feminine." She explains:

> I see the Feminine defined as a reconnection to the Self, a commitment to the wildness within—our instincts, our capacity to create and destroy; our hunger for connection as well as sovereignty, interdependence and independence, at once. We are taught not to trust our own experience.[3]

In her book, *When Women Were Birds: Fifty-four Variations on Voice*, Terry Tempest Williams asks what is necessary for a woman to have a voice. She names "Courage. Anger. Love." and "Something to say. Someone to listen."[4] "Courage. Anger. Love." are what lead us to become activists. Feminists see themselves as members of a sisterhood. Women who have a sense of sisterhood embody the archetype of Artemis whether they know it or not. Artemis is the archetype that was liberated by the women's movement, liberation meaning that girls and women are "free to be"[5] their focused, competitive, sometimes mystical, protective of others, curious selves—to realize that there is in them the indomitable spirit that characterizes this archetype. Exploration and venturing into the wilderness of nature, or into the unknown terrain of the psyche calls to women in whom the Artemis archetype lives.

These qualities were evident in the circle of women who came to the workshop I was leading at the Feathered Pipe Ranch in Montana, which borders on wilderness country where black bears are common in the rugged surrounding terrain. The workshop included a descent into a deep cave—part of an extensive cave system, with artifacts that suggest that it could be the oldest site of human habitation in North America—a sweat lodge, and being in women's circles with a sacred center. The theme of this women's retreat was "Path with Soul: Following an Inner Compass." Of the eight goddess-archetypes that I described in *Goddesses in Everywoman*,[6] this description would appeal mostly—maybe only—to women in whom Artemis is an active archetype.

In the preceding week, I had finished going through the final text of *Artemis: The Indomitable Spirit in Everywoman*[7] and I had also been musing as well upon Terry Tempest Williams words as I recalled them: "Anger. Courage. Love. Something to say. Someone to listen." I began our first meeting with this quote, emphasizing the cadence. Her actual words are "Courage. Anger. Love. Something to say; someone to speak to; someone to listen."[8] My version became a theme, and a song with a strong beat was composed in this workshop. These are the elements that energized the consciousness-raising groups that grew into the Women's Movement of the late sixties and seventies. They are present in the analytic container, and spur individuation. Stories about the goddess Artemis, the mortal Atalanta, the mother bear, and examples of them were alive in me, as I told myths and expanded their symbolic and metaphoric meaning. They served to mirror personal experience and evoked memories in women that now could be shared in small circles with a sacred center (metaphorically, Hestia, goddess of the hearth and temple, is at the center of the circle). Women's circles then become a *temenos* or sanctuary. In them, a woman who has "Something to say," has a sisterhood of others, who by listening and sharing their own experiences, validate each other's reality and insights, and serve as midwives to the dreams and intentions of each other.

ATALANTA UNDER THE PROTECTION OF ARTEMIS

There are two major stories about Atalanta: as a hunter in the Hunt of the Calydon Boar in which her courage and bow and arrow drew the first blood, and as the runner in the Footrace and the Three Golden Apples in which men who raced her forfeited their lives if they lost to her. She resembled Artemis in many ways, but as a mortal suffered loss and grief, and the wrath of a divinity. The bear is a powerful symbol associated with both the goddess and mortals. In classical Greek mythology and Ovid's retelling, when Atalanta was born, her father was so enraged that she was not the son and heir he expected that he abandoned her on a mountain, where she was left to die from the elements or wild animals. Instead, it was said that she "was under the protection of Artemis," because a mother bear found her, suckled, and raised her.

It is interesting to note that the ferocious protective power of the bear is an attribute of Artemis, who was a virgin goddess, not the Greek mother goddesses, who were powerless to protect themselves or their children from male predators and abusive partners. In fact, in Greek mythology and in the history of the Western civilization that owes so much to the Greeks, women have neither been empowered nor equal to men, however Olympian their social status. The patriarchal world of Zeus was in retrospect, a rape culture.

Bear Mothers

Mother bears are ferociously protective and extraordinarily nurturing. Good advice to people headed into the wilderness is *never* to get between a mother bear and her cubs! Mother bears have qualities that make them really good mothers. They are notably fierce in defense of their young; they are also good caretakers. Bear cubs are born in the winter months—usually in January and February, while the mother bear is in hibernation. Newborn bears are smaller than newborn human babies, weighing around ten ounces at birth. They can't open their eyes and are kept warm in their mother's fur and by her breath. They suckle instinctively and grow rapidly on the fat-rich milk, emerging only in early spring when they are big enough and strong enough to walk, run, and explore.

A mother bear sleeps only when her babies sleep. Initially, the cubs nurse every ten minutes. They are noisy, make humming noises when awake and suckling, and cry when they need something. The mother bear washes them often with her tongue, and puts them on a teat when they can't find one. Once the cubs leave the den, the mother will continue to suckle them until they are weaned. She then teaches them what berries they can eat, how to catch fish, and how to hunt. The cubs learn to climb trees for safety when there may be danger on the ground. They have little to fear when they are in their mother's sight— the biggest exception being the dangers posed by bad actors of their own species. Predatory male bears eat cubs.

When the cubs are able to take care of themselves, the mother bear makes them independent of her. She sends them up a tree, just as when she was teaching them to climb to safety, only this last time, she doesn't come back for them. They are old enough to be self-sufficient; now they must climb down and fend for themselves.[9]

Bear as an Artemis Symbol

The bear is a symbol of the protective aspect of Artemis. Artemis is particularly protective of girls and women. She is characterized as a virgin goddess and is never a mother. Yet she is the goddess to whom young pre-pubescent girls were dedicated; they were then referred to as the *arktoi* or "little bears." During the year that young girls were sanctified under Artemis' protection, they were safe from early marriage and had the freedom from women's constrictions in dress and behavior. They could play as boys did and were free to be outdoors—very much like nine- to twelve-year-old "tomboys."

I look back on summers at Girl Scout Camp and realize that these were *arktoi* experiences for me. The camp drew children from the Los Angeles area, busing us up to Big Bear Lake—to terrain dear to the goddess Artemis—where there were meadows, forests, mountains, lakes, and streams. We learned how to make campfires, use a compass, tie knots, carve with a knife, and recognize star constellations, trees, and various flora and fauna. We hiked a lot, sang together around the campfire, and while hiking, slept under the stars, showered sometimes, wore wrinkled nondescript clothes (except for the "greenie tops" that had a somewhat uniform look), and stowed our stuff away in a shared tent in case of rain. We were from many parts of the city and surrounding areas. At camp, we did not have to live up to any image we had at school; we didn't spend time concerned about our reflections in mirrors or in how boys saw us. We learned about ourselves and each other, and shared confidences. While our parents sent us away to camp the first time, we returned there by choice. It was meaningful and fun because we had the Artemis archetype in common—the archetype of sister. When this is an active archetype in a girl or woman, she has a sense of sisterhood and an affinity to feminist causes.

ARTEMIS THE GODDESS OF THE HUNT AND MOON

Artemis is twin sister to Apollo. While Apollo is God of the Sun, with his golden bow and arrows, Artemis is Goddess of the Hunt and Moon, with her bow and arrows of silver. She is also called Artemis *Eileithyria* and is the goddess of childbirth and the divine midwife, because she helped her mother, Leto, through the longest and most difficult labor in mythology. Leto was impregnated by Zeus, the chief god in Greek mythology, and bore the twins, Artemis and Apollo. Because Zeus's wife, Hera, was angered by the pregnancy, no one dared offer Leto shelter or aid.

Artemis is born first. After her delivery, Hera causes Leto to suffer and go into prolonged labor. But divinities are not like mortals, and newborn Artemis becomes her mother's midwife, helping to deliver Apollo. Consequently, in ancient Greece, women prayed to Artemis for swift delivery from the pain of childbirth. Contemporary midwives and women who choose obstetrics and gynecology as medical specialties to help women and reduce their fear and pain in childbirth are thus being true to this aspect of Artemis. *Artemesia* is the herb used to ease labor pain.

Artemis is the only goddess who often came to the rescue of women in other circumstances. She saves Arethusa from being raped; she protects or avenges her mother's honor when a giant tries to rape her and when a mortal woman demeans her. In these stories, Artemis is fierce in her protectiveness, like a mother bear. Or like activists who rescue trafficked girls from brothels and provide gynecological and psychological care to rape victims. Or like those who lead demonstrations to seek justice for raped girls and women in India, or lobby the United States Congress to pass the Violence Against Women Act, or advocate for a United Nations World Conference on Women. Or like anyone, in fact, who works toward equality for women and the protection of mothers and children.

GIRLS AND MOTHER BEAR

Girls raised metaphorically by mother bear are children nurtured by Mother Nature. They may be drawn to animals and find solace outdoors. They may feel safer and more at home under a tree or currying horses in a stable than in a home where they may be neglected or abused. When these girls find mother bear in themselves and find the support to be themselves in the archetype symbolized by the protective mother bear, they may become activists or competitors in the world. It is the archetype of Artemis that comes to the aid of these girls who, in some significant way, were abandoned and then found, in nature or with animals, the parents that they did not have at home. It may also be their nature as an Artemis to prefer to be in the woods, uninterested in staying at home or in doing womanly or girlish things.

I have known many women in my psychiatric and analytic practice and in my life who, like Atalanta, were psychologically abandoned and then raised by "mother bear." As girls, they came from families where parental figures neglected, rejected, or abused them emotionally or physically, or where parents, because of illness, death, or circumstance, could not be fully present. As a result, at a psychological and spiritual level, they had to raise themselves. They also instinctively kept up appearances, worked at making good grades or excelling at sports, and acted as if their home lives were normal. It is natural for their Artemis nature to follow examples we see in nature. Nature provides animals with protective coloration so they don't stand out. When animals are wounded or weakened, they know to hide their vulnerability to avoid becoming prey.

Gloria Steinem wrote of herself: "I remembered feeling sad about navigating life by myself, working after school, worrying about my mother, who was sometimes too removed from reality to know where she was, or who I was, and concealing these shameful family secrets from my friends. . . now as then, I turn away sympathy with jokes and a survivor's pride."[10] Artemis is the archetype that protects the young girl who instinctively hides her vulnerability during the years of middle school and high school.

Girls who are not under the protection of Artemis may reveal rather than hide vulnerability, which can mark them as potential victims to be preyed on, bullied, or made scapegoats. Recent media attention focused on two young girls, ages fifteen and seventeen, who hanged themselves. It's an old story: Girl has too much to drink at a party and passes out; boys take turns having sex with her; her name is passed around at school; then other boys want her to "put out" for them, too. She becomes known as a "slut" and is shunned by the "good" girls. A new variation on the theme makes it worse: While one of the young men is fucking her (what else can it be called?), there are "clicks" as another or others use their mobile phones to take photos or videos that are posted online and circulated around the school. Eventually, and in despair, the two young girls killed themselves.

I mentioned hearing about these two teenage suicides at the Pacifica Writers' Conference in Santa Barbara and learned from Donna DeNomme, author of *Ophelia's Oracle*,[11] about an "Artemis girl" who did not accept being a victim and whose story had a very different ending. What she told me warmed my heart and was the best kind of encouragement, since I was writing at that time about the Greek myth of Atalanta, a mortal woman identified with Artemis. Rejected by her father, Atalanta was left to die when she was born. She survived, the storytellers say, because she was under the protection of Artemis. My hope was that the story of Atalanta would help women to see themselves in this myth—younger women especially.

Donna described the situation in an email to me:

> One less-than-popular girl was thrilled to be included by her girlfriend with an invitation to attend a party.
>
> At that party her delight turned to terror as she was raped. Her so-called girlfriend filmed the violation and uploaded the video to the Internet. When the victim arrived at school on Monday, she was taunted by classmates for what they may have thought was consensual sex. The traumatized girl, who had been given *Ophelia's Oracle* by her grandmother a few months before, said it was the story about the boldness of Artemis in the book that gave her the courage to press charges against the boy who raped her, the girl who filmed the rape, and the mother of one of the teens who bought beer for the kids and then left them alone in her house. She told her grandmother: "Artemis would want me to do this."[12]

Like Artemis, Atalanta is at home in forests and associated with animals, the mother bear in particular. In one version of Atalanta's myth, hunters who think they are rescuing her kill the mother bear. In another version (preferred by readers who feel a connection with bears and Atalanta), the hunters come upon Atalanta when she is alone in the bear's cave and take her back to their camp. In both versions, Atalanta is, for a time, raised by men, from whom she learns language and proficiency with bow and arrows and spear. She no doubt gets approval and encouragement from these men, taking to everything they teach. Atalanta would have felt special, cared for, and supported during this phase of her life, as do girls in the mold of Artemis who have fathers who are delighted with their spunk and abilities.

It is easy to think of Atalanta as a high-spirited, confident girl who, small as she is, stands toe to toe with these hunters, insisting on what she thinks is true and protesting when something is not fair. Men like these take pride in such daughters. They are "Daddy's best buddy" or "Daddy's little girl." This kind of relationship often comes to an end as puberty approaches and it's time to establish physical and emotional distance from the budding woman the daughter is becoming. This transition may go smoothly or may be tempestuous and fraught with emotional outbursts. A best-buddy phase with a father who is admired and a good role model supports give-and-take, encourages assertiveness, and recognizes developing skills. These young women tend to become like their fathers or father figures in certain ways that give them a sense of pride, because their fathers are proud of them.

With Artemis as a guiding archetype, a little girl who reacts instinctively with "it's not fair!" when it clearly is not, can grow into a feminist with the protective outrage of a mother bear, who stands up for social justice, for the equality and empowerment of women, for the protection of children, animals, and the environment. Artemis activists are passionate about their causes, they are outraged at bullying and taking unfair advantages. They tap into the archetypal energy of the mother bear, a symbol of Artemis.

In *The Hunger Games* Katniss Everdeen is sixteen when the trilogy begins.[13] The happiest time in the week for her is when she goes with her father into the woods, lakes, and meadows outside the District-12 fence, beyond which citizens are forbidden to go. There, he teaches her to hunt with a bow and arrow, to bring down food for the family, and to hunt game to trade. Katniss has both instinct and skill; her arrows fly where she sends them. After her father's death, Katniss becomes the sole provider for her mother and sister. Her mother withdraws into her grief and stops functioning, and it is up to Katniss to look after the family.

Both Atalanta and Katniss excel as hunters, taught by their fathers or father figures to be competent and survive on their own. Katniss clearly identifies with her father and takes over as provider and protector as much as she can at his death. Her mother is clearly not a role model. In fact, both Atalanta's and Katniss' mothers are ineffectual.

And, although Atalanta's father rejects her and orders her exposed on a mountaintop to die, in psychological terms, both are "fathers' daughters." They are women who are decisive, can act swiftly, choose targets or goals of their own, and have the focus and skill to hit what they aim for. Their worlds are outside the household that is the realm of "mothers' daughters."

In the United States toward the end of the 1960s and 1970s, consciousness-raising groups became the foundation of the Women's Movement. Here, women learned about sexism and inequality. They became determined that this had to change, and they encouraged each other to make a difference. Women shared information, wrote, marched, testified, had demonstrations, and entered formerly all-male enclaves and professions. *Ms. Magazine* began publication. Couples worked to create egalitarian relationships and families. As a result, girls with Artemis qualities circa 1970 and after were likely to have parental approval to be active and confident. Spirited three-year-old girls with minds of their own could express what they wanted and felt, and still bask in the approval of their fathers and mothers. No more Little Miss Muffetts sitting on tuffets eating their curds and whey. Now, far from being scared away by the spider, these emancipated girls could be free to investigate and explore all the critters and creatures in the outdoors with interest. Indeed, little *Ms.* Muffett was "free to be you and me," and sang the songs to prove it!

Girls in the mold of Atalanta are often very independent, but not very good at intimacy with friends or partners. The forging of emotional bonds becomes challenging to them and to those who love them. Intimacy grows through mirroring, reciprocity, empathy, compassion, and thoughtfulness. Atalanta the adult may be a woman who did not learn how to look after the feelings of others and who may not know her own emotional needs or feelings. She cannot learn this from bear mother/Mother Nature or the Artemis archetype. This she can only learn from other human beings.

In *Goddesses in Everywoman*, I provided exemplars of each of the goddess archetypes that were public figures. Gloria Steinem, as a founder of *Ms. Magazine* and a beautiful spokesperson for feminism, was a natural choice for Artemis. Her concerns for girls and women, her competency and courage to stand for and stand up for equality and empowerment of women, are clearly those of the archetype. However, Gloria—like all women—is more than an embodiment of one archetype. While one archetype may be the strongest, all of the others are potential sources of meaning in every woman. And not every facet of the strongest archetype has to be lived out or felt in each woman. Gloria is like a mother bear in her protectiveness and in responding to appeals for help from women, but she is hardly noted for being a woman in the wilderness.

Julia Butterfly Hill, on the other hand, spent two years living in an ancient redwood tree exposed to the elements in order to prevent the logging of an old-growth forest in Northern California.

She is a symbol of an environmental activist who embodies this aspect of the archetype.

Film actress, UN High Commission on Human Rights Goodwill ambassador and Special Envoy, Angelina Jolie, in her real life and in many of her onscreen roles, embodies a number of Artemis qualities. She is a fiercely concerned humanitarian and activist, noted for going where the needs are great and often dangerous, is in an egalitarian partnership with Brad Pitt, with numerous adopted children. Her noteworthy onscreen roles are as an action star.

GODDESS OF THE MOON ASPECTS OF ARTEMIS

While an activist becomes proactive in response to or in protest against something happening in the outer world, the goddess-of-the-moon aspect of the Artemis archetype explains the capacity for reflection—to draw back from activity, to think about motivation and meaning, to see by moonlight or reflected light. In the wilderness, moonlight illuminates; there is beauty and mystery—a oneness I experienced as a Girl Scout in the wilderness that became the source of later understanding that I drew on in writing *The Tao of Psychology*.[14] Sleeping outdoors under the nighttime sky with the Milky Way overhead, paying close attention so that I might see a shooting star (probably a comet) to make a wish on—*these experiences prepared the way for me to slip into an altered state of consciousness*. They prepared me to recognize that I was part of everything out there. They brought me an inner certainty, even before I had words for or knew of the concept of oneness that underlies all visible manifestations. It was mystical insight, and so very Artemis.

To be able to take to the woods, to turn to animals or to books, to have a rich imagination, or to be nourished by solitude are solitary activities that feed self-sufficiency—a quality needed and strengthened in girls who have to raise themselves because of inadequate, absent, disabled, or abusive parents. Artemis can be alive in the inner lives of girls and women when there is no room for autonomy, education, or protest in the world they live in. In the inner world of the imagination, a girl can be heroic; she can have a place in her psyche that identifies with global expressions of feminism that are condemned or ridiculed. She has an archetypal connection with

Artemis, even if she must remain obedient or subservient, and is forced to marry young. I suspect that this accounts for the women who demonstrated during the Arab Spring against dictatorship, surprising the world with the fact that they even existed.

Infant girls and toddlers who survive illnesses that were expected to kill them—or were abandoned shortly after birth and then are found alive, or who survived terrible physical assaults—have an inherent or archetypal will to live. They draw upon an indomitable spirit, a characteristic of Artemis that shows up early when it has to. One amazing true story of survival, found in *The Girl with No Name*, tells of a five-year-old toddler who was probably kidnapped and then abandoned in the Colombian jungle.[15] The child stayed on the periphery of a troop of Capuchin monkeys, eating what they ate. She was taken in by the monkeys and grew up feral and walking on all fours until she was found and maltreated by humans, which began another whole saga of survival. The child's birth name was never discovered; she now goes by the name Marina Chapman. Marina made me wonder if Atalanta could have been a real person about whom stories were told—a little girl who became a mythical figure, a girl thought to have been suckled by a bear and found by hunters.

When women in India take to the streets to protest official disregard of rape, when women dance in the streets in an outpouring of support for Eve Ensler's One Billion Rising demonstrations to stop violence against women and girls, when the number of Non-Governmental Organizations (NGOs) working toward empowerment and equality for women and girls grows exponentially, women across the world are rising up, led by feminists for whom Artemis and mother-bear activism are deep sources of meaning, even when these forces are not named. And when they are, there is an immediate "aha!" because these are archetypal energies that are found in many cultures.

Send Word, Bear Mother

Helen Stoltzfus, author of and principal performer in the award-winning documentary film *Send Word, Bear Mother* based her work on her own true story, a saga that began with her illness and infertility.[16] She had seen many specialists without success over many years. With symptoms of fatigue and infertility, and no satisfactory explanations for either, Helen joined a support group for people with life-threatening and chronic illnesses. In an exercise in which she was supposed to tap into inner sources of healing and imagination, a skeptical Helen unexpectedly began having a series of profound encounters with a mother grizzly bear spirit who appeared to her in dreams and came to her unbidden in fantasy. She experienced these as powerful visitations from the spirit world. They empowered her to try one more specialist in her effort to get pregnant.

This doctor diagnosed Helen as having endometriosis—a condition in which cells that are part of the lining of the uterus that are normally shed during menstruation can grow anywhere in the peritoneum (the space that holds all our internal organs below the diaphragm)—and recommended surgery. Helen had the surgery, but there seemed to be no satisfactory explanation for her condition. So she began to search for possible causes. She learned that environmental toxins, dioxins in particular, had been linked to endometriosis. Meanwhile, the mother grizzly bear visitations continued. This prodded her to learn all she could about bears, including that bears are threatened by the same toxins as humans.

The bear-mother spirit persisted relentlessly in Helen's psyche, calling her to go to Alaska where the bears live. As soon after her surgery as she could, she heeded the call and went to Denali National Park by herself. She did not feel well. The effects of chronic fatigue and the operation had sapped her energy, and travel took even more out of her. She went, like sick people going to Lourdes, with the hope of being healed. Immediately upon entering the park, a mother grizzly with two cubs walked across the road in front of the tour bus. (In Denali, tourists are driven on buses through the park, while bears roam freely.) This was like a powerful waking dream to Helen. The real and the symbolic came together. While Helen may have appeared to be just another tourist, for her this was truly a pilgrimage.

No logical or practical decision brought Helen to Alaska, but rather a persistent and compelling message to come. The mother-bear symbol showed up over and over—not just in dreams and thoughts, but also in outer experiences. Helen encountered bear images in various art forms and in references in conversations. Suddenly, the idea or symbol of bear seemed to be everywhere. The urge or compelling desire to see real bears in their natural setting grew and set her on course for Denali. Only after going to Alaska did she come to understand the connection between what toxins had done to her body and the similar dangers they held for bears—as well as the larger implication of the danger to the wilderness and to Mother Nature herself.

The spirit of the bear gave an urgency to Helen's desire to do something with her new knowledge. She found her means of expression in her work. She wrote and staged a one-woman performance piece that became the basis for the film *Send Word, Bear Mother,* in which she played the principal role. Through this film and in the work that came from her inner/outer journey, Helen became an activist with a personal mission to foster an awareness of the connection between toxins, infertility, and the danger of the disappearing wilderness. And what's more, she became pregnant one month after she came back from Denali. Nine months later, her daughter, Lydia, was born.

"Send Word, Bear Mother" was Helen's personal healing chant, one that she adapted from a Sioux chant.

> Send word, bear mother
> Send word, bear mother
> I'm having a hard time
>
> Send word, bear mother
> Send word, bear mother
> I'm having a bad time.

Helen's encounters with the mother-bear spirit had a she-who-must-be-obeyed energy about them that persisted until she heeded the message, went to Alaska, and saw real bear mothers. The bear had a grip on her imagination. The chant was a plea for help to the bear-mother spirit. Her inner compass directed her to literally travel north to Alaska, in doing so she was enacting a pilgrimage. Simultaneously, she was going deeper into the Self, the sacred feminine, to mother bear and Artemis, where meaning and healing were to be found.

NOTES

1. Terry Tempest Williams, "Undressing the Bear," in *An Unspoken Hunger: Stories from the Field* (New York: Vintage, 1995), p. 58.
2. *Ibid.,* p. 52.
3. *Ibid.,* p. 53.

4. Terry Tempest Williams, *When Women Were Birds: Fifty-four Variations on Voice* (New York: Picador, 2012), p. 44.

5. Marlo Thomas, *Free to Be . . .You and Me* (Philadelphia: Free To Be Foundation, 35th Anniversary edition, 2008). Note: In Marlo Thomas' classic children's book *Free to Be, You and Me*, young readers read about growing up in a land where girls would become the women they were meant to be, and boys would become the men they were meant to be.

6. Jean Shinoda Bolen, *Goddesses in Everywoman* (San Francisco: Harper & Row, 1984); Harper's Colophon, paperback edition, 1985. Thirtieth Anniversary paperback edition (with new Introduction), New York: HarperCollins, 2014. "Artemis," pp. 46-74.

7. Jean Shinoda Bolen, *Artemis: The Indomitable Spirit in Everywoman* (San Francisco: Conari, 2014).

8. Williams, *When Women Were Birds*, p. 44.

9. A source of information and documentary filming of bears, mother bear, and newborn cubs in hibernation is www.covebear.com.

10. Gloria Steinem, *Revolution From Within* (Boston: Little, Brown and Company, 1992), p. 37.

11. Donna DeNomme and Tina Proctor, *Ophelia's Oracle* (Golden, CO: Inlightened Source, 2009).

12. Donna DeNomme, personal communication, quoted with permission, May 31, 2014.

13. Suzanne Collins, *The Hunger Games* (New York: Scholastic Press, 2008). First in the trilogy.

12. Jean Shinoda Bolen, *The Tao of Psychology* (Harper & Row, 1999; twenty-fifth anniversary edition, New York: Harper One, 2004).

13. Marina Chapman, with Vanessa James and Lynne Barrett-Lee, *The Girl with No Name* (New York: Penguin Books, 2013).

14. Helen Stoltfus *Send Word, Bear Mother*, documentary film. Co-producer and director, Lynn Feinerman, www.bearmother.com.

The Chinese story of Guanyin and the European tale of The Handless Maiden illustrate a universal path for women to heal the wounds of patriarchy and recover wholeness. In their mythical journeys both figures face severance and solitude before transformation in loving relationship that is beyond personal boundaries. The modern day stories of Aung San Suu Kyi, Mary Oliver, and Sonia Sotomayor reflect examples of wise women who have walked a similar path of individuation and compassionate action.

GUANYIN AND THE HANDLESS MAIDEN:
A FEMININE PATH OF AWAKENING

DEBORAH BOWMAN

The central role of the bodhisattva vow, to relieve the suffering of others, is a definitive quality of Mahayana Buddhism, the form of Buddhist practice that developed and flourished in China. Miracle stories were one of the factors that drove its development, including the tenth-century story of the transformation of Guanyin into a feminine figure. Her sinification was also accomplished in stories that gave her earthly roots, as Chinese gods more commonly began as humans, in contrast to western or Indian myths in which a god more frequently descended from the heavens to incarnate as a person.[1]

Among woman, the story of Princess Miaoshan's transformation into Guanyin is one of the most popular stories of Chinese mythology. There is speculation that the seed of the myth may have sprouted around the life of a daughter of a local king during the seventh century. Spread by publications and word of mouth, her miraculous conversion became the hope and salvation of Buddhists throughout much of East Asia. Here is one of the more frequent versions of the story:

Deborah Bowman, Ph.D., is a clinical psychologist, photographer, and professor at Naropa University where she founded the Transpersonal Counseling Psychology and Wilderness Therapy programs. She has been in private practice as a psychotherapist for twenty-seven years. Deborah served on the board of the C.G. Jung Society of Colorado for nine years, is certified as a Gestalt therapist, and a trained meditation instructor. She is the author of *The Female Buddha: Discovering the Heart of Liberation and Love* (2012), *The Luminous Buddha: Image and Word* (2007), and *When Your Spouse Comes Out: A Straight Mate's Recovery Manual* (2007). For four years she has published and presented articles on Buddhism and psychology at the International Association of Buddhist Universities conferences in Thailand. For more information about her work, see www.thefemalebuddha, www.luminousbuddha, and www.thefemalebuddha.wordpress.com.

Born a daughter of a King, Princess Miaoshan was drawn to Buddhist practices, enjoyed chanting, and would not eat meat. When she was of age, the king chose a husband for her who would increase his wealth. The idea was abhorrent to her and she said she would only marry someone who could alleviate the suffering of the sick, aging, and dying. He refused her suggestion and she asked to be sent to a nunnery so she could further her Buddhist practice.

While the king complied with her outer wish, he instructed the nunnery to only allow her to work as the most lowly maid. While she scrubbed night and day, her cheerful attitude made the flowers bloom, and the animals helped her with innumerable jobs. In his fury, when her father heard this news, he burnt the nunnery to the ground. Without being burned she put the fire out with her hands. Frightened by her supernatural powers, he sent an executioner to kill her.

She mysteriously deflected every blow of the executioner. Realizing the dreadful fate of a man who could not carry out her father's wishes, she allowed him to kill her and exchanged her karma for the executioner's. He was immediately redeemed of all his sins, and she went straight to hell with the burden of his sins. Nevertheless, her kindness relieved the suffering of the many beings in the hell realm and released them to heaven.

Yama, the god of death, was appalled as she was transforming the underworld into a place of redemption and threw her out of his realm before she destroyed it completely. Miaoshan was transported to the Purple Bamboo forest where she spent many years in quiet meditation. When she heard that her father was dying, she disguised herself as a monk and went to him to suggest he could be cured by ingesting the eyes and hands of one pure of anger. Unbeknownst to him, she was the one who provided the eyes and hands, and he was completely cured.

For the first time in his life, the king was filled with gratitude and traveled to thank the person whose body was offered to cure him. She was deep in meditation when he found her, and he fell to the ground when he recognized his daughter. At this moment of connection she was completely transformed into the goddess Guanyin with a thousand hands and a thousand eyes.[2]

Guanyin's story both challenges and fits the Confucian values that were dominant as Buddhism spread throughout China. On one level, her refusal to obey her father's wishes ran contrary to the obedience a child would unquestioningly offer her parents. In this way, she represented a radical departure from the standards of the day. Buddhism challenged the Confucian norms in that it placed greater value on the awakening of the individual. Her story emphasizes the value placed on being true to one's unique path of individuation. In choosing to defy patriarchal norms at the cost of her life, her actions are radical for her day.

True to the deeper values of Confucianism and its reverence for the bonds of family, she ultimately gave her body for the welfare of her father. True to Buddhist teachings, her act symbolized the ultimate truth of interdependence. In this way she performs the ultimate sacrifice and represents the realization of no-self. While her act represents the traditional sacrifice in China a child would offer a parent, it also symbolizes what a mother would do for the life of her child. She transitions from maiden to mother in the offering of her eyes and hands. In her final exchange with her father where both are renewed, she manifests as Guanyin, symbolizing the transforming energy of the Great Mother.[3] The role reversal between parent and child is complete when her father is reborn to a loving relationship.

COMPARING GUANYIN TO THE HANDLESS MAIDEN

The many symbolic themes of the story of Miaoshan have significant correspondences with the fourteenth-century European tale of the Handless Maiden. Both heroines are youngest daughters who face the terrible demands of fathers more interested in material wealth than the physical and emotional welfare of their daughters. Both suffer hellish experiences, remove themselves from the negating demands of the patriarchy, and seek solitude and renewal in the forest. While one is dismembered without choice and the other makes a conscious choice to offer her limbs, both losses represent a sacrifice before a re-membering of their true selves in relation to another. Among the many renditions of the story of the Handless Maiden, this one captures the central qualities of her suffering and ultimate transformation:

> A Miller is facing increasing hardship as his crops diminish in the face of a drought. One day he is visited by the devil who offers to change his fortune if the Miller is willing to give him whatever he requests. The devil gestures towards a

tree to indicate what he wants from the Miller and the Miller consents. Behind the tree is the Miller's daughter and the devil demands her hands as the terms of their agreement. The young maiden's hands are chopped off, and the mill begins to turn again as the crops flourish.

Despite the new wealth of her family and the many gifts that are offered the daughter, she grows increasingly unhappy with her state. She eventually leaves the mill and barely survives by snatching pears with her teeth in an orchard she discovers in her wandering. She is noticed by the orchard tender and reported to the owner, the King. Because of her beauty, the King is brought to view her desperate acts and immediately falls in love.

The marriage of the King and the Handless Maiden is cause for great celebration throughout the land, and she is fashioned beautifully crafted silver hands so as to never again attend to any task or care. She has a multitude of servants and every need is attended to by another. Their child is born, and the king cannot understand her laments that she cannot hold her baby. There is no consolation for her loss, and she weeps in sorrow.

The Handless Maiden wanders into the forest again. As she is sitting by a stream, her toddler wanders a few feet away and falls in the water. In panic, she cries out but no one can hear her pleas for help. Plunging her silver hands into the water, she grabs her child as he begins to sink beneath the surface. As the Maiden pulls him out, her hands are recovered and the vitality of her life renewed.[4]

In the story of Miaoshan-Guanyin and in the story of the Handless Maiden, a young girl is embedded in her family, subject to the selfish demands of the father, and loses innocence through the experience of suffering. As youthful feminine figures, they represents the feeling function that is crushed by the driven quality of the patriarchy and its endless desire for control and material goods.[5] Ignored are Miaoshan's values to connect through healing as represented by her wish to marry someone who could alleviate suffering. In a setting where her choices are limited before she knows her own values, the Handless Maiden expresses a sadness that cannot be lifted as long as she is subject to male dominance. Her ability to connect to life and provide a mother's touch is severed.

Miaoshan refuses to obey her father and is punished twice for her defiance. While she eventually puts out the fires when the monastery is burnt to the ground, the loss is very great and all five hundred nuns die. Miaoshan faces the fire a second time when she descends into hell, yet is able to manifest her basic loving nature in acts of kindness that liberate others. She is fearless in the face of great torment and is without the heat of anger. When she offers her clear vision and gentle touch through the transmission of her eyes and hands to her father, she also procures his release from the afflictions of greed and selfishness that are his own personal hell.

Twice in deep despair, the Handless Maiden separates herself from the subjugation of others, first from her family and then from the King. Intuitively she acts to restore wholeness when she seeks the solitude of the forest. Her suffering represents the loss of the feminine capacity to connect with others in a meaningful and heartfelt way. When she is challenged by the potential loss of her son, her strength is restored and she reaches out with the full force of her being to save him. Her loving human nature is recovered after having been cut off through years of subservience, artificiality, and denial by the dominant masculine culture.

After her experience in hell, Miaoshan finds solitude in the forest and practices meditation for several years until word of her father's illness. The depth of her practice allows her to release her hands and eyes as her senses are no longer necessary to rest in wisdom, the nature of her own mind. The forest is also a natural setting for the Handless Maiden to discover who she is without the outer world defining her. Quiet retreat in nature offers a contemplative setting to shed healing tears and recover a sense of wholeness.[6] The power of solitude is the medicine that heals the wounded feminine and is the precursor to wisdom.[7]

Miaoshan and the Handless Maiden complete the individuation process as they clear the path to their unique destinies. Encounters with the archetype of the Self are reflected in mystical events for both women. The Handless Maiden wanders into the garden of the Kingdom, a symbol of the Self, where her fate advances the development of her motherly and relational instincts.[8] Her hands are mysteriously recovered when plunged into the healing waters of life. Miaoshan develops into a bodhisattva as she puts out fire with her hands, saves souls in hell, and manifests with a thousand eyes and arms.

Both paths reflect an inward and transformative journey leading to fulfillment. The Handless Maiden recovers her humanity by reclaiming the feminine side of her nature. Handless, she represents the loss of the feeling function in our culture that is denigrated by an over-emphasis on the masculine and outer development. The feeling function knows what to value, not through logic, but by an inner process of knowing that the hands express through touch. A mother instinctively reaches for her child without having to think what is best.

Miaoshan expresses the struggle of the feminine to be recognized in the world. In her transfiguration into Guanyin, she represents the flowering of humanity into its fullest realization of wisdom and compassion. She asserts the feeling function denied by a lopsided authoritarian control and becomes a feminine Self-figure, bringing healing and affiliation to women and men.

The story of the Handless Maiden reminds us of the depth of the wound to the feminine and the feeling function when a child is subject to dismemberment before she or he has the opportunity to make choices. Having been hardened and denied his relational nature, the father makes a deal with the devil. The stress of impending poverty puts him over the edge. The daughter's hands represent the ability to reach out and make contact with the world in a way that binds together despite hardship. The feminine, an essential ingredient for eros to thrive, can overcome the greatest odds.

Miaoshan is born a princess, has the advantage of choosing her path early in life, and confronts the tyranny of her father at a stage in development reflecting greater consciousness. The signs of her preference for a life of quiet reflection and bodhisattva activity are displayed as a child. Grounded in the feminine and her feeling function early in life, Miaoshan is able to take a radical stand against her father's dominance. Outwardly, she is subject to his power to enslave or threaten her life. Inwardly, she maintains an attitude of lovingkindness and her caring actions radiate from her center. Her sacrifices appear overwhelming yet in the end are her salvation.

The deeper meaning of sacrifice is to give up something lesser for something greater. Women have been trained to sacrifice in a way that does not reflect this sacred meaning: to release what is no longer necessary to mature on the path. The devil's procurement of the hands of the Maiden is an act of stealth and reflects how the underbelly of society unconsciously robs both women and men of the power to feel.

What is taken is greater than what is given in return. When Miaoshan offers her hands and eyes to her father, she consciously chooses to release an outer life that is no longer relevant to her inward development of wisdom. Her feeling function is robustly centered in her heart and mind, and her sacrifice is a sacred exchange reflecting the need to advance the spiritual growth of both her father and herself.

When the Handless Maiden chooses a life of solitude and leaves her family behind, she begins the process of moving toward what will nourish her development of consciousness. Her encounter with the King marks the beginning of her good fortune, albeit with strings attached in the form of silver hands. The constellation of her new family is not outwardly ruthless, yet the understanding of her need for an embodied connection to her child is disregarded by her husband. The hands that tie her to an artificial life are made of a cold and precious metal.[9] She has been given the royal appearance of wholeness without the deeper experience she longs to know. The separation from her infant represents a tear in the fabric of life that the bond of mother and child symbolizes.

The contemplative life that Miaoshan seeks in the nunnery is tarnished by her father's anger at her disobedience and his efforts to punish her. Although she is given the lowliest jobs, her irrepressible cheerfulness brings allies to her side. Like Psyche, who is given impossible tasks, Miaoshan draws animals from the natural world to assist her. Nature, a mirror of the display of eros, proclaims she is on the affirming side of life. Guanyin is intimately associated with the natural world, and sacred sites dedicated to her include springs, oceans, trees, and mountains.[10]

In her trial in hell, Miaoshan has only compassion for the souls she meets who suffer unbearable pain for their sins against humanity. She understands that somewhere along their journey they lost their connection to the feelings that cause love to weave us together. With everyone she touches in the underworld, Miaoshan offers a healing connection through her compassionate presence.[11] This encounter alone releases them from their hellish experience of separation and pain.

The healing quality of relationship is emphasized in both stories. When the Handless Maiden reaches for her child, the two are brought back from the brink of death, one psychic and the other literal. Her love for her child reawakens eros and brings her out of a deadening depression. In the Maiden's thrust for life, the feminine drives eros to nurture and care. The moment Miaoshan's father recognizes his daughter as the one who saved his life through the sacrifice of her hands and eyes is the moment she transforms in Guanyin. In gratitude, he now fulfills his destiny as a true King in the offering of his wealth to the temple and to those in need. He humbly embraces his sacred mission as King in the realization of interdependence. Symbolically he has received her vision and capacity to offer a helping hand. The polarity of good and evil between daughter and father collapses, and her realization is thus complete.

FEMININE ARCHETYPE OF NO-SELF

A bodhisattva cannot leave the earth realm until all sentient beings are released from hell. Miaoshan's task is most significant when it comes to her father, her closest family member, and the relationship which is marked by the greatest personal distress. The story reminds us this is our most crucial and challenging work—to love those who are closest to us and who can make our lives hell. Nevertheless, we are reminded in the story that compassion does not mean blind obedience that is contrary to our basic Buddha nature. The crucible she faces demands she attend to the work she has set out to do, making her stand radically opposed to the consensual and patriarchal standards of the day.

Buddhanature is a term used to connote our basic goodness, the Buddha qualities we have within us to realize. In understanding our inseparability and impermanence, we naturally experience compassion because our hearts and minds are open to the entire universe and every new situation we encounter.[12] We have no "I" to protect, just as Guanyin has no eyes and hands that she would call her own.[13] The only given in her story is her destiny to unfold as a Buddha, and veering from this path would be counter to her nature as a conscious being with choices to express.

As a symbol of the Self, in her full capacity to comprehend and heal the suffering of the world, Guanyin is an archetype of No-self.[14] The Handless Maiden embodies the same capacity in the instant she reaches for her child. She momentarily forgets her limitations and reaches beyond what is possible. Her wholehearted effort is aligned with her maternal instinct and her truth. Guanyin with a thousand eyes and a thousand arms represents a continuous state of compassionate action flowing out of clear perception. Her final manifestation as a Buddha-to-be is said to be the completion of many lives of honing these traits until they form an unceasing chain of merciful activity.

Our stories remind us that it is only possible to awaken to our true nature through loving connection. This is our nature, to be intimate with all things. Anything less than this is suffering, the false understanding that we are self-contained, alone and fixed in our predicament. The understanding of impermanence allows for the acceptance of change and cultivates the urgency to love all the more. The Handless Maiden's sorrow is compounded by the narrowness of her perceived options. Not until she wanders outside the stifling perimeters of her family home does she begin a journey of healing. It is in her solitude that she begins to build the self-knowledge and strength to connect from her center.

No-self is not void of awareness, in fact, it is awareness itself.[15] It is just not filtered through the lens of personal desire and gain. Centered awareness is not self-centered or other-centered. It is grounded in a body rooted in the earth and in a community of beings. Guanyin embodies centered awareness analogous to the good mother who is continually alert and looking out for her children. As the good mother, she listens for where she may be needed and is ever ready to offer her body and mind for the benefit of all beings. As a goddess of no-self she represents a transpersonal consciousness beyond the limitations of the personal ego.

Guanyin is a goddess figure not only in the Buddhist pantheon; Taoists worship her as do individuals in China not aligned to either religion. Her compassion is available to anyone and is without limit. In the largest sense she is considered an inner figure, a mirror within each human being of our compassionate and enlightened mind. The outer image of Guanyin is a projection of our need for gentleness and mercy.[16] Throughout the world people pray to Guanyin as someone who can intervene on their behalf. She is supplicated and revered as a goddess, religious deity, savior, and friend.[17] The story of Miaoshan becoming Guanyin demonstrates realization as a human journey, not a bequeath from a God that can be meted out or taken away.

The moving remembrance of Chun-Fang Yu, a Chinese-American professor at Columbia University, demonstrates the inner and outer dynamic of a spiritual relationship to the figure of Guanyin.[18] As a young girl in China, Yu shared her bedroom with her grandmother, a woman who offered incense, chanted, and prayed at a personal altar to Guanyin. Yu remembers her grandmother talking and sharing her worries with Guanyin, represented on her altar by a female figure holding a baby.

At the end of World War II, when Yu's family was waiting to catch a boat on a riverbank, the grandmother had a vision of Guanyin in the river signaling them to not board. Grandmother insisted they not board. Watching the boat depart, they witnessed it hit a mine and sink before their eyes. Her siblings were only two and five years old, and Yu reflects that none of them would have survived.[19] The grandmother's spiritual practice connected her to a wisdom and knowing beyond normal understanding. The experience at the boat dock was one of the driving forces in Yu's life-long scholarly investigation into the Chinese understanding of Guanyin and the many miracle stories of the devoted.

We can understand a supplicant's prayers as the small self in conversation with the larger Self, which is connected to a transpersonal knowing beyond what is available to the personal ego. A practitioner who devotes his or her life to trust in the power of compassion has developed a strong self-Self relationship and may experience mercy in its most transcendent form. A Buddhist understanding would attribute all knowing flowing from the larger sense of Mind which is clear and aware and without personal boundaries. Guanyin is the personification of this big Mind and her benevolence flows out to all beings as she represents the love that arises when the indivisibility of life is realized.[20]

LIVING FEMALE BODHISATTVAS

While Guanyin represents the full flowering of the bodhisattva ideal, many women throughout history have walked a path marked by similar challenges and lines of development, meeting adversity with wisdom and compassion. The patriarchal wound to the feminine is healed through a process not dissimilar to the themes in the Handless Maiden and the story of Guanyin. Their stories are not unlike our own where "the father-daughter wound is a condition of our culture and, to that extent, the plight of all women and men today."[21] Encountering hellish circumstances, women have come to know their own preferences and capacities through leave-taking, seeking solitude, acting on their truth and transformation through a healing relationship. Their choices reflect a natural maturation beyond self concerns to a greater concern for the benefit of others. The following examples of three remarkable women— Aung San Suu Kyi, Mary Oliver, and Sonia Sotomayor—represent an affirmation of feminine principles balancing circumstances overly weighted toward patriarchal dictates.

Life-threatening and traumatic incidents are often the catalyst for the transcendence of individual boundaries. Aung San Suu Kyi, considered a living bodhisattva by the people of Myanmar, lost her father at three years of age when he was struck down by an assassin's bullet. He had been a military leader supporting the democratic movement, and she followed her father's footsteps as a political leader of the same cause over forty years later. She would have become prime minister following her party's successful election but was put under house arrest by a despotic military junta.

Aung San's life of solitude spanned over eighteen years that were punctuated by contact with the outer world on few occasions. A meager diet made her hair fall out, and she was prone to illness with no access to health care. She saw her two children only twice during this period; they were raised in England by their father. Utilizing her time to study, she also learned to meditate with the guidance of a book by one of the great Buddhist masters of her country. She transcended her suffering and later wrote that his writing was the "main source of spiritual support during those intensely difficult years."[22]

Devoted to her people, Aung San chose to stay incarcerated in Burma when she could have escaped with her family. She lived a life devoid of outer liberties but dedicated to freedom from tyranny and a cause larger than herself. For years she was the only hope of millions of people, many of whom kept her alive in their hearts with glimpses of her photo they kept in their homes, hidden from the authorities. The corrupt patriarchy she stood against was not her father, but his murderers. Aung San chose solitude where she developed an inner fortitude expressed in feminine grace. She was awarded the Nobel Peace Prize, and the international pressure surrounding her release was no doubt a critical cause in the opening of her country to the outside world and the beginnings of a democratic process.

The Pulitzer prize-winning poet, Mary Oliver, grew up in a home where her father sexually abused her and her mother sided with her husband when Oliver shared her trauma.[23] As a young girl she was left to sort things out on her own, sought the solace of the woods, and "built a world out of words" as a refuge from her pain.[24] The disempowerment resulting from sexual abuse is well documented. Children suffer loss of self-worth and live in a veritable hell, sometimes choosing to end their lives when their coping strategies fail or they have no one who will intervene.

Oliver discovered the beauty and fascination of the natural world as her salvation. From a young age, she wrote about transcendent experiences, and published her later poems of praise as an adult. Her gifted work is a spiritual transmission, a bodhisattva activity offering tangible access to the divine to her readers. In the beginning of her poem, *In Blackwater Woods*, Oliver invites us to enter her exquisite vision of the "luminous bodies of trees," while reminding us in the middle of her poem that her most significant learning has been in the "fires of loss."[25] In the final capstone verse, she tells us to:

> Love what is mortal,
> Hold it against your bones
> Knowing your whole life depends upon it,
> And when the time comes to let it go,
> To let it go.

Oliver's inspiring words reflect her hard-won wisdom in the most sublime and straightforward manner. She touches the rapture of relationship, our interdependency, and the inevitable confrontation with death we must accept if we are to be fully human. In 2012, in an interview with Maria Shriver, she describes her intense loneliness after her partner of forty years died. Afterward, Oliver felt she had a choice to become a hermit or unlock her door to the outside world. She choose the latter and with no regrets now enjoys the companionship of many friends. She sought psychotherapy at the age of seventy to heal the final wounds of abuse that despite her partnership, left her with profound feelings of isolation.[26]

Sonia Sotomayor suffered from her father's incapacity to provide for her basic well-being. While he was not a tyrant, he was lost to alcoholism and could not provide the physical care she needed when diagnosed with diabetes. At seven years of age, she took it upon herself to learn how to sterilize needles with boiling water and gave herself insulin shots.[27] Her father had made an attempt to give her a shot as his hands were shaking uncontrollably, and she realized she was on her own to take care of herself. While her mother was away working long hours as a nurse, in one afternoon she made sure Sonia could safely follow the precise procedure. Sotomayor marks this event as the beginning of a life of self-sufficiency that would serve her and, despite the love of an extended family, also caused her to suffer an inner loneliness for many years.[28]

When she was nine her father died of alcohol neuropathy, and she was thrown on her own resources to help support the family. She had an uncommon intelligence and ability to rise above her circumstances of poverty, excelling at school and taking jobs that honed her capacity to find meaning in serving others. She later came to see that she drew great lessons from her many hardships, including discrimination as a Puerto Rican growing up in the barrios of the Bronx.

Sotomayor's autobiography is unusually personal for a judge on the Supreme Court. In her writing, she felt it was important to share the gritty details of a life that might inspire others. She names her self-sufficiency as a barrier to reconciling a marriage that failed. The anger and distance Sotomayor felt with her often-absent mother would only be healed later in life as she came to understand the circumstances of her mother's life and learned to reach out. She now measures her own life by the many blessings she received and the impetus those blessings now impel her to serve.[29]

Aung San, Oliver, and Sotomayor all suffered personal wounding by the patriarchy, whether induced by a tyrannical system, an abusive or alcoholic father, or racial discrimination. Each set out on a path marked by solitude that was painful yet led to the development of inner knowing and feminine strength. The flowering of Aung San's devotion to her people is captured by her tremendous contribution to an entire country's release from oppression. Oliver's transcendent poems are punctuated by her personal transformation, helping her readers to absorb the depth of her insight. The same motif is evident in Sotomayor's journey, where the healing of her most personal relationship parallels her empowerment as a wisdom holder of a nation. Each of these women's lives reflects a pilgrimage of severance, solitude, and return to community, culminating in fulfillment and greater purpose, a heroine's journey.

ENLIGHTENED MOTHERS AND MODELS OF COMPASSION

Guanyin represents a timeless truth, that our personal path of individuation is intrinsically joined to our realization of our basic goodness, our Buddhanature. The development of the feminine necessitates a contemplative, inner journey to understand one's relative nature and the absolute reality of a self that is not separate or permanent. The story of the Handless Maiden is a carrier of the same universal themes: the wound to the feminine, overcoming strictures of the patriarchy, sacrifice, and awakening to one's true nature through loving connection. Both women recover their limbs and full capacity to serve life through reaching out to others, embodying the qualities of selflessness in their spontaneous acts of love.

When Guanyin is without eyes or hands she manifests as the dark feminine, a frightening image without an ultimate understanding of the indivisibility of life. The Handless Maiden wanders in a dark depression until she recovers her true nature. They both act in an enlightened state of wholeness when death threatens their kin.

As archetypes of the heroine, Guanyin and the Handless Maiden remind us of the central role of coming to voice and individuation in women's development. Both myths point to the significance of their maternal role, the Handless Maiden embodying the awakened and selfless instinct of the Mother archetype and Guanyin manifesting as the Great Mother in her incarnation as the bodhisattva of compassion.

These stories, reiterated in lives of women today, remind us that the wounds of the patriarchy can be healed with contemplative solitude and loving connection. We are blessed with mythical and living models of wisdom and compassion to inspire our lives.

NOTES

1. Chun-Fang Yu, *Kuan-yin: The Chinese Transformation of Avalokitesvara* (New York: Columbia University Press, 2001), p. 295.

2. *Ibid.*, p. 293-294.

3. Erich Neumann, *The Great Mother: An Analysis of the Archetype* (Princeton, NJ: Princeton University Press, 1955), p. 8.

4. Robert Johnson, *The Fisher King and the Handless Maiden: Understanding the Wounded Feeling Function in Masculine and Feminine Psychology* (San Francisco: HarperOne, 1995), pp. 57-94.

5. *Ibid.*, p. 79.

6. Linda Schierse Leonard, *The Wounded Woman: Healing the Father-Daughter Relationship* (Boston: Shambhala Press, 1982), p. 136.

7. Johnson, *Fisher King and Handless Maiden*, p. 79.

8. *Ibid.*, p. 81.

9. *Ibid.*, p. 85.

10. Sonoko Toyoda, *Memories of Our Lost Hands: Searching for Feminine Spirituality and Creativity* (College Station, TX: Texas A&M University Press, 2006), p. 88.

11. Stephen Levine, *Becoming Kuan Yin: The Evolution of Kindness* (San Francisco: Weiser Books, 2013), pp. 33-36.

12. Deon van Zyl, "Self/No-Self, the Transcendent Function, and Wholeness," in Dale Mathers, Melvin E Miller, Osamu Ando, eds., *Self and No-Self: Continuing the Dialogue Between Buddhism and Psychotherapy* (London: Routledge, 2009), p. 13.

13. Miyuki explains the transcendence of the boundary between "I" and the "world" as a function of the transcendent function synthesizing opposites. He explains from a Buddhist point of view that its full completion as a psychic process would be considered enlightenment. M. Miyuki, "The Ideational Content of the Buddha's Enlightenment: A Jungian Approach," in J.M. Spiegelman and M. Miyuki, *Buddhism and Jungian Psychology* (Delhi: New Age Books, 1994), p. 131.

14. The Buddhist experience of the center of consciousness is understood to be a continuously changing process without a fixed point of reference. Miyuki explains how a great deal of confusion has arisen as this has been inadequately translated as non-self or non-ego without a Western understanding of the psychological implications of these terms. M. Miyuki, "A Jungian Approach to the Pure-Land Practice of *Nien-Fo*," *Journal of Analytical Psychology,* Vol. 25, Issue 3, pp. 265-274, 1980; Spiegelman and Miyuki, *Buddhism and Jungian Psychology*, p. 141.

15. Chogyam Trungpa Rinpoche, a Tibetan lama, utilized the term ego to describe a neurotic process based on a solidified sense of self that is separate and self-referential and as such is the cause of suffering. He saw the projections of the ego as an incorrect understanding of the interdependent nature of reality and the primary obstruction to clear seeing and compassion. Chogyam Trungpa, *Glimpses of Abhidharma* (Boulder, CO: Prajna Press, 1978), p. 7-8.

This Buddhist interpretation, distinct from the strictly psychological definition, can now be understood as a unique understanding of the word ego and its counterpart non-self, describing the lack of a permanent, singular, and independent self. Deborah Bowman, *Slang, Freud and Buddhist Psychology: Clarifying the Term "Ego" in Popular, Psychodynamic and Spiritual Contexts* (UNDV Conference Volume/Buddhist Psychotherapy, The International Buddhist Conference, Thailand, 2011), p. 1.

16. Deborah Bowman, *The Female Buddha: Discovering the Heart of Liberation and Love* (CO: Samadhi Publications, 2012), p. 11.

17. Sandy Boucher, *Discovering Kwan Yin, Buddhist Goddess of Compassion* (Boston: Beacon Press, 1999), p. 14.

18. Yu, *Kuan-yin,* p. iv-v.

19. *Ibid.*

20. J. Blofeld, *Bodhisattva of Compassion: The Mystical Tradition of Kuan Yin* (CO: Shambhala Publications, 1977), p. 126.

21. Leonard, *Wounded Woman,* p. 25.

22. Sharon Salzberg, *Faith: Trusting Your Own Deepest Experience* (New York: Riverhead Books, 2002), p. 140.

23. Maria Shriver, "Maria Shriver Interviews Famously Private Mary Oliver," *O Magazine*, March 9, 2011. Accessed May 16, 2014, http://www.oprah.com/entertainment/Maria-Shriver-Interviews-Poet-Mary-Oliver.

24. *Ibid.*

25. Mary Oliver, *American Primitive* (Boston: Little, Brown and Company, 1978), p. 82.

26. Shriver, "Shriver Interviews Mary Oliver."

27. Sonia Sotomayor, *My Beloved World* (New York: Alfred A. Knopf, 2013), p. 4.

28. *Ibid.,* p. 279.

29. *Ibid.,* p. 254.

"Love and be Silent" follows the theme of the historical silencing of women's voices through literary texts. Beginning with Telemachus' muzzling of his mother in Homer's *Odyssey,* the personal-domestic and the public-political implications of this silencing are explored, as well as ways in which women have subverted their enforced silence and made their voices heard in and through the silence.

"LOVE AND BE SILENT:"
LITERARY REFLECTIONS

JOSEPHINE EVETTS-SECKER

When I was a post-graduate student in London, I did some substitute teaching in an impoverished school in a dismal inner city, now an upmarket London borough. Most of the children were sorely disadvantaged. The most notorious lad in the class called himself "Carrot Boy." We formed a bond (I myself a reformed early miscreant) and for me he always behaved "well," if eccentrically. It was clear to me that his aggression was equalled by his vulnerability. After school one day I was supervising Detention, when the students were supposed to be writing lines as punishment, as many hundred as one cared to demand of them before they could leave. "I must not ... I must not ... I must not ..." Instead of that mindless punishment, I asked them to write for me something about silence. Carrot Boy sat quietly for a full hour, seeming reluctant to depart. He handed in his "essay." It said starkly: "Silence is noises you don't usually hear." I have wondered over many decades what this scared and scarred lad really wanted to say. My worst fear for Carrot Boy is that following the trajectory already set, he will have spent many isolated, silent hours in prison cells, still unable to speak, paralyzed, perhaps, by his inner noise.

Josephine Evetts-Secker is a Jungian analyst in Britain, who studied at the University of London. She is an ordained priest in the Anglican Church, and a former professor of English literature at the University of Calgary. A graduate of the Jung Institute in Zürich, she has served on the council of the London Independent Group of Analytical Psychologists' (IGAP) training program and lectures regularly at the International School of Analytical Psychology in Zürich (ISAPZURICH). She is the President of the Association for Graduates in Analytical Psychology (AGAP), formed sixty years ago for Jungian analysts trained in Zürich. She is the author of *At Home in the Language of the Soul: Exploring Jungian Discourse and Psyche's Grammar of Transformation* (Spring Journal Books, 2012).

It may seem very odd to begin a reflection on the silencing of women with such an anecdote. But I start with the premise, as did Terry Tempest Williams, that silence speaks volumes.[1] And I suggest that not only women have been silenced, though theirs is a special case and tells a story that I want to recapture from the perspective of one who has never been conscious of being actively, explicitly, or instrumentally silenced. In fact, I have always been urged to speak by encouraging teachers or mentors. My own resistance to making my voice heard derived from fierce insecurity about having anything of value to say. The source(s) of that kind of inner silencing I hope to illuminate. It can take years of analysis to enable women like me to take the risk, a risk that all who speak must take.

However, two typical instances experienced as more subtle silencing occurred in ancient groves of Academe. At my first undergraduate Shakespeare seminar, I dared to speak, trying to differentiate between jealousy and envy. Not only did I panic and speak of "Desmedina," but I introduced my struggling formulation with the intellectual *faux-pas*, "I feel that ..." The retort from a superior male professor came like a sword: "We are not interested in what you feel, Miss Evetts." I never opened my undergraduate mouth again in seminars. Then many years later, teaching in a university arts faculty, I was enthusing about a class in which I'd just taught Johnson's *Rasselas*, perhaps an unusual text for freshmen to have been excited about. A senior fellow professor, an eighteenth-century bibliophile, interrupted my flow, asking what edition of the text I had been using. So irrelevant was this information to me at that time that, dumbfounded, I muttered ... "I don't remember ... it was red." Another *faux-pas*, revealing my mental frivolity, and no doubt by extension, that of most female students, at best, mere amateurs. Such seemingly innocuous disparagements are internalized, to be experienced as a "crippling inner voice."[2] Times have certainly changed, but some of the silencing mechanisms have not. Color was clearly more important to me than bibliographical exactitude, and I own responding to the world through feeling. Jungian psychology validated my experience and thereby my entangled sense of self. I was most encouraged years later when asked to act as external examiner of a Ph.D. thesis that arose from, and was formulated explicitly, from confessed feeling-knowledge.[3] By the end of the last century, feeling was consciously admitted to the Academy. I am convinced that Jung played his part in the cultural shift, in his insistence on the value of the feeling function as rational and discriminatory.

Nevertheless, some of the benefits of this thinking were threatened by Jung's typically disparaging judgments of female "animus," most intensely, the "animus-possessed woman," whose symptomatology, whose pathology, was allegedly reflected in verbosity and strength or volume of voice, as much as her limited thinking, her inferior logos. This has needed significant modification. Demaris Wehr suggests that most distinctively, for Jungians, "the source of personality is found largely in archetypal factors writ large in society, archetypal factors transcending time and space."[4] Historical social context is often overlooked or underestimated. The archetypal and the social factors need to be held in balance.

Traditional Jungian thinking about animus and anima has been significantly expanded and refined. In his pioneering work in this area, we now see how much Jung himself was shaped by negative thinking about the feminine when involved in life in any way not congruent with the way of Eros, and a limited concept of Eros at that. So early thinking about "animus-possession" might be seen to reinforce and exemplify what Wehr describes as "internalized oppression and invalidation of women."[5] She took Jung to task for his insufficient understanding of the social oppression of women, and judged that his work was therefore liable to reinforce patriarchy's longstanding negative assumptions. With that in mind, she accepts the value of the brave exploration of gender Jung offers and accepts it with the important proviso, that it was not legitimate "as the negative pole of a cosmic principle."

In the ensuing reflections on literary texts, I will illuminate the shifting contexts within which women have struggled to find a voice, to trust it, and have it heard, respected, and understood.

Shakespeare's female characters enact many of women's dilemmas enigmatically, as do many other fictional figures. Some literary women and some of their creators felt that their speech would only be heard if they spoke as men, *vide* Portia or George Eliot. Even Queens of England have suffered in this way. Legend has it that in speech to her fighting men at Tilbury, Elizabeth the First declared: "I know I have the body of a weak, feeble woman, but I have the heart and stomach of a king, and of a king of England too."

I go first to Shakespeare's drama, *King Lear,* a play about speaking and silence. An aged, weary, and foolish king wants to "creep unencumbered towards death." He has three daughters who must be married off to suitably royal husbands. Most importantly, he needs a male partner for one daughter who can reign in his stead. He prefers his youngest child, Cordelia, clearly always treated as his favorite. Lear demands an affirmation of his daughters' love, unwisely determined to reward each according to the amount of love declared. Goneril and Regan, the two older sisters, speak glibly and disproportionately. False words come easily. They represent something recognizable to Shakespeare's audience ... the unreliability of female speech. This is not lost on Lear himself. As Cordelia listens to her sisters' protestations, her asides reveal the inner crisis: "What shall Cordelia speak? Love and be silent."[6] Further, she muses,

> Then poor Cordelia,
> And yet not so, since I am sure my love's
> More ponderous than my tongue.[7]

When she is required to speak, she confesses,

> Unhappy that I am, I cannot heave
> My heart into my mouth. I love your majesty
> According to my bond, no more nor less.[8]

She is rebuked by her father: "Mend your speech." She cannot offer what he demands, that is, *all* her love. That would be calming to him but false, emotionally and psychologically inappropriate. So she is deemed to offer nothing. She can say nothing. And so she is left unrewarded, for "nothing will come of nothing."[9] She will only be rewarded by the patriarchy if she offers what is demanded of her as unequal partner. Total surrender, subjugated dependence, and unremitting service to "the Fathers." Cordelia's response in this impossible predicament is to "love and be silent." The speech required would be self-betrayal, for as she pleads, "... I want that glib and oily art/To speak and purpose not ...."[10] Kent, a transforming patriarchal figure, wise statesman, and friend to the king, later assures her that she is a "maid,/That justly think'st and hast most richly said."[11] Nevertheless, she is condemned to nothingness.

Reunion and reconciliation of chastened father and wise daughter come only in the final act. But it is not to be enjoyed, for Cordelia is killed, finally victim of patriarchal power, assumed by two overlooked and perhaps justifiably jealous sisters who have adopted avowedly masculine behaviors to satisfy their own ambition. The enlightened "foolish fond old man" now grieves for his lost child, paradoxically now valuing the very thing he condemned. Silenced by death, Cordelia's voice is now heard. But even in tribute to her honor and honesty, Lear reveals the ageless prejudice against the voice of conventionally invented woman. He remembers:

> Her voice was ever soft,
> Gentle and low, an excellent thing in woman.[12]

Cordelia is finally valued not for her truthfulness, her love, and her integrity, but for the quality of a voice that did not compete with man's, deemed to be deeper, more resonant, and naturally carrying authority. "Love and be silent," Cordelia's course of action to preserve her authentic being, is the solution that seems to have been adopted by, or forced upon, many women throughout their long history of suppression.

How often this has been the story: women do the loving and men do the talking, as attested even in current social life, though often disguised. This division of behavior and attitudes has been explained in popular ways—women from Venus, men from Mars. Mary Beard, a contemporary Cambridge don and classics scholar, has spoken outspokenly on many issues, and when any woman speaks with conviction, she is typically described as "outspoken," as though such speech is "out of place" and "over the top." On twitter and social networking sites Beard has been vilified, insulted, and threatened in most obscene ways. Yet still she speaks. She has been verbally abused and in crude fantasy, raped. In ancient myth, no doubt she would have suffered the fate of Philomela, having her tongue cut out. She recently gave a lecture on the silencing of women and, speaking from her first-hand knowledge of classical literature, she described what she claimed to be the first recorded example of telling women to shut up.[13] She then pursued the implications of this Homeric moment for Greek political and social philosophy.

In Book One of the *Odyssey,* the loyal and domestic Penelope questions why her unwelcome suitors are being entertained by a bard, who sings about the difficulties suffered by the heroes' efforts to return home from Troy. She speaks openly in the great hall of Ithaca's palace. "Wise" Telemachus, her maturing son, reacts:

> Mother ... go back to your quarters and take up your own work, the loom and the distaff ... speech will be the business of men, all men and of me most of all, for mine is the power in this household.[14]

She obeys. This is a crucial episode, for it establishes that the female's voice is not meant to be heard in the public sphere. Beard points out that,

> Growing into manhood involved taking control of public utterance and silencing the female. Speech is men's business. The Greek word here is *muthos,* that is, authoritative public speech, not chatting.[15]

In this context, public speaking may be thought to have defined masculinity itself. What has followed on from that for centuries is that women have always paid a huge price to be heard beyond the immediate family circle, if at all. Consider the fates of the suffragettes who fought for women's suffrage, that is, for a political voice. In the Greek political system, a woman revealing her voice publicly was tantamount to stripping off her clothes to reveal her body. Today too many women remain covered and silenced in this way.

Greek myth illuminates the refusal of such a woman's voice in such tales as that of Io, or Philomela, Procne or Echo. Io was turned into a cow, left only with the poignant sound of moo-ing. Procne was changed into a swallow. Philomela into a nightingale. Both left only with the sweet voice of birdsong. Philomela is raped by her brother-in-law, then her tongue cut out to prevent her telling her story. Shakespeare's raped Lucrece identifies with Philomela as she prepares to kill herself, and as the nightingale sings of the ravisher in her cry, *tereus,* she determines that she will "hum on Tarquin," her lascivious rapist. These mythic female figures have no political agency to make known their anguish, but as Lucrece laments, "[we can only] tune our heart-strings to true languishment."[16]

In the case of Cassandra, who had been given the gift of prophecy by Apollo himself, she was punished when she refused to submit to him sexually, her fate being that she would be heard, but never believed.[17] This also enforces silence. What is the point of speaking if what one says is dismissed as untrue or unreliable? Echo is left unable to speak in her own voice, only able to repeat the words of another. In contrast to this pattern of silence, it is one of the joyful and liberating experiences in analysis to find that one is heard, one's story is listened to, one is believed. At last, one finds a witness who grants the validity of one's story and is able to translate one's various vocalizing sounds into legitimately voiced human experience.

Centuries after Cordelia's refusal to reassure her father that he is loved, we see another female character following Cordelia's advice, to love and be silent. In the novel *To the Lighthouse,* Virginia Woolf depicts Mrs. Ramsey as a domestic goddess of the hearth, cherishing feeling, tending souls and bodies with her enigmatic care. Her philosopher husband, "incapable of untruth," is absurdly admired, having that "splendid mind" that can reach Q in logical, meticulous philosophical thinking.[18] His topic, his wife marvelled, was "the influence of something on somebody,"[19] so revealing the "admirable fabric of masculine intelligence."[20] Speech was denied her in that articulate household, full of verbal men ... and one questing young female artist. Speaking his thought to an audience was Mr. Ramsey's sphere of influence. And yet, his wife is constantly called upon to assure him of his excellence, reassure him of his worth. As she sits knitting, she knows this to be her task.

> Mrs. Ramsey flashed her needles. ... It was sympathy he wanted, to be assured of his genius first of all ... then to be taken into the circle of life, warmed and soothed to have ... his barrenness made fertile again.[21]

But Mrs. Ramsey could not always rise to this imperious demand, and at such times Mr. Ramsey experienced his wife's "sternness."[22] There were times when she could not give herself away, and though she never could withdraw her love, she would remain silent, despite the anguish this caused her:

> He wanted something—wanted the thing she always found it so difficult to give him; wanted her to tell him that she loved him. And that, no, she could not do. He found talking so much easier than she did. He could say things—she never could. So naturally it was always he that said the things, and

then for some reason he would mind this suddenly and reproach her. A "heartless woman" he called her; she never told him that she loved him. But it was not so—it was not so. It was only that she never could say what she felt. Was there no crumb on his coat? Nothing she could do for him. ... She knew what he was thinking ... Will you not tell me just for once that you love me? ... But she could not do it; she could not say it. Then, knowing that he was watching her, instead of saying anything she turned, holding her stocking, and looked at him. And as she looked at him she began to smile, for though she had not said a word, he knew, of course he knew, that she loved him. ... [23]

We see two vital elements in women's arsenal here: her silence and, traditionally, her needle.

After Philomela had her tongue cut out, she spoke through her embroidery, and women's history is replete with examples of this strategy. In Rozsika Parker's splendid study, *The Subversive Stitch*, she traces the history of sewing and the place of women in this craft, which was considered an art form only when men were involved in the making of tapestries.[24] She paints vivid pictures of women sitting silently, plying their needle(s), their outer peace discordant with their raging inner life. Olive Schreiner comments pithily and ominously:

The Poet, when his heart is weighted, writes a sonnet, and the painter paints a picture, and the thinker throws himself into the world of action; but the woman who is only a woman, what has she but her needle? In that torn bit of brown leather brace worked through and through with yellow silk, in that bit of white rag with the invisible stitching. Lying among the fallen leaves and rubbish that the wind has blown into the gutter or street corner, lies all the passion of some woman's soul finding voice-less expression. Has the pen or pencil dipped so deep in the blood of the human race as the needle?[25]

As I observed in a paper on the "prick of consciousness," pen and pin (and penis) are related, and today the pen is as likely to be taken up by women and men to make their voice heard through print, no longer relying on the subversive use of their needles.[26] But earlier female writers and scholars were sometimes violently discredited. Get back to the distaff and shut up!

Women who would not be silenced were disparaged as scolds and
the social history of the "scold" vividly illustrates the story of the voice
of outraged women. The "scold" was the assertive woman who would
not be silenced. She was punished and humiliated by being fitted with
a scold's bridle, a "brank's bridle." Shutting up here was entirely lacking
in nuance: it was literally an iron fixture, a chastity belt for the mouth.
(See the image at the end of the paper.) The talkative woman was locked
into it. Or she was imprisoned in the ducking stool and immersed in
cold pond or river. This was also considered to be a penitential aid,
urging the women to repentance! The stool of repentance, the cucking
stool, was used very occasionally for the punishment of dishonest
tradesmen, but it was reserved especially for troublesome women.
Though the scold was considered ribald and argumentative, the word
originally was associated with Old Norse "skald," a poet.[27] Certainly,
it was a sense of the lampoon rather than the lyric mode; nevertheless,
it suggests creative possibilities. The word lost any such positive sense
and came to be exclusively judgmental, a condemnation of the brawling
female. There is a rich vocabulary to designate such women, their voices
always "shrill," and always having qualities of the "shrew," in need of
taming. The wild shrew might seem mouse-like and weak, but it was
associated with the devil at worst and with malignancy and poison at
best. These words were always terms of abuse.

The fear of a woman's voice and word has been rife in the Christian
Church and lingers on. The twelfth century *Decretum* of Gratian, a
systematization of church law declared that,

> Woman's authority is nil; let her in all things be subject to the
> rule of men ... and neither can she teach, nor be witness, nor
> give guarantee, not sit in judgment.[28]

This echoed the Patristic certainty of St. Jerome, who, commenting
on the epistle to the Ephesians, declared:

> As long as woman is for birth and children, she is different
> from men as body is from soul. But when she wishes to serve
> Christ more than the world, then she will cease to be a woman
> and be called a man.[29]

The appropriate life for girls was formulated also by Vives, the famous
sixteenth-century humanist, who typically associated feminine

ignorance with innocence, and seeing female talk as a threat to chastity. Silence fostered virtue. This social "rule" remained a powerful weapon in the silencing of women, lingering into the nineteenth century when women who sought entrance to the universities were condemned/mocked as indecent "blue-stockings." This term was marginally more flattering than that for unconventional girls mocked as "hoyting girls," again aligning them with the masculine. So the speaking or writing woman was ridiculed or condemned as betraying her "fair sex." As in centuries before, "Their self-esteem was called vanity and their courage impertinence, while their desire to communicate was interpreted as exhibitionism."[30]

John Taylor (known as the "water poet") celebrated silent, sewing maidens in his poem, "In praise of the needle," which prefaced the popular book, *The Needle's Excellency*, 1624. He reflected:

> And for my countries quiet, I should like
> That woman-kinde should use no other Pike,
> It will increase their peace, enlarge their store,
> To use their tongues less, and their needles more.
> The Needles sharpness, profit yields and pleasure
> But sharpness of the tongue, bites out of measure.[31]

Two centuries later, Louisa May Alcott caught the American "March girls" girls in the same imprisoning conventions, as they sat knitting in the twilight in cloying domestic harmony. Each girl is trapped in a different modality. Jo, "who was a bookworm," cries out "in a gentlemanly manner … I'm dying to go and fight with papa, and I can only stay at home and knit."[32]

These are still the values articulated by the Renaissance humanist Juan Luis Vives, who wrote and thought in the circle of Thomas More and Erasmus. Despite Vives' revolutionary ideas about education, his *Education of a Christian Woman* promulgated the conventional dictates for feminine behavior, from childhood through to widowhood. He too believed that women should stay at home, always with eyes cast down, retiring and silent, so that "others may see her but none will hear her." In a chapter about what might be read and what was prohibited reading for women, he insisted:

> A young woman cannot be easily of chaste mind if her thoughts
> are occupied with the sword and sinewy muscles and virile

strength. What room do these thoughts leave for chastity, which
is defenceless, unwarlike and weak?[33]

The requirement for chastity, defined by Vives as "integrity of mind
which extends also to the body," was seen to be the foundation for all
other feminine concerns. It did, of course, underlie issues of legitimacy
of offspring and the laws protecting inheritance and property. Vives
encouraged the education of women despite his insistence that chastity
was "a woman's only care," while men's need for education was more
various. But female education should be concerned only with "those
part of philosophy that has assumed as its task the formation and
improvement of morals." Certainly, Vives was far from the tirades of
the *Malleus Malificarum* that hammered the female sex as being the
cause of original sin, "woman," so conceived, not being made in God's
image, a "truth" propounded in Gratian's *Decretum*. Vives did not accept
its dogma that "when woman thinks alone, she thinks evil," but he
often reveals secret sympathy for Gratian's conviction that "woman
signifies weakness of mind." Yet he was among those thinkers who were
introducing in a serious way the "*querelle des femmes*," which became a
central area of controversy up to the twentieth century.

     Vives was followed by another formative thinker on what was
called "the woman question." In his *Lettres Persanes*, Montesquieu wrote
robustly about harem life and the fate of women enslaved there.[34]
Importantly, he saw the relationship between the slavery problem and
the servile constrictions placed on women, but he was reluctant to follow
it through. His enlightened thinking about slavery was therefore
limited. He actually used the extreme example of the Harem to defend
the "marital regime" of masculine governance in the domestic sphere,
and though he understood the values of mutuality in marriage, it seemed
only to have validity so long as it served male superiority. Nevertheless,
Montesquieu had the integrity to admit:

> We use every sort of stratagem to demoralize [women], their power
> would be equal to ours if their education was also.[35]

This has been proven to be true. Women have found their place in the
universities and even in the fortress of the church.

     Twenty years ago the Anglican Church finally gave voice to women,
ordaining them despite much resistance. Today, the consecration of
women Bishops is accepted by all but a tiny minority of Anglicans.

Such silencing is now unthinkable and women's voices are already making a massive difference. Nevertheless, women politicians still feel that to reach the top, they must toe the line and never appear eccentric. Many find it easier to remain or become patriarchal daughters. In Church and State there is residual truth in Addison's eighteenth-century judgment that embroidery was crucial for women since it kept them out of affairs of government: "Whig or Tory will be but seldom mentioned where the great dispute is, whether Blue or Red is more proper Colour."[36] There is always a supposedly benevolent justification for silencing women.

When women demanded a literal voice, as in their strenuous efforts to gain electoral suffrage, they were ridiculed and imprisoned for breach of the peace, then violently force-fed if they refused food as their only means of protest. But the female voice had begun to be heard significantly from the seventeenth century onwards, when women began to seek publication for the written word. They had always been writing vociferously for as long as they were able to read and write, but their literary domain was the private poem, the domestic journal or the private letter. Aristocratic women had long functioned as patronesses for articulate men, but they now claimed their own literary voice. Dr. Johnson notoriously remarked to Boswell of any female speaking publicly, especially in a pulpit, that a woman preaching was like a dog walking on it hind legs. This could not be done effectively, but it was shocking to find it done at all.

Some women revealed the same attitude themselves. When they did turn to verse, for example, they were continually hampered by a sense that it was not only unseemly to write, but that it was impossible to compete with men especially in the field of prosody.

It is sobering to leaf through Germaine Greer's anthology of seventeenth-century women's verse, significantly entitled, *Kissing the Rod*. Much of the writing is genuinely pathetic, written during pregnancy to imagined surviving children, in case of death in childbirth; or to husbands, protesting love and faithfulness, with a plea for the defense of surviving children against step-mothers after his probable future re-marriage. Such wives and mothers accepted a life of suffering or death with grace and courage. But increasingly they question, with increasing passion, "Shall none but the insulting

Sex be wise?" In the same poem, "The Emulation: A Pindarick Ode," the anonymous, female poet exalts,

> We'll tune and cultivate our fruitful Hearts.
> And should Man's Envy still declare,
> Our Business only to be fair;
> Without their leave we will be wise,
> And Beauty, which they value, we'll despise.
> Our Minds, and not our Faces, we'll adorn.
> For that's the Employ to which we are born.[37]

"Wanting" "language to dresse my Fancies in" (*wanting* in both senses, lacking and desiring) the Duchess of Newcastle agonizes that she must rely on those of her witty poet-husband, "whose Braine is Fresh and Pleasant, as the Spring."

> There ofte I leane my Head, and listning harke,
> To heare *his* words, and all *his* Fancies mark;
> And from that Garden Flowers of Fancies take,
> Whereof a Posie up in Verse I make.
> Thus I, that have no Garden of my owne,
> There gather Flowers that are newly-blowne.[38]

Pseudonymous "Philo-Philippa" also triumphs in being the "envy of men," who cannot bear the brightness of her "bright pen," for,

> It dazles and surprises so with light,
> To find a noon where they expected night.[39]

So women found new voices and broke through identity barriers, no longer content to stay imprisoned in the roles of inspirers and admirers of men's literary accomplishments. Nevertheless, Greer's anthology demonstrates more than anything else what she describes as "Mnemonics for female magnanimity," the sentiments most acceptable from women. As one analysand once remarked, "someone has to do the loving." For that, her voice was finely tuned!

The patriarchal rod kissed by women for centuries, even in submission to masculine metrical forms, was rudely kicked aside in a female folk tradition. Angela Carter brings together from the four corners of the globe the earthy story of feminine subversion.[40] Her mischievous collections enact the truth formerly articulated by men, that when a woman speaks much, she becomes unchaste. These are not aristocratic women and the tales affirm the richness of low culture. They are bawdy and vivacious; the humor scatological. Carter retells stories of "strong minds and low cunning," "black magic and dirty tricks." Here women have the last word, humiliating and rendering men speechless or foolish. They subvert with wit any move to beat a wife "to make clear who is master."[41] Men are stripped of masculine body hair in their sleep, left smooth as girls,[42] or even worse, tricked into having their heads thrust down the toilet, while women shit in baths.[43] Suitors are deprived of the bridewealth by clever subterfuge, daughters assuring mothers "that is how I want it."[44] In their pursuit of women, men are made to suffer numberless ordeals and insults. Wives persist in "always wanting the opposite of their husbands," and they get their way![45] When a husband leaves home, the "wife never missed a chance to betray him."[46] One imagines the telling and sharing of such tales providing space and opportunity to entertain and relieve oppression. Marina Warner suggests that we hear Carter "snatching stories for women out of the jaws of misogyny itself." The tales expose the myriads of ways in which a woman-as-trickster refuses collusion with their universally imposed subjection, "breaking new ground for women in occupying the male voice of narrative authority."[47]

Twenty-first century women writers are now confidently eminent in the literary canon of poets, novelists, and scholars. Feminist writers like Carter have contributed in eccentric and robust ways to this hard-won equality. When Carter died, Salmon Rushdie mourned, "With Angela's death English literature has lost it high sorceress, its benevolent witch queen, a burlesque artist of genius and antic grace."[48]

I have been writing this reflection in a week described by news readers as "brutal for women," with rapes, hanging, and kidnapping, culturally approved executions and refusals of female rights. The horrors of such violent oppression and slavery are scarcely credible in the west. But subtle forms of oppression continue; the wounds of such subjugation still to heal. This truth is lived in our daily praxis. How many women "find their voice," literally and figuratively, through analysis. I conclude with two such cases. In neither was physical harm or abuse experienced, but psychic damage was considerable.

The first woman was the daughter of a well-respected teacher and eminent citizen. She remembers the anguish of weekend family outings.

There was no choice about these exertions and when a child might plead hunger or the need for rest, father would consult his watch and then pontificate, "You are not yet hungry." His authority was absolute and the child was not even allowed to voice the realities of her own physical and feeling experience. She married a similarly dictatorial man and came to analysis as a terrifying act of subversion. Like so many of the exemplary women I have celebrated in this paper, she was an excellent needlewoman, especially productive in knitting her own beautiful garments. They were intricate and finely executed. We talked about the satisfaction the craft gave her. I was full of admiration. But she also revealed, through a dream, a fantasy of not following a set pattern, but creating her own design. In this woman's circumscribed existence, that would really be risking failure, terror, and defiance. How dare she? What could she possibly produce out of her own soul and imagination? *Mirabile dictu,* the analysis ended with her turning up for a final session wearing an amazingly colored, simply but exquisitely designed sweater/cardigan. She had found her voice, her own voice, finally able to transform her need for the set pattern, the fastidious observance of which had felt dictatorial. She was free. A dream reinforced this. She was in a prison and had been languishing there helplessly. Suddenly … that subversive prick of consciousness … she was moved to go over to the cell door. She discovered that the door was not actually locked. She could go free. This motif of finding the imprisoning door open has been brought to my practice several times by women dreamers.

Another woman, mercilessly shaped by dictatorial father, found her own voice with equal suffering and fear. A gifted woman but voiceless in so many ways, she immediately found relief and release in being able to talk about her life and be heard. This being heard was the necessary means to her own speech. Her father was musical and she had been coerced into music throughout her childhood. There was no choice. She did in fact love music, and was clearly a gifted musician. But there was no possibility of engaging this love, this talent, because if she did, even as a mature, married adult, she felt that immediately her father (perhaps her mother too, also shaped by the patriarchy) would claim it as her inheritance from them, so depriving her of it, making it their speech, not hers. She could not afford to please parents in this way; it was silencing. She discovered that I sing in choirs and there was poignant longing in her references. After painful sessions, realizations of loss and deprivation, she decided that she could not let them rob her of this experience of herself any longer. She dared to audition for a choir after taking a couple of voice lessons. She was utterly terrified of being heard singing, and elated when she was successful. This finding of her voice and the thrill of music-making was the high point of the analysis.

I end this paper, as I began it, with communications from silence. Terry Tempest Williams created fifty-four different interpretive voices from her mother's empty journal volumes. Each offered a different space from which each individuated voice could be heard through the daughter's memories and projections. The silencing mechanisms that operated in Mormon life did not allow an intelligent and imaginative mother to articulate her rich inner world, but the daughter produced the speech her mother was denied. She imagined the unspoken story, spoken on every bare page.

The literary and personal experiences explored in this paper illuminate the discovery of the voice of passion and the passion of voice. They affirm Williams' insight that "finding one's voice is a process of finding one's passion."[49]

NOTES

1. Terry Tempest Williams, *When Women Were Birds: Fifty-four Variations on Voice* (New York: Picador, 2012).

2. See Demaris S. Wehr, *Jung and Feminism: Liberating Archetypes* (London: Routledge, 1987), p. 121.

3. See Patricia A. Clifford, *Here There be Dragons: De-literalizing the Margins of Educational Thought and Practice* (Calgary, Canada: University of Calgary, Dept. of Educational Policy and Administrative Studies, 1996). Most salient are her comments about the fate of girls in primary education, most often taught by self-replicating females teachers, who "reject in themselves the very compliance, obedience and passivity that we, as educators, are called upon to instil in young children," p. 150ff.

4. Wehr, *Jung and Feminism*, p. 14.

5. *Ibid.*, p. 18ff.

6. William Shakespeare, *King Lear* (London: Thomson, The Arden Shakespeare, 1997), Act 1, Scene 1, l.62.

7. *Ibid.*, 78ff.

8. *Ibid.*, 91ff.

9. *Ibid.*, l.90.

10. *Ibid.*, 226ff.

11. *Ibid.*, l.184.

12. *Ibid.*, Act V, Scene 3, l.270.

13. Mary Beard, "The Public Voice of Women," in *London Review of Books Winter Lecture*, 2014, at www.lrb.co.uk/winterlectures (accessed June, 2014).

14. As quoted in *ibid*.

15. *Ibid.*

16. William Shakespeare, "The Rape of Lucrece," in *The Poems* (London: Routledge, The Arden Shakespeare, 1990), l. 1141.

17. See Laurie Layton Shapiro, *The Cassandra Complex: Living with Disbelief, A Modern Perspective on Hysteria* (Toronto: Inner City Books, 1988).

18. Virginia Woolf, *To the Lighthouse* (New York: Harcourt Brace, 1927), p. 53.

19. *Ibid.*, p. 5.

20. *Ibid.*, p. 159.

21. *Ibid.*, p. 59.

22. *Ibid.*, p. 98.

23. *Ibid.*, p. 184.

24. Rozsika Parker, *The Subversive Stitch: Embroidery and the Making of the Feminine* (London: The Women's Press, 1984).

25. Olive Schreiner, *From Man to Man* (London: Virago, 1982), Chapter 4.

26. Josephine Evetts-Secker, "The Prick of Consciousness: On the Psychology and Art of Arousal," in *Harvest: Journal for Jungian Studies*, 1993, Vol. 39, pp. 16-36.

27. *Oxford English Dictionary* (Oxford: Oxford University Press, 1971).

28. *Decretum*, cited in *Not in God's Image*, eds. Julia O'Faolain and Lauro Martines (New York: Harper & Row, 1973), p. 130.

29. St. Jerome, cited in Mary Daly, *The Church and the Second Sex* (Boston: Beacon Books, 1968), p. 210.

30. Germaine Greer, *Kissing the Rod: An Anthology of Seventeenth Century Women's Verse* (New York: Noonday Press, 1988), p. 20.

31. John Taylor, "In praise of the needle," cited in Parker, *The Subversive Stitch*, p. 86.

32. Louisa M. Alcott, *Little Women* (London: Penguin Books, 1967, first published, 1868), p. 20.

33. Juan Luis Vives, *The Education of a Christian Woman: A Sixteenth Century Manual*, ed. and trans. Charles Fantazzi (Chicago & London: University of Chicago Press, 2000), Chapter V.

34. Charles de Secondat, Baron de Montesquieu, *Lettres Persane* (*Persian Letters*), eds. Andrew Kahn and Margaret Waldon (Oxford: Oxford World Classics, 2008).

35. *Ibid.*, Letter 36, "Ricca to Ibben, in Smyrna," p. 49.

36. Joseph Addison, in *Spectator*, No. 606, 1716, cited in Parker, p. 115.

37. Anonymous, "The Emulation: A Pindarick Ode," in *Triumphs of a Female Wit, in Some Pindarick Odes, or the Emulation. Together with an Answer to an Objector against Female Ingenuity and Capacity of Learning*, cited in Greer, p. 311. The very titles of these volumes are significant of the spirit in which they have been risked to the world's eye and ear!

38. Cited in Greer, from *Poems, and Fancies* (1653), pp. 173-4.

39. Philo-Philippa, in *Poems by the most deservedly Admired Mrs Katherine Philips, The Matchless Orinda* ... (London: Printed by J.M. for H. Herringman at the Sign of the Blew Anchor in the Lower Walk of the New Exchange, 1667), cited in Greer, p. 204.

40. Angela Carter, *The Second Virago Book of Fairy Tales* (London: Virago Press, 1993).

41. *Ibid.*, p. 163.

42. *Ibid.*, p. 18.

43. *Ibid.*, p. 20.

44. *Ibid.*, p. 24.

45. *Ibid.*, p. 29.

46. *Ibid.*, p. 20.

47. *Ibid.*, p. xv.

48. Quoted in the publisher's note at beginning of Carter, *The Second Virago Book of Fairy Tales*.

49. Williams, *When Women Were Birds*, p. 85.

Figure 1: 17th century Scold's Brace "[Scottish Bridle]," from the collection of the Wellcome Foundation Library

The Diary of Anne Frank is the most well-known published diary. It is also considered one of the most sophisticated and well-written personal memoirs by formal writing standards, an astonishing fact since it was written by a fourteen-year-old girl during one of the most tumultuous historical periods and under the most horrific living conditions. What follows is an attempt to explain how Anne Frank was able to write a diary that is now considered a literary triumph and an inspiration for countless millions.

WRITING FOR THE WATCHER:
HOW ANNE FRANK WROTE THE
MOST FAMOUS DIARY EVER PUBLISHED

JIM KLINE

> "A holy spirit dwells within us, a scrutinizer and guardian of our good and evil."
>
> —Seneca

For over half of my lifetime, I have been keeping a personal journal. I am fully aware that much of what I have written in these journals is not considered well-structured, grammatically correct prose suitable for publication. However, much of my journal writing is what I consider my best writing. And, surprisingly, many passages are well written by formal English composition standards. Most importantly, numerous entries capture and express a unique voice, a singular point of view, a core identity.

Before some of my more formal writing efforts were accepted for publication, the act of writing in a journal helped feed my fantasy of being a real—i.e., published—writer, even though I knew deep down that journal writing wasn't considered real writing by the literary and academic establishment. In some college English composition texts, journal writing is referred to as "pre-writing,"

Jim Kline earned his Ph.D. in Psychology with a Jungian Studies Specialization from Saybrook University, San Francisco. He has contributed articles to *Spring Journal*, *Psychological Perspectives*, and the *San Francisco Jung Library Journal*. Most recently, he served as Dean of Humanities at Mt. Hood Community College in Gresham, Oregon. He currently teaches as an adjunct instructor for the Engaged Humanities and the Creative Life program affiliated with Pacifica Graduate Institute. He lives in the Pacific Northwest with his wife Beatriz and their four cats: Bastet, Fiona, Clarissa, and Little Red.

as if the only people who considered this type of writing a legitimate literary genre were preliterate Neanderthals.

I was familiar with personal journals published by major publishing houses, but the vast majority of these journals were written by well-known, established authors and were considered supplemental products to the authors' other more formal writings.

There was, however, one great, extraordinary exception, a diary which was considered one of the most significant and influential autobiographies ever published. It had sold untold millions of copies, been translated into dozens of languages, inspired movie and play adaptations, documentaries, biographies, even art and history exhibitions.

The diary was so well written, not only by formal structural standards but also because of its achingly honest and perceptive insights into the writer's view of her life, that there were many people who doubted that the author—a fourteen-year-old girl—could have written it. Even her father, when he first read it after she died at the age of fifteen—a victim of the Holocaust—couldn't believe his daughter had penned such nakedly revealing, insightful observations about herself and the two-year ordeal she and the rest of the family had gone through together—hiding from Nazis in the backroom offices of her father's business warehouse in Amsterdam during the final years of World War II. Her father, Otto Frank, was so overwhelmed by the beauty, honesty, and maturity of his daughter's personal writings that shortly after he finished reading the diary, he began to seek out ways to publish it.

As he struggled to find a publisher, Otto Frank gave a copy of the manuscript to a writer friend of his, Jan Romein, who had the same astonished reaction to the diary's amazingly sophisticated contents. Jan Romein was so impressed by the diary he wrote an article about it for an Amsterdam newspaper. The article, called "A Child's Voice," appeared in the April 3, 1946 edition of *Het Parool:*

> By chance a diary written during the war years has come into my possession. The Netherlands State Institute for War Documentation already holds some two hundred similar diaries, but I should be very much surprised if there were another as lucid, as intelligent, and at the same time as natural....It is written by a Jewish girl who was thirteen years old when she went into hiding with her parents and an older sister and began this diary,

and it ends one wretched day more than two years later when the Gestapo discovered her family. One month before the Liberation, she died in one of the worst German concentration camps, not yet sixteen. ...

If all the signs do not deceive me, this girl would have become a talented writer had she remained alive...[showing] insight into the failings of human nature—her own not excepted—so infallible that it would have astonished one in an adult, let alone in a child. At the same time she also highlighted the infinite possibilities of human nature, reflected in humor, tenderness and love, which are perhaps even more astonishing, and from which one might perhaps shrink, especially when they are applied to very intimate matters, were it not that rejection and acceptance remain so profoundly childlike....[1]

On the strength of this first formal review of the diary of Anne Frank, Otto Frank was able to get his daughter's diary published. The world-wide reaction to the published diary confirms the original response to its brilliance by those who first read it. But, it also confirms the opinions of those who doubted that a fourteen-year-old girl could have written it. Even though there is not a shred of doubt about the diary's authenticity, many still rightfully raise the question: how was Anne Frank at such a young age able to write the most well-known, well-regarded, well-written diary ever published?

THE WATCHER AS CORE AUDIENCE AND CORE IDENTITY

Anne Frank discovered and perfected an approach to personal journal writing that I began to apply to my own personal writing after having filled up dozens of journals for twenty-plus years. It had taken me that long to finally realize something so basic to this approach to writing—and to writing in general—that I was embarrassed to admit the delay in insight: the writing audience for my journal entries.

It might seem ridiculous to even bring up such an obvious point. Naturally, a journal writer's audience is the journal writer. But, when one writes strictly for oneself, with the idea that no one else will read the words being written, this insular context of silence can be deafening and self-defeating. Because the journal writer is not addressing a formal audience, because what is being written is not meant for publication or approval or criticism, the absence of these traditional compositional guidelines and restrictions can sometimes alienate the writer from the words being written.

It takes a conscious effort to admit that one's journal writing audience is actually oneself. But, even this conscious acknowledgment isn't enough. Because we all have multiple selves, various personas we adapt and present to the world depending on the setting, context, and the people we are with, when it comes time to sit down and write exclusively for oneself, it is sometimes hard to determine which self or persona we are writing to.

When I first began to keep a journal, sometimes I would find myself writing such sentences as "You won't believe what happened today," or "You should have been there to see this," or "You really blew it that time." Sometimes after realizing that I was addressing myself as "you," I would pause, smile, and then write, "Who *are* you?"

The approach I developed over the years to journal writing also puzzled me. After a while, I got into the habit of including minute details, background information, and clarifying references to well-known people and past incidents in order to give each entry a sense of formal compositional structure. It was almost as if I weren't jotting down random thoughts and impressions for myself, but instead composing interconnected mini-essays for the benefit of a distant someone who needed these extra details and background information to better understand what was going on at that moment in my life. Because I was so determined to write as clearly and completely as possible, I also rewrote and revised some of my journal entries, crossing out words or blotting out passages and including a more clarifying phrase or sentence or paragraph in a side margin.

Although I had never bothered to consciously envision my journal writing audience, I took for granted that this audience would accept anything I chose to write and find all my entries interesting. No matter if I were writing about the most boringly mundane personal habit or complaining for the umpteenth time about some annoyingly pointless work routine, I knew this audience would not think of me as boring or mundane just as long as I was sincere and clear in expressing my point of view. Also, because I had entrusted this audience-friend for years with so much of my life, I knew that whatever I wrote, I couldn't falsify any details of an event or distort an opinion in a vain attempt to make myself appear faultless or smarter than I was. I had to tell the truth, or at least make the effort to do so, because my audience would always know when I was lying. More importantly, I wanted to make the effort to capture the truth of an event or an insight. Deep down, I knew that when I was successful in expressing the essence of an experience or a deeply felt opinion in an entry, this pleased my friend more than anything else.

I continued to develop this approach to journal writing for over two decades, writing faithfully to this vague but loyal someone who seemed to exist somewhere out there. Then, one day, I came across a short essay written by Michael Ventura. It was actually one of a series of letters Ventura had written to his friend, James Hillman, included as part of a book the two had written together, *We've Had a Hundred Years of Psychotherapy and the World's Getting Worse*. Ventura entitled this letter/essay, "What About the Watcher?" As I read this excerpt, a startling realization began to grow inside me:

> ...[Don't] you sometimes feel accompanied, especially when alone, in a way that you usually take for granted...? I'm thinking of something I now call "the Watcher...." [It's] that sense of a common companion, which is you and yet more than you, and who seems always with you, watching from a slight distance....It's not exactly passive but rarely active. Its action is to watch....
>
> [My] experience of the Watcher is that it's not within you, it's a little off to the side....(Or it's above; a friend of mine told me that as a child he pictured his Watcher as a television camera that followed him off to the side....)
>
> [Some] people have endured horrors because their Watcher is...a companion....You may not like yourself at all, yet your Companion is calm and doesn't disapprove, and your solitude can be sweet at times because of this....[My] Companion, my Watcher, is patient—not condoning nor even reassuring, just patient....
>
> [According] to the people I compare notes with, the sense of a Watcher is so common it's taken for granted. My conviction is

that during a bad time one's relationship with one's Watcher is crucial; it may be all one has....[2]

After reading Michael Ventura's comments about the Watcher, I wrote the following entry in my journal:

Wednesday, Nov. 13, 1996

...I think Ventura is right about the Watcher. The Watcher doesn't judge a person or prod a person. The Watcher just hangs out, accepts the individual completely, totally.

Ventura's mentioning of his friend who described his Watcher as a TV camera following him around and dispassionately filming every detail of his life sent a shock wave of recognition through me. For years, beginning when I was around six, I began to imagine all the events of my life being filmed by a hovering TV camera. The camera followed me everywhere, filming everything I did, recording every moment of my life, even my dreams. As the camera dispassionately filmed my life, sometimes I provided narration, talking to myself, internally explaining the significance of a scene or a moment for the benefit of an invisible, all-accepting TV-viewing audience.

The omnipotent TV camera fantasy remained a favorite up until my early twenties. I still indulge in it from time to time, but it's lost most of its appeal for me. It's been replaced by another one, the "Journal fantasy."

After reading Ventura's article, I now know who I've been writing to in my journals all these years. It's my Watcher, the part of me (or *is* it a part of me?) that accepts me completely, the part of me that never passes judgment, never questions the quality (or banality) of my journal entries, never questions my sanity (or lack of), never does *anything* really. Except watch. And listen.

Since writing down my initial reaction to Michael Ventura's ideas about the Watcher concept, I have revised my own ideas about this intriguing, omnipotent, companion-eye entity. Ventura emphasized that the Watcher is outside of a person, "always with you, watching from a slight distance." Although this was also my initial, vaguely conceived concept of my Watcher—the distant friend to whom I had been writing my journal entries—I now believe that the Watcher is not only out there, but also in here, both without and within a person.

The Watcher remains outside of me when I first begin to write an entry in my journal. The outside Watcher is my sympathetic audience of one who encourages me to open up and confess anything I want; after all, he is my best friend and will accept anything I share with him without passing judgment. Normally, when I begin to write an entry, I have a topic in mind, but because the Watcher doesn't care what the topic is, he encourages digressions. In fact, I can't remember ever writing an entry that stayed completely focused on the original topic I had in mind when I first began writing the entry. However, after I have poured out words upon a page and feel that I have reached a stopping point, I reread the entry, keeping in mind that my outside Watcher might not understand some of the vague references I have made or realize the connection between the original topic and passages that stray from this topic. So, I begin to add, cross out, and insert comments that help to add continuity to the references and digressions. If there are awkwardly worded phrases, I try to rephrase them to improve their meaning. I then try to add a conclusion that attempts to wrap up the entry as a whole.

When I am satisfied with the wording and substance of the entry, I begin ingesting the significance of what I have written, letting it resonate within me, noting its style, completeness of thought, and relevance to my life. After I have taken the time to allow an entry to make an impact on me, I know that what I have written is for the Watcher within, the part of me that encourages honesty of expression, clarity, and completeness in detailing the events and passions of my life in order to make clearer to myself my own individuality, who I really am, and how I view the world in which I live.

The Watcher, therefore, is both my core audience and my core identity. As a writing audience, it encourages clear and honest self-expression because it wants the writer to reveal the Watcher within.

ANNE FRANK AND HER WATCHER

Making a conscious acknowledgment of the existence of a part of oneself that encourages honesty and clarity in self expression is the first step a person must take if the person wants to consider journal writing a serious literary genre. Acknowledging this writing audience gives the writer not only a sympathetic audience for confessing the truth, but an approach to writing that helps to make these confessions understandable, comprehensible, and worthy of preserving.

The dominant culture has constructed approved ways for satisfying the autobiographical impulse, which to a large degree shuns the journal writing genre. Approved modes of expression usually favor exaggeration, sensationalism, exhibitionism, and self-promotion rather than blunt, introspective honesty. The emphasis is more on capturing the interest of the biggest public audience rather than satisfying the demands of one audience: the writer's Watcher.

There is no better illustration of this great conflict between the personal desire for fame and success as a writer and the desire to satisfy the demands of the Watcher within than the diary of Anne Frank. Anne's diary is also the best illustration of a person struggling to find the right audience for her self-confessions, and how this discovery not only brought to light the writer's core identity but also vastly improved the author's writing.

Anne began writing her diary in June 1942, shortly after her thirteenth birthday, and only a few months before she went into hiding from the Nazis with her father, mother, older sister, and another family. Anne's earliest diary entries reflect her young age, dealing with such typical juvenile subjects as boyfriends, school concerns, and gossipy banter shared with her girlfriends. After she was forced into hiding, it appears that Anne wrote in her diary primarily to keep herself sane as she struggled to adjust to the terrifying reality of her new claustrophobic living conditions.

One of the ways Anne attempted to cope with her life in hiding was to create a more comforting, insular fantasy world by writing her diary entries as if she were writing letters to former schoolmates and to fictional characters from some of her favorite juvenile fiction books. In fact, it was the epistolary or letter-writing style of one series of juvenile fiction books, *Joop ter Huel,* by Dutch writer Cissy van Marxveldt, that inspired Anne to adopt the letter-writing format for her diary entries.

Many of Anne's early, fanciful letters to her friends are hastily written and filled with vague references about her living situation, as if she were actually sending letters that she thought might be intercepted by the Nazis.

Other letters written around this same time to fictional characters from *Joop ter Huel* are more openly descriptive of her living situation and filled with humorously exuberant passages that mask Anne's underlying fears and sense of claustrophobic entrapment:

Sept. 27 1942

Dear Pop,
Another scribble, today I took a really peculiar bath, like this, first I carry a small washtub downstairs to the large W.C. [i.e., toilet stall], then I go and put my feet in it, meanwhile sitting on the W.C. and start to wash myself, but of course it all splashes everywhere and later when I'm clean, I have to wipe everything up with a dirty mop. At home, I would never have believed that one day I'd be taking a bath in a W.C., but it isn't all that bad, for it could still happen that I might have to live in a W.C. one day, then I'd have a little bookshelf made and a little table and use the W.C. as a chair, but there wouldn't be anywhere to sleep, I'd have to push everything out of the way and that couldn't be done. There is a light as well and you can also black the place out. Well Pop the family has arrived, with the cat, and now I am being distracted, because I want to go and look. Kindest regards to Kees, and love from Anne Frank[3]

Using an unsophisticated writing style that is more like stream-of-consciousness freewriting, these early entries illustrate Anne's struggle to find an approach to writing that could give expression to the overwhelmingly unsettling events of her life.

Gradually, after Anne began to adjust to her new living conditions, her writing began to lose much of its fantasy aspects and its juvenile tone. Then, after nearly two years of living in her office-room hideaway, Anne began to rewrite some of her earlier entries. She had been inspired to do so by her growing confidence as a writer, believing she might be able to publish some of her diary entries in book form after the war.

The rewritten passages display a revelation in style, startling in their clarity of expression, their skillful and sophisticated use of language, and their perceptive insights into her own character and her unique living situation. These entries are all written as letters to a fictional character. But, in the first revised entry, written from the perspective of her life just before going into hiding, Anne revealed for the first time who this character was:

20 June, 1942

It's an odd idea for someone like me to keep a diary; not only because I have never done so before, but because it seems to me that neither I—nor for that matter anyone else—will be interested in the unbosomings of a thirteen-year-old schoolgirl....I want to write but more than that, I want to bring out all kinds of things that lie buried deep in my heart....[However,] as I don't intend to show this...diary to anyone, unless I find a real friend, boy or girl, probably nobody cares.

And now I touch the root of the matter, the reason why I started a diary; it is that I have no such real friend....

I don't seem to lack anything save "the" friend. But it's the same with all my friends, just fun and joking, nothing more. I can never bring myself to talk of anything outside the common round or we don't seem to be able to get any closer, that is the root of the trouble. Perhaps I lack confidence, but anyway there it is, a stubborn fact and I don't seem to be able to do anything about it. Hence, this diary. In order to enhance in my mind's eye the picture of the friend for whom I have waited so long, I don't want to set down a series of bald facts in a diary like most people do, but I want this diary, itself, to be my friend, and I shall call my friend Kitty.[4]

After nearly two years of dutiful diary writing, during which time she experimented with various writing styles and writing audiences, Anne discovered her true writing audience: her Watcher. She gave her Watcher a name and a personality, then began to write her entries as letters addressed to this best friend, knowing that, by writing as honestly, openly, and clearly as she could, this friend would give her the comfort and encouragement she needed to help her cope with the unsettling madness swirling around her. Describing this madness to her friend whom she imagined was far removed from her own predicament also gave Anne the emotional distance she needed to more objectively record the events of her life for her sympathetic audience.

Comparing some of Anne's revised entries with her earlier entries reveals the transformation in Anne's writing after she began observing her life for the benefit of her Watcher. Here is a revision of the earlier "taking a bath in the W.C" entry, written for Kitty over a year after she wrote the original version, but dated around the same time as the original entry:

Tuesday 29 Sept. '42

Dear Kitty,
Extraordinary things happen to people who go into hiding. Just imagine, as there is no bath, we use a washtub and because there is hot water only in the office (by which I always mean the whole of the lower floor), all 7 of us take it in turns to make use of this great luxury. But, because we are all so different and some are more modest than others, each member of the family has found his own place for carrying out the performance. Peter [Van Daan] uses the kitchen in spite of its glass door. When he is going to have a bath he goes to each one of us in turn and tells us that we must not walk past the kitchen for half an hour. He seems to think this is sufficient. Mr. Van Daan goes right upstairs; to him it is worth the bother of carrying hot water all that way, so as to have the seclusion of his own room. Mrs. Van Daan simply doesn't bathe at all at the present; she is waiting to see which is the best place. Daddy has his bath in the private office, Mummy behind the fire guard in the kitchen, [my sister] Margot and I have chosen the front office for our scrub....

However, I don't like this place any longer, and since last week I've been on the lookout for more comfortable quarters. Peter gave me the idea that was to try the large office W.C. There I can sit down, have the light on, lock the door, pour my own bath water away, and I'm safe from prying eyes. I tried my beautiful bathroom on Sunday for the first time and although it sounds mad, I think it is the best place of all....[5]

Unlike the original entry, which is easily recognizable as the jottings of an imaginative yet self-absorbed thirteen year old, the entry written for Kitty displays an amazing maturity of style and substance. The revised entry is not so much a reworking of the original but a more fully, all-encompassing re-observation of the act of taking a bath in this unusual living environment, written for the benefit of Anne's distant friend who needs the extra details and clarifying references in order to better understand Anne's life in this unusual setting.

As Anne revised older entries, she continued to compose new entries for Kitty. The vast majority of these entries—both the rewritten and the unrevised ones—dramatically demonstrate a style that is much more mature than the typical output of a young teenager. Anne also wrote fictional stories during this time—fable-like tales and sentimental romances—which she freely shared with the rest of her family. But, she never let anyone get near her diary.

Although Anne's motivation for rewriting certain entries was to have them published after the war, she remained conflicted over whether or not she would ever share any of her diary entries with anyone other than Kitty. In some entries, she hinted that she would rather destroy the diary than let anyone else read it. Her reasons for this fierce, protective stance toward outsiders reading her most private confessions are revealed in the diary's final entry, an unrevised draft written only days before Nazis finally discovered her family's hiding place:

Tuesday, 1 August, 1944

Dear Kitty,
...I've already told you before that I have, as it were, a dual personality. One half embodies my exuberant cheerfulness, making fun of everything, my high-spiritedness, and above all, the way I take everything lightly. This includes not taking offense at a flirtation, a kiss, an embrace, a dirty joke. This side is usually lying in wait and pushes away the other, which is much better, deeper, purer....

I'm awfully scared that everyone who knows me as I always am will discover that I have another side, a finer and better side....I'm used to not being taken seriously but it's only the lighthearted Anne that's used to it and can bear it; the deeper Anne is too frail for it....Therefore, the nice Anne is never present in company, has not appeared one single time so far, but almost always predominates when we're alone. I know exactly how I'd like to be, how I am too...inside. But alas I'm only like that for myself. And perhaps that's why, no I'm sure it's the reason why I've got a happy nature within and why other people think I've got a happy nature without. I am guided by the pure Anne within.... [6]

It is impossible to know whether or not Anne Frank would have ever followed through with her plans to publish portions of her diary. Her father—the only member of Anne's family to survive the Holocaust—made that decision for her. Even her father remained conflicted over his success at having published his daughter's most private writings, believing he had betrayed Anne's trust by revealing her "better, deeper, purer" side to the world; after he died in 1980, several new pages from Anne's diary came to light which Otto Frank had kept hidden from the public, ones in which Anne boldly claims the contents of her diary are meant to be read by no one but her.

However, what is undeniable is that the inner Anne, what she believed to be her true self, would have remained unknown even to Anne herself if she had not found a way to first discover it and then give expression to it in her diary writing. What is also undeniable is the brilliance of Anne's writing. Although thousands of other people went into hiding during World War II, and hundreds kept written accounts of their experiences, the diary of Anne Frank remains the most deeply moving, beautifully written personal chronicle of this nightmarish period in human history. It is also one of the most insightful, emotionally powerful personal memoirs ever written. Because she succeeded so brilliantly in finding, acknowledging, and giving expression to her "finer and better" side, her core identity, Anne Frank proved that writing for the Watcher to reveal one's true self to oneself can have a profound impact not only on the individual, but can also result in making the world a finer, better place.

NOTES

1. Jan Romein, "A Child's Voice," in David Barnouw and Gerrold Van Der Stroom, eds., *The Diary of Anne Frank: The Revised Critical Edition* (New York: Doubleday, 2003), p. 67-68.

2. James Hillman and Michael Ventura, *We've Had a Hundred Years of Psychotherapy and the World's Getting Worse* (New York: HarperCollins Publishers, 1993), pp. 83-89.

3. Anne Frank, *The Diary of Anne Frank*, p. 278.

4. *Ibid.,* p. 200-201.

5. *Ibid.,* p. 277-278.

6. *Ibid.,* p. 719-721.

CLEARING

Grace rushes in, bright wind,
finding the least chink in ruins,
whirls through destruction,
rimming with light
the edges of what was,
what might have been.

Grace rushes in, scouring,
not older than but other than
the visions broken, the
lives hurt, the dead promises,
given and meant.

Grace rushes through and through
for all the world as though
what remained were livable,
despite destruction.

Grace tears pain open. Grace seals
the raw wound of despair.
Its fire inflames the air,
blessing our makeshift love,
our lived entanglement,
tangential to intent.

Robin van Löben Sels

FILM REVIEW

Philomena, 2013. A film directed by Stephen Frears. Adapted screenplay by Steve Coogan and Jeff Pope, based upon the book, *The Lost Child of Philomena Lee,* by Martin Sixsmith. Starring Judi Dench and Steve Coogan.

PHILOMENA:
A FILM, A WOMAN, A RECLAMATION OF RESPECT

REVIEWED BY JANE ALEXANDER STEWART

> I walked a mile with Pleasure,
> She chattered all the way;
> But left me none the wiser
> For all she had to say.
> I walked a mile with Sorrow,
> And ne'er a word said she;
> But oh, the things I learned from her
> When Sorrow walked with me.
> — Robert Browning Hamilton, "Along the Road"

I could have been the main character played by Judi Dench in *Philomena.* I had a close friend who found herself in a similar position. To be an unmarried pregnant teenager in the 1950's in America as well as in Ireland was not simply frowned upon, it was a

Jane Alexander Stewart, Ph.D., a psychologist in Los Angeles, writes about mythic themes in film. Her popular essay, "The Feminine Hero in *The Silence of the Lambs,*" originally published in *The San Francisco C.G. Jung Library Journal* (Vol. 14, No. 3, 1995), also appeared in *The Soul of Popular Culture* (1998) and *The Presence of the Feminine in Film* (2008) as well as in *The British Association of Psychological Types Quarterly* (1996) and the *National Organization of Women Times.* Currently, she is a staff writer reviewing films for http://newtopiamagazine.wordpress.com. A collection of her reviews and other writings can be found at her website, www.Cinemashrink.com. She can be reached at: Jane@Cinemashrink.com.

slip from grace. Philomena Lee, upon whose story the film *Philomena* is based, was given shelter and educated at the Sacred Heart Catholic Convent in Roscrea, Ireland. When she was found pregnant by the nuns, it was firm evidence of her fallen soul. For the rest of us, we simply suffered the shame of being a girl with sexual desires. There was no "girls will be girls" impetus for adults to look the other way with an approving smile of recognition as there was for boys. No get-out-of-jail-free card. No respect.

No rights.

The road to respect, in the capable and gifted hands of director Stephen Frears, receives a romantic, innocent beginning in *Philomena*. Philomena Lee is a young teenage girl who, having gotten pregnant in a happenstance moment of pleasure at a county fair with a boy her own age, loses the rights to her child. She is, after all, a ward of Roscrea Convent and she has sinned. Her three-year-old son, put up for adoption by the nuns, disappears from her life. All her attempts to find him are thwarted by devilish, punishing Catholic rules regarding adoption. Yet, Philomena is still a deeply faithful Catholic at sixty-five as she lights a votive candle for her lost son's fiftieth birthday. When Philomena confesses the birth and her despairing search for her son to her grownup daughter, she breaks the silence of a secret kept to herself for so many years. Her daughter responds sympathetically—and with a next-generation determination, she sets out to ease her mother's grief. When she overhears a man at a party saying he's a journalist, she is not shy about appealing to him to help her mother find her lost son.

In *Philomena*, the man at the party is Martin Sixsmith, a noted journalist recently fired from his position as political advisor in Tony Blair's administration on a dubious slander charge. He's feeling a loss of identity and self-esteem, so he only half-heartedly agrees to help Philomena because a human-interest story is far from front-page news. A visit with Philomena to the convent where she gave birth yields little. But photos of well-known adoptive parents, like Jane Russell, on the wall stir his investigative instincts. Suspicious of the convent's adoption history, he does a bit of research that warrants pitching Philomena's story to a friend in broadcasting. Perhaps unconsciously, his own fall from prominence in the Blair administration makes him susceptible to another who has suffered a similar blow, albeit from a very different kind of authority. And he needs a project.

With a commission for a television news magazine piece and a slim lead that the boy was adopted by Americans, Philomena and Martin board a plane for Washington, D.C. to uncover the son's whereabouts and attempt a reunion. When Philomena begins to realize that Martin may make her dream come true, she knocks on his hotel door late at night to speak to him about his being fired from his job with the Blair administration. Spoken with a sense of urgency as if he needs to hear it, she tells him, "Their loss is my find." But this is not a documentary. Philomena's "find" did not accompany her to the States in real life. He did not write *her* story. Martin Sixsmith wrote a book entitled *The Lost Child of Philomena Lee*, about *her son*, a gay man who grew up to be an important advisor in the Reagan administration.

It is Stephen Frears, Steve Coogan (who also co-starred in the film), and Jeff Pope who in their adapted screenplay turn Philomena's secret into Philomena's own story. The narrative power of *Philomena* reaches out to women who recognize its truth as their own. The relationship between Philomena and Martin imaginatively calls to mind what might have been between Philomena and her own son. It makes an invisible loss visible. The cinematic mirroring of a "could have been" mother-son relationship in *Philomena* arouses empathy for the breadth and depth of a mother's grief. A lifetime of missed moments is irreplaceable, not to be set aside as a lesser wound than the one crushing scene when Philomena, as a girl, watches her son disappear in a car with strangers. The abandoned child is common fare in literature, fairy tale, and myth. A mother's lingering loss is rarely seen.

The charismatic Judi Dench transforms Philomena Lee into a stand-in for women who lived through—and past—the stigma of being an unwed mother. As a woman and actress, Judi Dench also provides living testimony to the changes for women experienced in one generation. Dame Dench is playing leading ladies at age seventy-nine. Forget being cast as a technical consultant in the film *Marigold Hotel*, she is a world class M, boss of OO7 in *Skyfall*! What Judi Dench brings to *Philomena* is an uncanny warmth and stoicism as she bears witness to contradictions that lay within every woman. When she turns her blue eyes toward us, we become knowing co-conspirators.

Many women have now shared their plight of being "caught" pregnant and the consequences of oppressive reactions. Each story has added insight and created a public community of empathy. But, more importantly, we watch *Philomena* a generation once removed. We know we were part of an immense change, and we can endow ourselves with respect, reclaim a heritage for ourselves.

Dench's fictionalized Philomena Lee did not so much see as want to see. Catholicism blocked her sight but fed her spirit. Her desire was not to expose but to discover what others knew. She didn't want to know the why of the nun's decision. That was left to Martin Sixsmith, the surrogate son. Philomena wanted a first-hand experience of what had been denied her. She wanted to feel her son's desire to be known to her. Throughout, she sticks to the choices meaningful to her.

Steve Coogan, the actor who plays Martin Sixsmith and co-wrote the screenplay, cast himself in the role of an investigator intent on getting to the bottom of Philomena's pain. Why, indeed, had she been denied information about her son's whereabouts? And why was she so nice about it, when he was so incensed? As director, Stephen Frears honors a feminine sensibility in Philomena, answering the latter question by showing how her grief is a part of a whole, a part of an inner sense of self. She's feeding her soul, not her anger, with her search.

However, the writers and director provide an effective conduit for the heart of Philomena's story to join public outrage. *Philomena* presents a full, multi-faceted reflection of a woman's ability to simultaneously be herself and a devoted mother. She doesn't seek change so much as completion. She genuinely wants to know what happened to her son, to know the unknown of his being snatched from her when she was helpless to hold onto him. Unexpected observations and a surprising understanding come forth from Philomena's simple persona. Perhaps keeping her secret to herself nurtured seeds of connection with her lost son.

As in life, light and humor lace the objectionable and the ominous in *Philomena*. We smile no less when she unbuckles her seatbelt to knock on the door of her son's lover than when she rattles on about an entire book she's been reading to Martin. Philomena Lee had a bit of a career as a nurse and shows evidence of having been an astute learner. She intuits her son is gay before she's told. The loving tone of her voice trumps any Catholic reserve. It's not his sexual identity that would lessen her intent nor stop her search. It's only if he never thought of her, never wondered about her or where he came from. If there's a chance to get closer to that truth, she will ask to be heard, be given details, shown photos.

Philomena's spirit prevails when she and Martin confront the aging Mother Superior, the one who kept mother from son, even as her son sought her in person while he was dying of AIDS. It is Martin who angrily pushes open closed doors to find Sister Hildegaard and demand an answer to the question, "Why?" He wants to know what drove such cruelty. Philomena protests, trying to protect the nun. But Martin presses, hard and angry. The nun's answer arouses a pathos in Philomena. The nun fiercely denounces a woman's sexual desire as "sexual incontinence," equaling moments of passion to an embarrassing loss of bladder control. Perhaps Philomena intuits that the nun has separated herself from a critical source of empathy with other women? As Philomena faces her oppressor, she stands on the other side of a rewarding outcome to her quest. She's learned, with Martin's help, that her son remembered her.

Philomena forgives the Mother Superior, but audiences gasp. No hands fly to mouth to muffle outrage. Such a clear vision of cruelty links to a growing momentum in a wider community of men and women who speak out against such opaque, high-minded religious authority.

Though the film suggests Philomena achieves peace of mind after visiting her son's grave and returns to her ways, it's not completely true. A conjunctio between the opposites of calm grace and sharp mind has occurred for her and for Sixsmith. The near atheist, Sixsmith, is moved to bring Philomena a small religious statuette to place on her son's grave and she, grounded in her newfound confidence, tells him a story from a book she's been reading about a woman who didn't know she was beautiful.

In fact, in real life, Philomena's story does continue. She joins a powerful community voice demanding fair laws regarding adoption practices. *Philomena* is providing a platform for Philomena Lee to be taken seriously in Washington, D.C. as she, at the age of eighty, fights for the rights of adopted children to access records of their biological parents. This is not a Hollywood ending. This ending comes from an evolution of respect rising from a far-reaching circle of women who, like Philomena Lee, have been steadfastly removing the mask of hidden realities that have been hurting girls and women for centuries.

> "…oh, the things I learned from her
> When Sorrow walked with me."

I could end here. But *Philomena* reminded me of a fairy tale that helped me respect sorrow for its guidance in a time when I was almost defined by it.

In the fairy tale, *The Handless Maiden*, a young woman whose hands have been sacrificed to the devil to save her father's mill happens to have the good fortune to marry a king. But when she learns she's pregnant after her husband leaves for war, the devil returns and using the ignorance of men about women, mixes messages and slanders her name. Tricked by his High Court, the king gives the order to banish his wife from the kingdom. In exile, she gives birth to a son and names him Sorrow. For seven years they live in the woods until one day, Sorrow finds a man sleeping on a wall nearby and, as the tale is told, awakens the man by lifting a handkerchief from his face. When the man visits the child's home, he finds a surprise. The silver hands he had crafted for his handless wife so many years ago when they married are hanging on the wall. He recognizes Sorrow's mother as his long-lost wife who he believed had abandoned him. Though she had, in the years intervening, grown her own hands (symbolic for becoming a capable woman in her own right), she had kept the silver hands as a reminder of the king's love for her. King and Queen are, of course, reunited and Sorrow revealed as an active hope for the future.

Fairy tales always have a moral. Sorrow empowers the young woman and clears the eyes of the mature man, bringing masculine and feminine elements together for a renewal of relationship and a formidable partnership against untoward forces. When the woman holds her own in *The Handless Maiden*, she gives birth to Sorrow, a spirit of truth capable of removing veils of deceit and promising to play a protective role in generations to come.

In real and cinematic life, Philomena stood fast through strokes of dark fate to emerge as a feminine hero, one who draws upon roots of empathic wisdom for her voice to impact public policy and relieve a baseless suffering known to many. Philomena's story inspires a new ending for an old fairy tale. Viewers are left with a note of resolve to never fall on the wrong side of love again.

As Philomena liked to say, "I didn't see that coming."

BOOK REVIEW

Irene Hardwicke Olivieri: Closer to Wildness, by Irene Hardwicke Olivieri. Pomegranate Press, 2014.

REVIEWED BY SUSAN AMONS

> "Your voice is the wildest thing you own."
> —Terry Tempest Williams, *When Women Were Birds:*
> *Fifty-four Variations on Voice*

One wintery day in Maine, Carl Little emailed me about a new art book, *Irene Hardwicke Olivieri: Closer to Wildness*, for which he wrote an Essay entitled "Irene Hardwicke Olivieri: The Mysterious Workshop of Nature." Knowing I have a passion for animal imagery in my own artwork, where I combine animal archetypes with the natural world, he thought, rightly, that Irene's work would speak to me. While working on this review, I was fortunate to have a conversation with Irene—artist to artist. Her words, both written and shared with me, are woven throughout this review.

Closer to Wildness is a lavishly illustrated, beautifully designed book. There are 152 pages divided into eight realms of imagery: Wildlife, Portraits, Transition, Love and Desire, Wilderness, Stories, Insects, and Underwater. The large format presentation allows us to experience each

Susan Amons is a nationally recognized artist residing in Maine. A graduate of the Massachusetts College of Art, she has received twenty Artist's Fellowships and is a member of the prestigious Peregrine Press in Portland, Maine and the venerable National Association of Women Artists in New York. Her art is represented by numerous galleries on the east coast and is included in many museum collections. For more information see: www.susanamons.com.

The cover art for this issue of *Spring* is a painting by Irene Hardwicke Olivieri called "Tail for blanket and pillow." It appears in *Closer to Wildness* on page 13.

Images from *Closer to Wildness* contained in this book review are reproduced in black and white with the permission of the artist.

of Irene's unique, visionary worlds. Her comments accompanying each image further expand and illuminate her work.

Irene Hardwicke Olivieri studied painting in Texas, Brazil, and Mexico, and graduated with a Master's degree from New York University. She comes from south Texas, has visited Mexico often, and traveled along the Amazon River, which may explain her attraction to fecundity and exotica. Irene also worked in the Cloisters and the New York Botanical Gardens, which provided her with a life-long passion for biology. Irene's father, a Rio Grande farmer, grew beautiful water gardens that appear often in her paintings. "Out of the ordinary"(p. 42), a semi-biographical homestead depiction, provides clues to the origin of Irene's preference for using domestic objects on which to paint. Among many other miniaturized details depicted in this painting are owl-headed adults, with a baby in an earthy kitchen surrounded by green.

In her artwork, Irene creates a very original combination of elements: the gem-like color of Persian miniature, the spiritual quality of "paleo" drawing, the storytelling component of indigenous cultures, and the mysterious messages of hand-scribed text. These tiny hand-written words inside the image have a dual purpose of providing information about the subject upon which it is inscribed, as natural or personal history, and of developing a word pattern which wraps around the forms, further defining shapes and volumes. In our conversation, Irene tells me she loves the process of painting the miniscule letters of each word, and the text reinforces memory, adds texture, and another level of meaning to each piece.

Visually, I am captivated by her use of vibrant color. In "How dare you" (p. 29), a female figure banded in cobalt blue is set against a field of emerald green and vermillion red (Figure 1). The woman is over-painted with wild animal images of caribou, lynx, rabbit, and fox. The figure's Rapunzel-like braids surround the animals, protecting them. Then, I notice tiny, hand-written messages inscribed on everything. The text describes the qualities of the animals. The title of this painting is Irene's message to the hunters who leg-trap wild animals: "How dare you"?

My next observation is the supports on which she paints: unique found objects such as old door panels, wooden bread bowls, cutting

Figure 1: "How dare you"

boards, ironing boards, and iron bedsteads. I ask her about the significance of these choices. What do they add to the overall mystery of the work? Irene tells me, "I am always looking for things to paint on so I have an interesting collection of pieces. Very often the shape or surface makes sense for the piece." When she wanted to paint a memorial to loved ones who had died, she chose a very old hand-carved, wooden bread-rising bowl for "Little house of my heart" (p. 119) because the bowl reminded her of a "primitive coffin shape." In her painting, the lower half of the rising bowl displays the underworld where her dead have gone. Ancient *Mimbres* bowls with holes to release spirits of the dead are brought to mind, as well as *Cinco de Mayo*, Mexico's Day of the Dead, when ancestors are offered their favorite snacks at graveside. Irene's paintings present a similarly comfortable connection between the living and the dead.

Painted doors are a favored surface. Irene says "I especially love old doors, they symbolize so much transition, maybe into a new place, maybe into the wilderness." Painted on a tall, narrow board, reminiscent of a coffin cover, "Wendy and Pato go boating" (p. 46) reveals another underworld vision (Figure 2). A pea-pod canoe carries a woman and black cat, like the Egyptian *Bastet,* across the River Styx. "Handfull of earth" (p. 31) painted on a door shows Irene's interests in flora, fauna, animal / human integrations, and textual messages. The female figure displays animal and botanical paintings on her skin, like beautiful tattoos.

Irene's painted ironing boards appear as domestic altarpieces, displaying a variety of well-matched feminine archetypes. Irene's collection of classic icons includes a rococo mermaid as Aphrodite the lover (p. 144), a bandoliered soldier wearing a painter's palette as Athena the warrior (p. 11), and "Now that you know" (p. 125), a caterpillar-clad woman as Circe the witch—appealing, but deadly (Figure 3). When asked if she is honoring women's relationship to this domestic item, she says she does think about that, but basically, she says, "I'd definitely rather paint on an ironing board than iron something."

There are so many powerful images conveying Irene's love of wildness, it is difficult to choose favorites. Among her favorite creatures are typically unappealing beetles, caterpillars, moths, and rats. But I found "Valentine for a cougar"(p. 23) to be one of the strongest, most resonant images (Figure 4). Painted on a wooden board, the cougar

Figure 2. "Wendy and
Pato go boating"

Figure 3. "Now that
you know"

Figure 4. "Valentine for a cougar"

with the woman inside calls to mind Rousseau's dreamlike "Sleeping Gypsy" with the lion, but in this case the human has already been comfortably consumed, embodied within the large cat. The woman's long wild braid combines with the cougar's tail, while her body reclines in the hammock of the cougar's belly. Below, a small artist/cougar offspring paints with her cougar tail. Irene says she has always had an inclination to combine animal and human forms in her work. "Perhaps," she tells me, "it is a way to be closer to the wild animals; to be intertwined with nature."

The wandering, hand-written text that flows across the cougar/woman describes the biological attributes of the big cat. Irene writes in her commentary, "I always tell friends I hike with: Please do not kill a mountain lion who might be eating me. I'd never want to end the life of such an extraordinary creature in order to save mine. If it were my time to go, I'd eagerly choose to be food for a cougar, to pay back the wild animals that have enriched my life and inspired my paintings." A deep ethics of exchange is evident in her attitude, her philosophy comparable to indigenous hunting cultures that make offerings to animals to thank them for becoming food. In his Essay, Carl Little aptly describes Irene as having a "profound empathy for animals" and an "extraordinary vision of coexistence." (p. 7)

Irene's unique use of text is a critical and original component of her work. I ask her, "Is this how you best express your voice?"

> When I begin a painting which is about a wild animal or some aspect of the natural world, it usually comes after time spent reading, taking notes and putting it into my own words, adding my own thoughts and observations. . . . Painting the tiny text helps me remember what I've learned as well as add texture and another level of meaning to the piece. I love this part of making my painting—physically I love painting the letters of each word and seeing it cover the surface of the piece. When the paint is dry I love to gently run my fingers over the miniscule lettering. I realize that many people might never read what I write in a painting, but I like knowing that if they do, they might find something interesting, like the text in one painting describes how to raise caterpillars, another describes aphrodisiac recipes around the world. When I'm working on a painting about something deeply personal like family secrets, the text happens organically—I'm feeling, thinking, painting.

Women's voices are often softly held. Sometimes tragic acts or injustices lead us to discover newly found powers. In *When Women Were Birds*, Terry Tempest Williams poses a rhetorical question: "What needs to be counted on to have a voice? Courage. Anger. Love. Something to say; someone to listen."[1] It is hard to imagine Irene was ever a quiet or reticent artist; she seems born with a fiery voice. Her positions regarding the treatment of wildlife and the environment are very clearly defined. In her painting, "Better Is the Ready" (p. 47), her warrior artist is armed with a paintbrush quiver, her bandolier is stuffed with artist's ammunition; tubes of paint, pencils and other art supplies (Figure 5).

Political figures are not immune from her painter's arsenal. In "Nature's Cleanup Crew" (p. 111), Irene portrays George Bush and Dick Cheney as vulture food (Figure 6). Visions of the Iraq war come to mind, with oil spills and black, burning deserts, a vast magnitude of environmental destruction. Irene

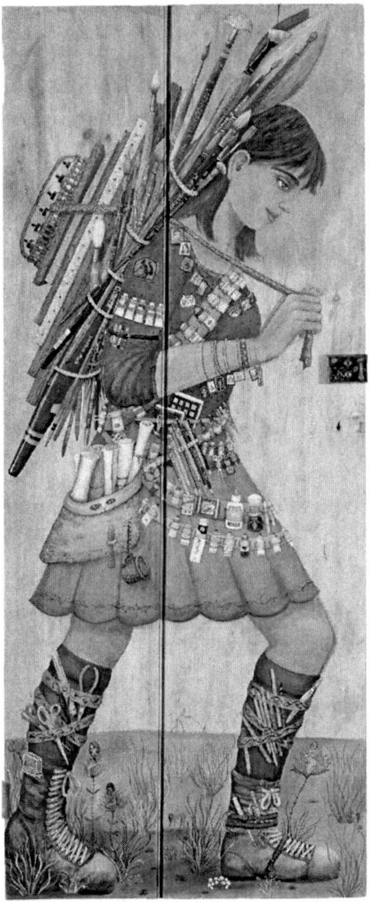

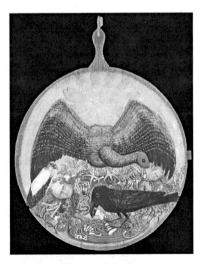

Figure 5. "Better is
the Ready"

Figure 6. "Nature's
Cleanup Crew"

smites her enemies with a vengeful brush, no quarter is given. Her platoon of vultures follows along for the cleanup. Irene tells us vultures are nature's recyclers, turning carrion into life energy.

Opposing the forces of destruction is creation. Irene's work includes many images of fecundity, pleasure, and restoration. "Some kind of wilderness" (p. 98) depicts the greening of our world; an enormous, green, plant-cloaked man emerges from the lake, signifying renewal and rejuvenation. It is unusual to have a male figure symbolizing rebirth, these attributes are generally associated with female powers. The green figure holds a small girl in a cherished manner. Perhaps Irene is restoring the presence of her beloved father, the water gardener, whose death was a traumatic loss for her. The painting process can indeed be a healing process. Adding to the richness of the painting is a tiny, concentric text, which covers the entire 5 x 5 foot painting surface. The text describes exotic lands, rich with flora and fauna.

"Providing the pollen" (p. 79) shows a female figure within a green pea-pod shape (Figure 7). Strings of text float across her, netting her into the pod (Figure 7a). The intricate text describes the banana plant as an aphrodisiac drink and as a source for food, clothing, medicine, and building materials. Pollen is the source of life which creates the remarkably useful, life-sustaining banana. Pollination can be viewed as an act of creation. The Muses are seen at the woman's ears, whispering creative secrets, pollinating her seeds of creativity (Figure 7b).

"Wildflowers grew while I waited for you" (p. 60) shows a Gaia-like, female figure, covered with botanicals, awaiting her special someone (Figure 8). Her body lies on the mossy earth, plants and flowers sprout from the surface of her skin, small creatures walk over her. She is a fertile ground, an iconic female, creative, fertility symbol. The image resonates with Terry Tempest Williams' observation: "In every culture the voice of the feminine emerges from the land itself."[2]

Many of Irene's paintings are curative, restorative, processing grief and loss, and celebrating recoveries and renewal. I ask if she considers the creative process itself to be healing? Irene replies, "Yes, painting is how I deal with everything and I could not survive without it."

We as a culture are searching for ways to restore what we have destroyed, our oceans of fish, our wild birds, our wandering herds, our tiny insects. The art and voice of Irene Hardwicke Olivieri call upon

Figure 7. "Providing the pollen"

Figure 7a. Image detail

Figure 7b. Image detail

Figure 8. "Wildflowers grew while I waited for you"

us to revere and stand up for some kind of wilderness; the one we have left. She asks us: "Who will save the secrets of the creatures? And what would they tell us if we could listen? How can we speak out for the trees, for those who stand tall and quiet?" (p. 21)

NOTES

1. Terry Tempest Williams, *When Women Were Birds: Fifty-four Variations on Voice* (New York: Picador, 2012), p. 44.

2. *Ibid.*, p. 9.

BOOK REVIEW

Kenneth A. Kimmel, *Eros and the Shattering Gaze: Transcending Narcissism*. Fisher King Press, 2011.

REVIEWED BY ROBIN McCOY BROOKS

OVERVIEW

K en Kimmel has made a unique contribution to the psychology of men through a Jungian perspective. His book focuses on heterosexual male narcissism, emphasizing his personal view of how male narcissism can be "transcended" through the love relation. He develops his theory using two major influential sources: Carl Jung, the analytical psychologist, and Emmanuel Levinas, the post-modern, post-phenomenological, and post-Heideggerian philosopher. He robustly enhances his text with references from the classical and post-Jungian tradition, and from works from the Kleinian, Self Psychology, Relational, and Lacanian schools. His proficient use of story telling enables him to relate points of view that might seem otherwise discordant from formal theoretical perspectives. Indeed, most of his text consists of the amplifications of his ideas through stories, in his words: "old, new, epic, personal, fictional and historic." (p. 5) He bridges many dimensions in his work—and his gift is relating these dimensions to one another so that they are not totally alien to each other.

Kimmel defines the focus of his concern as having to do exclusively with the "love problem" of individual heterosexual males. He organizes

Robin McCoy Brooks, M.A. and Trainer, Educator and Practitioner of Group Psychotherapy, Sociometry and Psychodrama, is one of the founding members of the New School for Analytical Psychology in Seattle, Washington. She is a Jungian psychoanalyst in private practice. Her written works attempt to clarify her interest in the phenomenology of subject formation, most especially the correspondences between the physical and metaphysical realms. Her interests include the intricate relationship between psychoanalysis and philosophy, political activism, post-Lacanian thought, and neuro-diversity.

his central thesis around interpreting the tale of "Eros and Psyche" that is embedded in the *Golden Ass* by Apuleius. He returns to this tale throughout his text using it as a "metaphorical entry-point" to each of its meaty sections.

Part One is entitled "Narcissism in the Romantic: The Mother, Her Son, His Lover." It explores a wounded man's ill-fated pursuit of the belated trace (*nachträglich*) of the lost (or never had) object of desire. This desire, Kimmel asserts, emerges from a primal reunion fantasy that can be played out in adult romantic relationships. The fantasy of containing wholeness splits him off from "the raw truth of human existence" of being in a world that is shot through with terrifying uncertainty (p. 5). He argues that defensive structures emerge to insulate men throughout their lives, while perpetuating the fantasy that such an inflated possibility (for re-union) exists. In this section, Kimmel focuses on developing various defensive forms of narcissism that include masochism, fusion, negative identification with the *puer aeternus* complex, and the devaluation of failed idealized love objects. Kimmel uses classical Jungian concepts as infrastructure for his conception of narcissism, such as soul (*anima*) projection, transcendent function, complex theory (mother, *puer aeternus*), and the *coniunctio*, as well as thought from multiple psychoanalytic traditions. In addition to Amor and Psyche, he weaves in his own fresh interpretations of aspects of the Arthurian legend of Parzival, the fairy tale *Hansel and Gretel,* and the ancient Greek tale of Attis and Cybele as well as clinical vignettes that amplify his central depictions of defensive narcissism.

Part Two, entitled "The Predator Beneath the Lover," explores examples of *destructive* narcissism, such as sadism, annihilation of the other, psychic encapsulation, and the personality's identification with the negative *senex* complex. Kimmel's application of the term "encapsulation" is a good example of how he integrates Jungian and Freudian concepts into his own formulation of this deadly defensive structure. He states:

> The revisioning of Freud's death drive, and the process of repetition compulsion that lies at its heart, hypothesize regression to fantasies of a preanimate existence in which the ego is encapsulated in a perpetual, pain-free state…The concepts set forth in Melanie Klein's *paranoid-schizoid* position and in

> Kalsched's description of the encapsulation of the wounded and
> aggressive internal child objects in the *self-care system* further
> elucidate this stabilizing yet agonizing repetition. (p. 176)

Borrowing from the thought of Symington, the author describes
a kind of "psychic autism" that is inaugurated from infantile trauma
that leaves the child like a "burn victim who perceives his primary
skin as exquisitely fragile and recoils from even the slightest touch."
(pp. 100-101) From what Kimmel calls the "burn wound of Eros,"
the child develops a "second skin" that *encapsulates* and becomes a
"fortress of despair" as a means of regulating primal anxieties that
are ignited from everyday human relatedness. (pp. 126-127) He
distinguishes *defensive* narcissism, as described in part one, with its
destructive neighbor, in that the latter is marked by a drive to destroy
all links to otherness (hence "encapsulation"), devolving into a
position of sadistic dominance (pp. 126-127). He powerfully
illustrates how this dark manifestation of psychotic (delusional)
woundedness can emerge into the political realm through the lens of
Theodore Dorpat's thoughtful psychoanalytic assessment of Hitler's
psychology in the text *Wounded Monster: Hitler's Path from Trauma
to Malevolence*. Additionally, he untangles James Hillman's depiction
of a negative *senex* and Kalsched's perspective of daimonic reality based
on Ferenczi's later work to highlight multiple theoretical dimensions
of a profoundly disturbing psychological disorder.

The culminating section of Kimmel's text is entitled "The
Shattering Other." He crucially argues for an extended version of the
Jungian "Self," one that includes both the inter-subjective element of
the Levinasian ethical relation, while retaining Jung's version of the
other—which is the Psyche. That is, through Levinas, Kimmel attempts
to incorporate an ethics of responsibility that can open up new
perspectives that contrast with the formulaic ways in which we tend
to understand the effects of and treatment for narcissism. While what
he proposes is commendable, even desirable, a fundamental gap
remains between the respective ontologies of analytical psychology and
the post-Heideggerian philosophy of Levinas that cannot so easily be
reconciled, even with the discussion about the differences that he has
included in his text. I will elaborate on this point below.

The cure for narcissism, according to Kimmel, is to establish a
capacity for love that can emerge by fully encountering what it means

to inhabit a world *with* others. Openness and responsiveness toward the affects that the other has stirred within me is a basic precondition for the ethical development of the subject. It is through bearing the suffering of others that the *subject comes to be*. The Levinasian ethical dimensions of subject formation that Kimmel's notion embraces is one that supports an openness to the repetitive and "passive movement of dying itself" that is inaugurated by the command of the other and my responsibility to him or her. This position is antithetical to the seductive defensive edifices of narcissism in all its forms. Narcissism, from this perspective, is the flight from one's own suffering—in Kimmel's term, a flight from the shattering gaze or presence of the other.

CRITIQUE

The author is gifted in his use of literary contextualization, and he includes masterful case illustrations. His potent rendering of the devastating manifestations of male narcissism was very psychoactive for me as I read the text, and that continued afterwards. This deepened my understanding of the material, and I suspect future readers will be similarly moved.

Kimmel skillfully builds a weight-bearing bridge between the disparate traditions of analytical psychology and psychoanalytic thought in the development of his theory of narcissism. He also manages to integrate complex philosophical concepts into his thinking about self-formation without over-burdening the reader with distracting neologisms. On the other hand, I found that the philosophical theory he does introduce was often lacking in reflection in two crucial areas: (a.) the key concepts used by Jung and Levinas clearly employ gender-biased metaphor, and (b.) there is a sometimes striking conflation of disparate theories that is under-addressed.

Levinas's notion of sensible alterity and Jung's notions of the soul are equally phallocentric. By that I mean that Jung's and Levinas's methodological normative binary conceptions of gender retain a masculine bias (masculine subject to feminine other or object) as if these conceptualizations of difference speak for themselves as "universal essences sharing consensual meaning."[1] How does one read their works as a woman without having to rigorously deconstruct and retranslate what is relevant to the experience of becoming a subject and what is not?[2] It is clear that Jung's association of the soul (*esse in anima*) with the feminine is problematic in many contemporary feminist critiques, especially since his foundational essentialism is contrary to the aims of his entire project of individuation.[3] Likewise, Levinas's conception of the transcendent is controversial with feminist academics on many grounds, but particularly because he associates alterity (Otherness) entirely with the feminine.[4] Levinas's association of the feminine with alterity can be viewed as a contradiction of his valorization of difference as the site of the ethical relation, especially when he engages in the kind of essentialism that his entire project rallies against. Jung and Levinas did not intend to designate the feminine as a biological reality and used a gender-biased metaphorical description of a reality that today is no longer convincing, in a world that has long since incorporated queer theory into its consciousness. Indeed, even though Kimmel is describing the experience of transcending "male" narcissism, he is working within the shadowy frame of the old tradition—where the *answers* to the questions of what it means to be a *human* subject have lost plausibility, not the questions themselves.

Kimmel does not clarify his own specific use of the term "transcendence." This is crucial because it is a key concept that both Jung and Levinas use in disparate ways even within their own corpuses. That Jung and Levinas both use the word is basically the only way in which their meanings are similar. Jung believed that he had indeed discovered the typos (pattern) of the *arch* (the primal substance) and by its very nature, the "psychoid" archetypes were the foundational principles of being and emissaries or emanations *of* the transcendent world soul that was situated within the *unus mundus*.[5] In contrast, the Levinasian ethical relation could not be systematized or reduced to an *archè* or basic ontology. For Levinas, the ethical relation, or the site of subjectification, occurs at the level of pre-reflective sensibility through the command of the actual outside "Other" which is very different from an activity of reflective consciousness that involves an archetypal presence engaging within an isolated mind. Levinas would have objected to Jung's reification or symbolic interpretation of material. He would have perceived that material as unthematizable and not reducible to archetypal or other "totalizing" concepts. Jung's ground of subjectification was situated in the gap between the phenomenal and transcendent realms via the psychoid archetype. Levinasian ground was inaugurated through the sensorial trauma of impotence in response to the other's suffering, or the nether space between being and beyond being that Levinas referred to as the "there is" [*il y a*].[6]

The author defines Jung's *coniunctio* as the "uniting of separated qualities or an equalizing of principles." (p. 278) In contrast, Levinas rejects a romantic conception of love that merges two souls into one. The locus of transcendence for Levinas is situated in an *asymmetrical* intersubjectivity incommensurable with unification.[7] Contra Jung, this perspective does not define "the feminine" in terms of its opposition to the masculine, but as something that has its own positive being. Levinas specifically rejected the notion that the feminine is what it is through its relation with its opposite, or as a duality.[8] Levinas viewed transcendence as deriving from a surplus of being, which is different from the mutual determination or synthesis of dialectic movement as is implied in Jung's transcendent function or in Kimmel's use of it.

It is commendable that the author attempts to assimilate Levinas's relational ethics into his project of healing narcissism, even though its basic assumptions are fundamentally opposed to Jung's foundationalist perspective. Other theoreticians have made similar attempts of rehabilitating Jungian theory by incorporating aspects of philosophical thought, such as Roger Brooks with Heidegger's *oeuvre* and Wolfgang Giegerich with Hegel's. Kimmel's mastery lies in his clinical acumen and his skillful ability to communicate his own deeply held understanding of and empathy for his patients. He movingly describes those who suffer from narcissistic blindness and insensitivity and the devastating effects this can have on love relations, including within the analytic couple. One has the clear sense in reading his text that he works closely with the revelation of impotent trauma with his patients. He is clearly able to stay in the nether space of the "there is" [*il y a*], wait for new directions to appear, and respond to his patient's terrible suffering in its primitive forms. Kimmel has borne not only his own impotence in the counter-transference, but also that *of* his patients again and again. And in so doing, the patient can possibly one day *take in* his own wretchedness, not unbearably alone but accompanied by Kimmel or other therapists with a similar perspective. This is a profoundly ethical relation.

I recommend this book without reservation to any analyst, therapist, student, or analytic candidate who is interested in deepening their clinical understanding of the dynamics of male narcissism through multiple perspectives.

NOTES

1. Sharon R. Green, "Embodied female experience through the lens of imagination," *Journal of Analytical Psychology* 55 (2010): 339-360.

2. See David Tresan's very personal account of his failed attempt to "corral" a metaphysical entity (Anima) into a "core definition." What emerges instead is an agonizing portrayal of his sensual awareness of a "soul that has now been forged" through suffering. Not once does he assign gender to what he instead refers to as "the discontinuous small energy that seemed to hover so lightly near me when I saw myself within." "David Tresan on the Process of Writing," *Jung Journal: Culture & Psyche* 8 (2014): 9-16.

3. Richly varied Jungian feminist critiques in the last twenty years include: Francis Gray, *Jung, Irigaray, Individuation: Philosophy, Analytical Psychology, and the Question of the Feminine* (London: Routledge, 2008) (some discussion of Levinas); Polly Young-Eisendrath, *Gender and Desire: Uncuring Pandora* (College Station, TX: Texas A & M University Press, 1997); Susan Rowland, *Jung: A Feminist Revision* (Oxford, UK: Blackwell Publishers, 2002); Lucy Huskinson, "The Self as Violent Other: The Problem of Defining the Self," *Journal of Analytical Psychology*, 47 (2002): 439-460 (includes a critique of Levinas).

4. Feminist critiques of the works of Levinas are also richly varied, and one can begin with: *Feminist Interpretations of Emmanuel Levinas: Re-reading the Canon,* ed. Tina Chanter (University Park, PA: Pennsylvania State University Press, 2001); Bracha Lichtenberg-Ettinger and Emmanuel Levinas, "What would Eurydice say?" in *Emmanuel Levinas in Conversation with Bracha Lichtenberg Ettinger* (2006), *Athena: Philosophical Studies*, 1: 137-145; Judith Butler, *Giving an Account of Oneself* (Bronx, NY: Fordham University Press, 2005).

5. Robin McCoy Brooks, "Un-thought out metaphysics in analytical psychology: a critique of Jung's epistemological basis for psychic reality," *Journal of Analytical Psychology* 56 (2011): 491-512; Ladson Hinton, "*Unus Mundus*–transcendent truth or comforting fiction? Overwhelm and search for meaning in a fragmented world," *Journal of Analytical Psychology* 56 (2011): 375-396.

6. Emmanuel Levinas, *Basic Philosophical Writings,* ed. A. Peperazak, S. Critchely, R. Bernasconi (Bloomington, IN: Indiana University Press, 1996), p. 110.

7. Emmanuel Levinas, *Existence and Existents,* trans. A. Lingis (Pittsburgh, PA: Duquesne University Press, 2001), p. 100.

8. Emmanuel Levinas, *Time and the Other,* trans. R.A. Cohen (Pittsburgh, PA: Duquesne University Press, 1987), p. 86.

BOOK REVIEW

Michael Vannoy Adams, *For Love of the Imagination: Interdisciplinary Applications of Jungian Psychoanalysis.* Routledge, 2014.

REVIEWED BY GINETTE PARIS

M ichael Vannoy Adams remains the undisputed champion of the basic and foundational insight of Jungian psychology: "we have to keep it simple, and *stick to the image.*"[1] The benefits of examining the inner images we live by (call them, if you wish, symbols, metaphors, myths, archetypes, narratives, scripts…) is the reason why Adams suggests that Jungian psychology is an *imaginology*—rather than a psychology. "For me, psychotherapy is essentially an affair of images— of how we imagine, and, more important, reimagine ourselves," writes Adams. (p. 3) This process of reimagining ourselves, Adams, in 2004, called the *fantasy principle*, and now, in 2014, he argues that it is more fundamental than either the pleasure principle or the reality principle. "The reason that I am a Jungian rather than a Freudian is that it seems to me that Freud wants to rectify the imagination—to require what I call the fantasy principle to conform to what he calls the reality principle." (p. 9) Adams's sharp critical judgment also applies to Jungians who only ask *what images mean*, while neglecting to ask *how they mean*. The *how* we construct—and deconstruct—reality is the core of a Jungian analysis.

Adams's *imaginology* is not only a way back to the essential Jung, it is also a way out of the tiresome hyper-theorizing that is typical of an aging, fading, dying, boring Jungian orthodoxy. For too long, the emphasis has been on the *interpretation* of the image—a left brain, logos

Ginette Paris, Ph.D., is a core faculty at Pacifica Graduate Institute. She is the author of several books that exemplify the archetypal perspective, among which are *Wisdom of the Psyche: Depth Psychology after Neuroscience* (2007) and *Heartbreak: New Approaches to Healing* (2011).

operation—while re-imagining is a right brain, Eros operation. Like an app that needs upgrading to function on new operating systems, what Adams calls the *Jungian app* needs to redress the balance between interpreting and imagining. Adams urges Jungians to leave the field of conceptual essentialism with its "vain definitional conflict over concepts that are intrinsically vague" to get back to the core task of analysis: the differentiation of imagination. "To me, the discovery that internal reality, psychic reality—or imaginal reality—is just as real as any external reality is the most important discovery of psychoanalysis." (p. 8)

Neuroscience would agree with such a statement. The new wave of left-brain/right brain research (summarized among others by Iain McGilchrist) demonstrates how inner images push neurons around. This biological reality underscores the necessity of a balance between right brain and left brain operations.

When Adams explores what he calls *non-ego images*, he reminds us how surprising they always appear, because they have a transformative power that may frighten the ego. For that very reason, we, like Adams, should be curious about non-ego images! This curiosity brings us to what Hillman believed Jungians should be doing: "We need an imaginal ego that is at home in the imaginal realm, an ego that can undertake the major task now confronting psychology: the differentiation of the imaginal."[2]

Adams's writing is doing "things with images that do things." (p. 68) He does it by seeing through many trends in our culture, for example, the conceptual *impossible purity* in Giegerich's discourse, or Hillman's brilliant renaming the unconscious as *the imagination*. He makes us see through the ideological stance that keeps our economy in the grip of the myth of the *invisible hand*, with its rigid ideology of the *bottom line*. He renews our imagination of political heroism, with Obama as Icarus: "the myth of Icarus does not say not to fly. The moral of the story is to fly just high enough and not fall." (p. 132) He invites us to visit Moscow's mythological unconscious.

Adams's imaginology is both original and a most-needed return to the basics, before conceptual jargon contaminates our whole field. Adams writes: "Ironically, it is not the unconscious that is unconscious. Rather, it is the ego-image that is unconscious, and what it is unconscious of is the imagination—the images that emerge continuously, incessantly from the unconscious." (p. 14) I read this great quote to also mean this: *Ironically, it is not so much the unconscious of the patient that is unconscious. It is the ego of the analyst that is unconscious, and what it is unconscious of is his imagination and that of the patient.*

NOTES

1. C.G. Jung, "The Practical Use of Dream-Analysis" (1966), in *The Collected Works of C.G. Jung*, vol. 16, ed. and trans. Gerhard Adler and R.F.C. Hull (Princeton, NJ: Princeton University Press, 1966), § 320.

2. James Hillman, *Re-Visioning Psychology* (New York: HarperCollins, 1977), p. 37.

Spring

A Journal of Archetype and Culture

Spring: A Journal of Archetype and Culture, founded in 1942, is the oldest Jungian psychology journal in the world. Published twice a year, each issue explores from the perspective of depth psychology a theme of contemporary relevance and contains articles as well as book and film reviews. Contributors include Jungian analysts, scholars from a wide variety of disciplines, and cultural commentators.

Upcoming Issues of Spring Journal

VOLUME 92 — WINTER 2014

Eranos—Its Magical Past and Alluring Future: The Spirit of a Wondrous Place

Edited by Nancy Cater and Riccardo Bernardini, Scientific Secretary, Eranos Foundation

Subscribe to Spring Journal!

2 issues (1 year) *within United States* ($40.00)
2 issues (1 year) *foreign airmail* ($65.00)
4 issues (2 years) *within United States* ($70.00)
4 issues (2 years) *foreign airmail* ($115.00)

To order, please visit our online store at:
www.springjournalandbooks.com

Spring Journal, Inc.
New Orleans, Louisiana USA

CPSIA information can be obtained
at www.ICGtesting.com
Printed in the USA
FFOW01n1609170115
10308FF